# Omar Sharif Jr.

*Bridging LGBTQ and Middle Eastern Advocacy – Unauthorized*

Ahmed Deng

ISBN: 9781779696373
*Imprint: The Dork Dictionaries*
Copyright © 2024 Ahmed Deng.
All Rights Reserved.

# Contents

Discovering His Identity    11
Navigating Two Worlds    18
The Road to Activism    28
Impactful Influences    37

**Chapter 2: The Rise of a LGBTQ Icon    45**
Chapter 2: The Rise of a LGBTQ Icon    45
The Coming Out Journey    47
Omar Sharif Jr Takes the Stage    56
Bridging Cultures    66
The Power of Education    78

**Bibliography    83**
Building a Legacy    91

**Chapter 3: Challenges and Triumphs    101**
Chapter 3: Challenges and Triumphs    101
The Price of Activism    103
Celebrating Victories    113
Impacting Policy and Legislation    122
Awards and Recognition    134
Lessons Learned    144

**Chapter 4: Beyond Borders: The Global Impact    153**
Chapter 4: Beyond Borders: The Global Impact    153
International Activism    157
Breaking Barriers through Media    167
Creating Safe Spaces    177
Public Speaking and Engaging the Masses    187

The Continued Journey  197

**Chapter 5: Legacy and Future Endeavors  209**
    Chapter 5: Legacy and Future Endeavors  209
    Leaving a Lasting Legacy  211
    Expanding the Middle Eastern LGBTQ Movement  219
    The Future of Activism  231
    Conclusion: A Hero for Our Times  241

**Index  251**

## 1 1 The Birth of a Star

In this chapter, we delve into the captivating journey of Omar Sharif Jr., a prominent LGBTQ advocate and a rising star in Middle Eastern advocacy. Omar's story is one of self-discovery, resilience, and breaking barriers within his traditional Middle Eastern upbringing. From his early years, marked by the influence of his famous grandfather, to his courageous decision to live authentically and embrace his LGBTQ identity, we follow Omar's path to becoming a shining beacon of hope for marginalized communities.

### 1 1 1 An Introduction to Omar Sharif Jr.'s Background

Omar Sharif Jr. was born into a world of glitz and glamour on April 20, 1983, in Montreal, Canada. As the grandson of the legendary actor Omar Sharif, Omar Jr. was destined to carry on the legacy of his iconic grandfather. From an early age, he was exposed to the entertainment industry, attending movie premieres, award ceremonies, and witnessing the captivating allure of the spotlight.

Growing up, Omar Sharif Jr. was a curious and compassionate child. Although surrounded by fame, he always maintained a down-to-earth spirit, driven by a genuine desire to make a positive impact on the world. As he ventured further into adulthood, he confronted the realities of his dual identity as both an LGBTQ individual and a member of the Middle Eastern community.

### 1 1 2 The Influence of His Famous Grandfather

Omar Sharif Jr. was undeniably shaped by the remarkable legacy of his grandfather, Omar Sharif. Known for his mesmerizing performances in classic films such as "Lawrence of Arabia" and "Doctor Zhivago," Omar Sharif was an international sensation and a true icon of the silver screen. His talent, charisma, and Middle Eastern heritage struck a chord with audiences around the world.

Inspired by his grandfather's accomplishments, Omar Sharif Jr. recognized the power of representation. He understood that by embracing his own identity, he could inspire others who were grappling with similar struggles. While holding onto his grandfather's memory, Omar embarked on a mission to redefine what it means to be a star and pave the way for LGBTQ rights in both the Western and Middle Eastern worlds.

## 1 1 3 Growing Up in a Traditional Middle Eastern Family

Omar Sharif Jr.'s upbringing was deeply rooted in his traditional Middle Eastern family. The values of honor, respect, and family unity were instilled in him from a young age. However, within this familial structure, he confronted the complex challenges of embracing his sexuality in a society that often deemed it taboo.

The duality of his life, navigating between the cultural expectations of his Middle Eastern heritage and his own authentic self, became a central theme in Omar's journey. It exposed him to the contrasting realities faced by LGBTQ individuals in the Western world and the Middle East. This contrast fueled his determination to bridge the gap between LGBTQ advocacy and Middle Eastern communities.

## 1 1 4 Early Signs of Activism and Advocacy

Even in his formative years, Omar Sharif Jr. exhibited a deep-seated passion for social justice and equality. As a teenager, he joined human rights organizations and became involved in powerful initiatives focused on advocating for marginalized communities. These early experiences awakened his activist spirit and set the stage for his future endeavors.

Omar understood the importance of using his platform and privilege to uplift voices that often went unheard. He recognized that activism could not be limited to personal struggles, but should extend to those facing discrimination and prejudice on a larger scale. Omar's journey was marked by his unwavering commitment to effecting positive change in the world around him.

## Unconventional Insight: The Power of Storytelling

One of the most powerful tools in Omar Sharif Jr.'s activism is storytelling. By sharing personal experiences and shedding light on the struggles faced by individuals within the LGBTQ community and the Middle Eastern world, he breaks down barriers and fosters empathy.

Through his captivating storytelling, Omar invites others to see the world through his eyes, encouraging dialogue and understanding. His ability to connect on a human level challenges stereotypes and fosters a sense of shared humanity. Storytelling has become the cornerstone of his advocacy, allowing him to bridge the gap between cultures and ignite conversations that lead to meaningful change.

## Example Problem: Challenging Stereotypes

Imagine you are tasked with challenging a stereotype about a marginalized group. Develop a powerful storytelling strategy that shares personal experiences and highlights the humanity behind the stereotype. Specify the key elements you would include to create an emotional impact and facilitate empathy.

## Exercise: Embracing Dual Identity

Reflect on your own identity and culture. Consider how you navigate the expectations and norms of your heritage while embracing your personal values and beliefs. Write a short journal entry exploring the challenges and triumphs of embracing a dual identity. Share your thoughts on the importance of self-acceptance and how it contributes to personal growth.

## 1.1 The Birth of a Star

In this chapter, we delve into the origins of one of the most influential LGBTQ activists and Middle Eastern advocates of our time, Omar Sharif Jr. His journey from a traditional Middle Eastern family to becoming a prominent figure in the LGBTQ rights movement is nothing short of extraordinary. Let's explore the events that shaped his path and set the stage for his remarkable activism.

### 1.1.1 An Introduction to Omar Sharif Jr.'s Background

Omar Sharif Jr., born on February 20th, 1983, in Montreal, Canada, was destined for greatness from the start. As the grandson of the legendary actor Omar Sharif, known for his iconic roles in films like "Lawrence of Arabia" and "Doctor Zhivago," Omar Jr. inherited a rich heritage of talent and charisma.

Growing up in an environment where art and creativity were celebrated, Omar Jr.'s passion for storytelling and expression took root at an early age. Inspired by his grandfather's on-screen presence and ability to captivate audiences, he dreamt of following in his footsteps and making a positive impact on the world.

### 1.1.2 The Influence of His Famous Grandfather

Omar Jr.'s famous grandfather, Omar Sharif, not only left a lasting impression on the cinematic world but also played a significant role in shaping his grandson's outlook on life. The elder Sharif's ability to transcend cultural boundaries and portray complex characters left a deep imprint on Omar Jr.'s artistic sensibilities.

From an early age, Omar Jr. was exposed to stories of his grandfather's travels and experiences as an international star. These tales ignited a curiosity within him to explore the intricate tapestry of cultures, breaking free from the constraints of societal norms and expectations.

### 1.1.3 Growing Up in a Traditional Middle Eastern Family

Despite being born and raised in Canada, Omar Jr. was intimately connected to his Middle Eastern roots through his family and their traditions. His upbringing in a traditional Middle Eastern household provided him with a unique perspective on the values and customs that shaped his cultural identity.

While his family cherished their heritage, Omar Jr. also recognized the contrasting realities faced by LGBTQ individuals within Middle Eastern societies. The duality of his experiences as both an LGBTQ person and a member of a traditional family laid the foundation for his ultimate mission: to bridge the gap between LGBTQ rights and Middle Eastern advocacy.

### 1.1.4 Early Signs of Activism and Advocacy

From an early age, Omar Jr.'s compassionate nature and sense of justice propelled him towards activism. His innate understanding of the struggles faced by marginalized communities, including LGBTQ individuals, fueled his desire to create a more equitable world.

Throughout his formative years, Omar Jr. actively engaged in initiatives that strove to break down barriers and promote understanding. Whether it was organizing fundraisers for LGBTQ youth organizations or volunteering at local community centers, his dedication to making a difference was unwavering.

As Omar Jr. grew older, he realized that his voice and platform could be used to effect change in a profound way. The fire of advocacy burned brightly within him, igniting a journey that would define his life's purpose.

### 1.1.5 The Decision to Live Authentically

One of the most defining moments in Omar Jr.'s life came when he made the courageous decision to embrace his true self and live authentically as a gay man. This choice was not without its challenges, especially considering the potential backlash and stigma associated with being LGBTQ in certain cultural contexts.

However, Omar Jr.'s unwavering commitment to his own happiness and well-being ultimately triumphed over the fear of societal judgment. Through self-acceptance and self-love, he found the strength to navigate the complex terrain of his identity while staying true to his roots.

In doing so, Omar Jr. became a beacon of hope and inspiration for countless individuals struggling with their own sexual orientations and the pressures imposed by society. His journey emboldened others to embrace their identities proudly, regardless of cultural or societal expectations.

### 1.1.6 Embracing His Dual Identity

With his LGBTQ identity at the forefront, Omar Jr. embarked on a journey to harmonize his Middle Eastern heritage with his activism. He recognized the importance of bridging these seemingly disparate worlds and the transformative power that could be harnessed by advocating for LGBTQ rights within Middle Eastern communities.

Omar Jr.'s ability to navigate the intricate complexities of cultural expectations, family dynamics, and LGBTQ activism sets him apart as a unique voice in the fight for equality and understanding. By embracing his dual identity, he not only challenged societal norms but also presented an alternative narrative that defied stereotypes and opened dialogue.

In the following chapters, we explore how Omar Sharif Jr. navigates the challenges and triumphs that lie ahead on his path to becoming an iconic LGBTQ activist and a beacon of hope for Middle Eastern advocacy. We delve into his personal struggles, his efforts to create change, and the legacy he is shaping for future generations.

## The Influence of His Famous Grandfather

Omar Sharif Jr.'s famous grandfather, Omar Sharif, was a legendary actor in the Golden Age of Egyptian cinema. Born Michel Dimitri Chalhoub in 1932 in Alexandria, Egypt, he later changed his name to Omar Sharif to appeal to the international film market. Omar Sharif's exceptional talent and charisma made him a global icon, and his influence on Omar Sharif Jr.'s life cannot be overstated.

From a young age, Omar Sharif Jr. was captivated by his grandfather's movies. As he watched his grandfather light up the silver screen with his magnetic presence, Omar Sharif Jr. felt a deep admiration and connection. He saw in his grandfather the power of storytelling and the impact that an actor can have on the world.

But it wasn't just his grandfather's on-screen success that shaped Omar Sharif Jr.'s worldview—it was also his off-screen persona. Omar Sharif was known for his charm, grace, and humility. He was a true gentleman, treating everyone he encountered with kindness and respect. This level of compassion and empathy became ingrained in Omar Sharif Jr.'s values and would later inform his own approach to activism.

Growing up in a traditional Middle Eastern family, Omar Sharif Jr. witnessed his grandfather navigate the complex dynamics of fame while staying true to his culture and heritage. Despite his international acclaim, Omar Sharif remained deeply connected to his Egyptian roots. He continued to support the local film industry and championed the representation of Middle Eastern culture in Hollywood.

This connection to his heritage was crucial for Omar Sharif Jr., who himself would grapple with the intersection of his LGBTQ identity and Middle Eastern background. Seeing his grandfather navigate these dual identities with grace and resilience showed Omar Sharif Jr. that it was possible to reconcile seemingly opposing aspects of oneself.

Omar Sharif Jr. often recounts a story his grandfather shared with him about the making of the film "Lawrence of Arabia." In the film, Omar Sharif played the role of Sherif Ali, an Arab leader in the revolt against the Ottoman Empire. The character was initially written as a villain, but Omar Sharif insisted on portraying him as a hero—a complex and layered character with depth and humanity. This approach not only elevated the film but also challenged stereotypes and provided a more nuanced representation of Arab culture.

This story left a profound impact on Omar Sharif Jr. It taught him the importance of using his platform to challenge stereotypes and misconceptions, not just about the LGBTQ community, but also about the Middle East. Like his grandfather, Omar Sharif Jr. recognized the power of representation in shaping public perceptions and advocating for social change.

In the footsteps of his famous grandfather, Omar Sharif Jr. has embraced his role as a bridge between LGBTQ and Middle Eastern advocacy. He acknowledges the immense privilege of his famous lineage and uses it as a catalyst to amplify voices that are often marginalized and overlooked.

The influence of his famous grandfather extends far beyond the realm of acting. Omar Sharif Jr. carries with him the legacy of a man who touched the hearts of millions and used his platform to bring people together. Through his activism and advocacy, Omar Sharif Jr. continues to honor his grandfather's memory and forge a path towards a more inclusive and accepting world.

**Excerpt from Omar's Diaries: Nourishing the Seed of Activism**

*Dear Grandfather,*

*Today, as I reflect on the impact you have had on my life, I can't help but feel an overwhelming sense of gratitude. You were not only a talented actor but also a beacon of compassion and understanding. You showed me that it's possible to embrace different parts of oneself and create change in the world.*

## Growing Up in a Traditional Middle Eastern Family

Growing up in a traditional Middle Eastern family, Omar Sharif Jr. faced unique challenges and experiences that shaped his journey as an LGBTQ activist. In this section, we will explore the cultural context of his upbringing, the influence of his family, and the early signs of his activism and advocacy.

### Cultural Context and Traditions

Middle Eastern culture is rich in history, traditions, and deeply rooted beliefs. Family, religion, and community play vital roles in shaping an individual's identity and values. In this context, gender roles and expectations are often strictly defined, and non-heteronormative identities can be seen as taboo or even forbidden.

Omar Sharif Jr. grew up in this cultural backdrop, where the importance of tradition and maintaining societal norms was emphasized. This environment created a complex landscape for him, as he had to navigate his own identity within this rigid framework.

## Family Influence

The Sharif family is well-known in the Middle East, particularly Omar's grandfather, the legendary Egyptian actor Omar Sharif. This iconic figure represented the epitome of traditional masculinity, and his fame amplified the pressure on Omar Jr. to conform to societal expectations.

Omar Jr.'s father and uncles also played significant roles in shaping his worldview. They instilled in him a deep sense of pride in his Middle Eastern heritage and upheld the values of honor, respect, and discipline. However, reconciling his family's values with his own journey of self-discovery was not an easy task.

## Early Signs of Activism

Even from a young age, Omar Sharif Jr. displayed a natural inclination towards speaking out against injustices and advocating for marginalized communities. While many children are encouraged to conform and prioritize conformity, Omar Jr. questioned the status quo, especially when he witnessed the oppression faced by LGBTQ individuals in his community.

His early experiences of witnessing discrimination and the struggle to be authentic in a traditional environment planted the seeds of activism within him. These experiences shaped his understanding of the privilege and responsibility he held to stand up for those who did not have a voice.

## Navigating Identity and Belonging

Growing up in a traditional Middle Eastern family meant that Omar Sharif Jr. faced the challenge of reconciling his LGBTQ identity with his cultural heritage. The expectation to hide his true self and conform to societal norms created a sense of isolation and internal conflict.

Despite these challenges, Omar Jr. found support and solace in unexpected places. He sought out like-minded individuals within his community and formed close bonds with allies who understood his struggle. These connections provided a lifeline and a reminder that he was not alone in his journey.

## Embracing Intersectionality

Omar Sharif Jr.'s upbringing also emphasized the importance of recognizing and embracing intersectionality. As a person of Middle Eastern descent and a member of the LGBTQ community, he witnessed firsthand the interconnectedness of various forms of oppression and discrimination.

His experiences taught him the significance of working towards solutions that addressed the unique challenges faced by individuals who belong to multiple marginalized groups. This understanding would later become a driving force in his advocacy work, as he strived to bridge the gap between LGBTQ rights and Middle Eastern advocacy.

## Breaking Cultural Barriers

One of the greatest challenges faced by Omar Sharif Jr. while growing up in a traditional Middle Eastern family was the cultural stigma and misconceptions surrounding LGBTQ identities. Being openly gay in such an environment was met with strong opposition and often led to ostracism.

However, Omar Jr.'s journey taught him to challenge these cultural barriers through patience, understanding, and empathy. He recognized that change could not be forced upon his family or community but required respectful dialogue and the gradual breaking down of stereotypes.

## The Power of Cultural Exchange

While growing up in a traditional Middle Eastern family presented its fair share of challenges, it also provided Omar Sharif Jr. with a unique perspective and an opportunity for cultural exchange. His exposure to Middle Eastern traditions and values allowed him to appreciate the richness and diversity of his heritage.

As Omar Jr. began his journey as an LGBTQ activist, he sought to bridge the gap between LGBTQ rights and Middle Eastern advocacy by fostering understanding and dialogue. He realized that change required finding common ground and highlighting the fundamental values of acceptance, tolerance, and love that exist across cultures.

Through his experiences growing up in a traditional Middle Eastern family, Omar Sharif Jr. learned the importance of authenticity, empathy, and cultural sensitivity. These values would become the foundation of his advocacy work as he embarked on a lifelong mission to bridge the gaps between LGBTQ rights and Middle Eastern cultures. His story serves as an inspiration to individuals around the world who face similar challenges and strive to create a more inclusive and accepting society.

## Early Signs of Activism and Advocacy

Growing up in a traditional Middle Eastern family, Omar Sharif Jr. was exposed to a culture that held conservative views on many social issues, including LGBTQ rights. However, even from a young age, there were early signs that Omar was destined for a life of activism and advocacy.

1. Unconventional Thinking:

From a young age, Omar demonstrated a sense of independent thinking and a willingness to question societal norms. He was never satisfied with accepting things as they were without challenging the status quo. This inquisitive nature would later prove instrumental in his journey as an LGBTQ activist.

2. Empathy and Compassion:

Omar had an innate sense of empathy and compassion towards others. He could deeply feel the struggles and pain faced by marginalized individuals, including those from the LGBTQ community. His natural inclination to help and support those in need laid the foundation for his future activism.

3. Sense of Justice:

Omar's strong sense of justice was evident early on. He couldn't stand the discrimination and inequality he witnessed around him. This righteous indignation fueled his passion for fighting for equal rights and social justice, particularly for LGBTQ individuals who were often marginalized and oppressed.

4. Artistic Expression:

Omar found solace and self-expression through the arts. Whether it was performing in school plays or exploring various creative outlets, art became a means for him to voice his thoughts and emotions. This artistic inclination would later play a crucial role in his ability to advocate for LGBTQ rights through media and entertainment.

5. Curiosity and Desire for Knowledge:

Omar possessed a thirst for knowledge and a curiosity about the world. He sought out information and engaged in meaningful conversations to broaden his understanding of different cultures, perspectives, and social issues. This intellectual curiosity would become a powerful tool in his advocacy work, helping him to challenge societal norms and educate others about LGBTQ rights.

6. Taking a Stand:

Even as a young person, Omar was unafraid to take a stand for what he believed in. Whether it was defending a classmate who faced bullying or speaking up against discriminatory practices, he demonstrated courage and a willingness to fight for justice. This early resilience paved the way for his future activism in the face of adversity.

7. Empowering Others:

Omar had a natural ability to inspire and empower those around him. He uplifted others with his words and actions, encouraging them to embrace their authentic selves and break free from societal constraints. This innate leadership quality enabled him to become a powerful advocate for LGBTQ rights, empowering others to do the same.

It is important to note that these early signs of activism and advocacy were not isolated incidents but rather a culmination of experiences and personal growth. They laid the foundation for Omar's journey towards becoming a trailblazer in LGBTQ and Middle Eastern advocacy. As we delve deeper into his story, we will explore the transformative moments and challenges that shaped his remarkable path.

# Discovering His Identity

## Coming to Terms with His Sexuality

Coming to terms with one's sexuality can be a challenging journey for anyone, but for Omar Sharif Jr., it was a particularly complex process. Growing up in a traditional Middle Eastern family, where homosexuality is often considered taboo and stigmatized, Omar had to confront his own feelings and navigate a path towards self-acceptance.

Like many LGBTQ individuals, Omar experienced internal conflicts and a sense of isolation as he tried to come to terms with his sexuality. As a young boy, he was aware of his attraction to other boys, but societal expectations and cultural norms made it difficult for him to express these feelings openly. This forced him to hide his true self and conform to the expectations placed upon him.

1. **Repression and Denial:** Omar initially struggled with denial and tried to suppress his true feelings. He believed that if he ignored his attraction to the same sex, it would eventually go away. However, this tactic only led to further confusion and inner turmoil.

2. **Exploration and Self-Discovery:** Over time, Omar began to explore his sexuality and seek answers. He delved into LGBTQ literature, online communities, and personal conversations with trusted friends. This process allowed him to gain a deeper understanding of his own identity and realize that his feelings were valid.

3. **Emotional Turmoil:** Coming to terms with his sexuality was an emotional roller coaster for Omar. He experienced moments of self-doubt, fear, and even guilt. He questioned how his family and community would react if they found out about his true self. These emotions tested his resilience, but they also fueled his determination to live authentically.

4. **Seeking Support:** Throughout this process, Omar sought support from individuals who had gone through similar experiences. LGBTQ support groups, counseling services, and online platforms became invaluable sources of strength and guidance. Finding a community that understood and accepted him played a crucial role in Omar's journey towards self-acceptance.

5. **Acceptance and Self-Love:** After much introspection and self-reflection, Omar came to understand that his sexuality was an intrinsic part of who he was. He realized that embracing his true self was not only necessary for his own happiness but also for the betterment of LGBTQ individuals in his community and beyond. This recognition allowed Omar to embrace his sexuality with pride and self-love.

Omar Sharif Jr.'s journey towards accepting his sexuality is an inspiring example of the resilience and courage required to confront societal norms and embrace personal truths. His story serves as a reminder that self-acceptance is a necessary step in the path towards advocating for LGBTQ rights and fostering understanding in communities worldwide.

**Example Problem:**

Omar is attending a family gathering where he knows he will face questions about his personal life, including his relationship status. He is concerned about coming out to his relatives, as he is unsure of their reactions. Omar approaches you, asking for advice on how to navigate this potentially challenging situation. What guidance could you offer him?

**Solution:**

Navigating family gatherings as an LGBTQ individual can be complicated, especially when dealing with relatives who may have different cultural or religious beliefs. Here are a few strategies that Omar could consider:

1. **Choose the right time and place:** Omar should consider having one-on-one conversations with family members who are more likely to be receptive and understanding. It is important to create a comfortable setting where open and honest dialogue can take place without distractions or interruptions.

2. **Educate and inform:** Omar can prepare resources such as articles, books, or documentaries that explain LGBTQ identities and issues in a relatable and accessible manner. This will allow him to address any misconceptions or stereotypes that his

family may hold.

3. **Express vulnerability and emotions:** Sharing personal experiences and emotions can help Omar's family members understand the significance of his journey towards self-acceptance. By expressing his vulnerabilities and fears, he can appeal to their empathy and foster a deeper understanding.

4. **Acknowledge cultural and religious beliefs:** Omar should be sensitive to the fact that his relatives' reaction may be influenced by cultural or religious beliefs. By acknowledging and respecting their perspectives, he can help open up a constructive dialogue that focuses on shared values of love, acceptance, and family.

5. **Seek mediators or allies:** Having supportive family members or friends who can act as mediators during these conversations can be beneficial. These individuals can help address any tensions, answer questions, and provide a different perspective that supports Omar's journey.

It is important to remember that each family dynamic is unique, and navigating these discussions requires careful consideration. While it can be challenging, approaching these conversations with empathy, patience, and an open mind can lay the foundation for greater acceptance and understanding within the family.

By following these strategies, Omar can create an environment where his relatives are more likely to understand and accept his sexuality, fostering a sense of unity and love within the family.

## Conclusion

Coming to terms with one's sexuality is a deeply personal and transformative journey. Omar Sharif Jr.'s courageous exploration and eventual acceptance serve as an inspiration to others who may be struggling with their own identities. By embracing his true self, Omar has been able to become a powerful advocate for LGBTQ rights and bridge the gap between LGBTQ activism and Middle Eastern advocacy. His story reminds us of the importance of self-love, resilience, and the need for a more inclusive world. The journey towards self-acceptance is ongoing, and Omar's unwavering commitment to his advocacy work stands as a testament to the transformative power of embracing one's truth.

## The Struggle of Hiding His True Self

In this section, we delve into the personal journey of Omar Sharif Jr. and the immense struggle he faced in hiding his true self. The battle between societal expectations and personal authenticity is one that many individuals within the

LGBTQ community face, but for Omar, it was further compounded by the cultural norms of the Middle East.

Growing up in a traditional Middle Eastern family, Omar understood from an early age the importance of conforming to societal expectations. The pressure to adhere to traditional gender roles and norms weighed heavily on him. Omar felt the weight of these expectations, which dictated that he must marry a woman and fulfill the duty of starting a family.

As a young boy, Omar displayed early signs of his true identity, but he quickly learned that these signs needed to be concealed and suppressed. He developed a chameleon-like ability to adapt to his surroundings, molding himself into the image that society expected of him. However, these constant efforts to hide his true self took a toll on his mental and emotional well-being.

The struggle to hide his true self became even more challenging as Omar Sharif Jr. gained recognition and success in the entertainment industry. As the grandson of the legendary actor Omar Sharif, the expectations placed upon him to uphold the family's legacy and adhere to traditional values became even more pronounced. The fear of disappointing his family and losing their love and support intensified his internal conflict.

The burden of hiding his true self began to manifest in different areas of Omar's life. He became surrounded by a constant state of anxiety, fearing that his secret would be exposed. The psychological toll of living a double life was challenging, as he had to constantly filter his thoughts, actions, and emotions in order to maintain the facade.

Furthermore, the fear of rejection from society reinforced the need to remain hidden. Omar experienced firsthand the deeply ingrained social stigma and prejudice against the LGBTQ community in the Middle East. The severe consequences, including legal repercussions and social ostracism, added another layer of complexity to his struggle.

Within this web of secrecy, Omar found solace in the few unexpected places where he could be his authentic self. Supportive friends who accepted him without judgment played a crucial role in helping him navigate this challenging journey. Moreover, he discovered online communities that provided a virtual safe space where he could connect with others facing similar challenges.

However, as the years went by, the weight of hiding his true self became increasingly unbearable. The toll on his mental health and overall well-being were undeniable. The decision to live authentically emerged as the only option for Omar if he ever hoped to find true happiness and fulfillment.

In the next section, we will delve into the pivotal moment when Omar Sharif Jr. made the life-altering decision to embrace his true self and live authentically, regardless of the consequences. It was a defining moment that would catapult him into becoming an iconic LGBTQ advocate both in the Middle East and on the global stage.

But first, let us pause for a moment and reflect on the immense courage it took for Omar to confront his fears, shatter the chains of hiding, and step into the light of his true self. It is a journey that resonates with countless individuals around the world, reminding us of the universal struggle for acceptance, love, and our fundamental right to be who we truly are.

## Finding Support in Unexpected Places

In Omar Sharif Jr.'s journey of self-discovery and acceptance, he encountered numerous challenges and hurdles. However, amidst the turmoil, he also found support in unexpected places. These experiences not only shaped his personal growth but also influenced his activism and advocacy for the LGBTQ community.

One unexpected source of support came from his extended family members. Growing up in a traditional Middle Eastern family, Omar initially feared rejection and alienation. However, to his surprise, he found solace in the acceptance and understanding shown by some family members. It was through their love and support that he gained the courage to embrace his identity and live authentically. This realization taught him a powerful lesson – that sometimes, the people we least expect to stand by our side can become our greatest allies.

Additionally, Omar discovered support in the LGBTQ community itself. When he started to explore his sexuality, he joined LGBTQ organizations and engaged with queer individuals who had gone through similar experiences. In these spaces, he found a sense of belonging, acceptance, and empowerment. The LGBTQ community became his chosen family, providing him with the strength to navigate the challenges he faced as a gay man in the Middle East.

Moreover, Omar found support in unexpected friendships. As he began to openly share his story, he encountered individuals from different backgrounds and cultures who stood by his side. These new friendships challenged his preconceived notions and shattered stereotypes. They showed him that support can be found in the most unlikely of places and that people's capacity for empathy and understanding transcend societal norms and cultural boundaries.

One particular example of finding support in an unexpected place was through his professional network. As Omar stepped into the public eye as an activist, he encountered individuals within the media and entertainment industry who were eager to lend their support. Through collaborations and partnerships, he was able to amplify his message and reach wider audiences. These unexpected alliances not only provided a platform for his activism but also helped challenge and change societal perceptions about LGBTQ individuals.

In reflecting on these experiences, Omar realized the importance of fostering empathy and understanding across different communities. His journey taught him that prejudice and discrimination can be overcome when people have the opportunity to connect on a human level, beyond cultural and societal expectations. He learned that when individuals from diverse backgrounds come together to support a common cause, the impact and reach of advocacy work can be far-reaching and powerful.

To illustrate the significance of finding support in unexpected places, consider the story of Sarah, a young LGBTQ individual living in a conservative society. Sarah, like Omar, faced challenges in accepting her identity and feared rejection from her family and friends. However, through a support group at her university, Sarah found solace in the stories and experiences of others who had walked a similar path. As she gained a sense of belonging and community, Sarah's confidence grew, and she became an advocate herself, working towards creating safe spaces for LGBTQ individuals in her local community.

In conclusion, Omar Sharif Jr.'s journey of self-discovery and advocacy highlights the importance of finding support in unexpected places. From his extended family to the LGBTQ community, from newfound friendships to professional alliances, these connections became sources of strength and encouragement. They reinforced the power of empathy, understanding, and unity in overcoming societal prejudice and discrimination. The journey of finding support in unexpected places is a reminder that sometimes, the greatest allies may be waiting in the most surprising corners of our lives.

So, my dear readers, never underestimate the potential for support and understanding, for it may emerge from the most unassuming of sources.

## The Decision to Live Authentically

In this section, we will explore the pivotal moment when Omar Sharif Jr. made the courageous decision to embrace his true self and live authentically. We will delve into the internal struggles he faced, the support he found, and the impact this decision had on his life and activism.

### Coming to Terms with His Sexuality

For Omar Sharif Jr., discovering his true sexual orientation was a journey of self-exploration and self-acceptance. Growing up in a traditional Middle Eastern family, he faced societal pressures and norms that often stigmatize LGBTQ individuals. As a young man, he grappled with his own feelings and desires that did not align with the heterosexual expectations placed upon him.

It was during his adolescent years that Omar began to realize his attraction to other men. This realization was met with a mixture of confusion, fear, and self-doubt. He questioned his identity and struggled with feelings of guilt and shame, fearing the consequences of living a life that deviated from societal norms.

## The Struggle of Hiding His True Self

In a society where homosexuality is often viewed as taboo, Omar understood the potential risks of revealing his true self. He realized that embracing his sexuality would mean challenging deeply ingrained cultural and religious beliefs. The fear of rejection, isolation, and even harm was a constant reminder of the societal barriers he faced.

Omar's decision to hide his true self was not easy. He lived a dual life, presenting a façade to the world while suppressing his authentic identity. This inner conflict took an emotional toll, as he yearned for acceptance and the freedom to be his true self. However, the fear of judgment and persecution kept him in a state of constant apprehension.

## Finding Support in Unexpected Places

Despite the challenges and fears he faced, Omar Sharif Jr. was fortunate to find support in unexpected places. He discovered allies who accepted him unconditionally and provided a safe haven for him to express his true self. These allies formed a network of friends, mentors, and organizations dedicated to supporting LGBTQ individuals.

One key aspect of Omar's journey was connecting with other LGBTQ individuals who had undergone similar experiences. Their stories of struggle, resilience, and triumph inspired him to confront his own fears and embrace his identity. These connections provided a sense of belonging and empowerment, reinforcing the courage to live authentically.

## The Decision to Live Authentically

The turning point in Omar Sharif Jr.'s life came when he made the life-altering decision to live authentically. This decision was not made lightly, as it required immense bravery, self-acceptance, and a willingness to challenge societal expectations.

Omar recognized that living authentically meant risking the loss of relationships, opportunities, and societal approval. However, he also realized that denying his true self would lead to a life filled with regret and unhappiness. With unwavering determination, he made the conscious choice to embrace his sexuality and face the challenges that lay ahead.

By deciding to live authentically, Omar opened himself up to a world where he could fully express his true identity. This decision marked the beginning of a remarkable journey towards self-discovery, personal growth, and advocacy.

**Impact on Omar's Life and Activism**

Living authentically had a profound impact on Omar Sharif Jr.'s life and activism. Embracing his true self allowed him to break free from the shackles of societal expectations and find genuine happiness and fulfillment.

From a personal perspective, living authentically enabled Omar to build stronger, more authentic relationships. It allowed him to foster a deep sense of self-acceptance and self-love, which radiated positively into all aspects of his life.

In terms of his activism, the decision to live authentically gave Omar a powerful platform to advocate for LGBTQ rights. By sharing his own story, he amplified the voices of countless individuals who faced similar struggles. His authenticity and vulnerability inspired others to embrace their own identities and paved the way for greater acceptance and understanding.

Furthermore, the decision to live authentically deepened Omar's commitment to bridging LGBTQ advocacy and Middle Eastern advocacy. By living as an openly gay Middle Eastern man, he challenged societal norms, shattered stereotypes, and worked towards dismantling the barriers that hindered progress in both communities.

In conclusion, the decision to live authentically was a transformative moment in Omar Sharif Jr.'s life and activism. It marked a shift from a life of hiding to a life of honesty and authenticity. Despite the challenges and risks involved, Omar's courageous decision brought immense personal growth, inspired countless others, and furthered the cause of LGBTQ and Middle Eastern advocacy.

# Navigating Two Worlds

## Embracing His LGBTQ Identity

In this section, we delve into Omar Sharif Jr.'s journey of embracing his LGBTQ identity in the face of cultural and societal challenges. We explore the importance of self-discovery, acceptance, and the courage it takes to live authentically.

## Understanding Self-Identity

Coming to terms with one's sexuality is a deeply personal and transformative process. For Omar Sharif Jr., this journey began with the exploration of his own self-identity. Growing up in a traditional Middle Eastern family, where homosexuality is often stigmatized, he faced unique challenges in accepting his true self.

## The Struggle of Hiding His True Self

Omar Sharif Jr. experienced the struggle of hiding his true self to conform to societal expectations. Like many LGBTQ individuals, he faced the fear of rejection, discrimination, and isolation. The pressure to conform can be overwhelming, particularly in conservative cultures where LGBTQ identities are often deemed as taboo or even illegal.

## Finding Support in Unexpected Places

Amidst the struggle, Omar found solace and support in unexpected places. Through his journey, he discovered allies who helped him navigate societal barriers and overcome the fear of self-expression. Finding a support system is crucial for LGBTQ individuals, providing the framework needed to nurture self-acceptance and embrace their true identities.

## The Decision to Live Authentically

After years of introspection and self-discovery, Omar Sharif Jr. made the brave decision to live authentically. In doing so, he embraced his LGBTQ identity and found the courage to challenge societal norms. His journey serves as an inspiration to many, encouraging individuals to stay true to themselves and never apologize for who they are.

## The Challenges of Being Openly Gay in the Middle East

As an openly gay individual living in the Middle East, Omar Sharif Jr. faced unique challenges. Homosexuality is highly stigmatized in many Middle Eastern cultures, leading to discrimination, marginalization, and even violence against LGBTQ individuals. However, Omar's journey of self-acceptance and advocacy highlights the importance of pushing for change and challenging cultural norms.

### Breaking Cultural Norms through Advocacy

Omar Sharif Jr. recognized the need to break cultural norms and challenge preconceived notions surrounding LGBTQ identities in the Middle East. Through his advocacy work, he has become a beacon of hope for LGBTQ individuals in the region, striving to create a more inclusive and accepting society. His efforts serve as a reminder that change is possible, even in the face of adversity.

### Balancing His Public and Private Life

Living openly as an LGBTQ individual comes with its own set of challenges, particularly for individuals in the public eye. Omar Sharif Jr. had to navigate the delicate balance between his public and private life. This includes managing personal relationships, addressing public scrutiny, and staying true to his values while advocating for LGBTQ rights.

### Finding Strength in Identity

Embracing his LGBTQ identity has not only transformed Omar Sharif Jr.'s life but has also become a source of strength and purpose. By embracing his true self, he found the power to advocate for LGBTQ rights, challenge societal norms, and drive change. His journey is a testament to the transformative power of self-acceptance and the resilience that comes with embracing one's true identity.

In this section, we explored Omar Sharif Jr.'s journey of embracing his LGBTQ identity. We discussed the challenges he faced, the importance of self-discovery and acceptance, and the transformative power of living authentically. Omar's story serves as an inspiration for individuals facing similar struggles, reminding us that embracing our true selves can lead to personal growth, empowerment, and the capacity to effect change.

### The Challenges of Being Openly Gay in the Middle East

Being openly gay in the Middle East comes with numerous challenges and obstacles. The region has a complex cultural, religious, and socio-political landscape that often places significant restrictions on LGBTQ individuals. This section explores the difficulties faced by LGBTQ individuals in the Middle East and highlights the importance of advocacy and support in overcoming these challenges.

## Oppression and Discrimination

One of the biggest challenges faced by openly gay individuals in the Middle East is the pervasive oppression and discrimination they encounter. Homosexuality is largely considered taboo in many Middle Eastern societies, with deeply rooted cultural and religious beliefs often fueling negative attitudes towards the LGBTQ community. This can lead to ostracism, social stigma, and even violence against LGBTQ individuals.

**Example:** In countries like Saudi Arabia and Iran, same-sex relationships are criminalized, and individuals can face severe punishment, including imprisonment or even the death penalty. This climate of fear and persecution makes it incredibly challenging for openly gay individuals to exist without constantly living in fear for their safety and well-being.

## Social Isolation and Rejection

Being openly gay in the Middle East often leads to social isolation and rejection from friends, family, and the broader community. LGBTQ individuals may face discrimination and prejudice within their own families, leading to a breakdown in relationships and a lack of support systems.

**Example:** Many LGBTQ individuals in the Middle East are forced to hide their true selves and live in the closet, unable to express their authentic identities. This isolation can have profound effects on mental health, leading to feelings of loneliness, depression, and anxiety.

## Lack of Legal Protections

Another significant challenge faced by openly gay individuals in the Middle East is the absence of legal protections against discrimination and hate crimes. Many Middle Eastern countries lack comprehensive anti-discrimination laws that safeguard the rights of LGBTQ individuals.

**Example:** In Jordan, while homosexuality is legal, there are no legal protections against discrimination based on sexual orientation. This leaves LGBTQ individuals vulnerable to mistreatment in areas such as employment, housing, and healthcare, further exacerbating their marginalization.

## Limited Access to LGBTQ Resources and Support

Openly gay individuals in the Middle East often have limited access to LGBTQ resources and support structures. Due to the hostile environment and lack of legal protections, many LGBTQ organizations and safe spaces are unable to openly operate in the region.

**Example:** Pride parades and LGBTQ community centers are virtually non-existent in most Middle Eastern countries. This lack of support leaves LGBTQ individuals without access to crucial resources, such as mental health services, peer support groups, and educational workshops.

## Silencing of LGBTQ Voices

The silencing of LGBTQ voices in the Middle East further compounds the challenges faced by openly gay individuals. LGBTQ individuals may encounter censorship, restrictions on freedom of expression, and limited opportunities to share their experiences and advocate for their rights.

**Example:** Online platforms and social media networks are often monitored or censored, making it difficult for LGBTQ individuals to connect with each other and share their stories. The fear of reprisal or backlash can silence LGBTQ voices, further perpetuating the invisibility and marginalization of the community.

## Advocacy and Support: Navigating the Challenges

Despite the challenges posed by being openly gay in the Middle East, there is a growing movement of advocacy and support that seeks to overcome these obstacles. LGBTQ individuals and their allies are working tirelessly to create safe spaces, challenge societal norms, and advocate for equal rights and protections.

**Example:** Organizations like the Arab Foundation for Freedoms and Equality (AFE) and Helem in Lebanon provide vital resources, support, and advocacy for LGBTQ individuals in the Middle East. These organizations play a crucial role in fostering a sense of community, providing legal aid, and promoting social acceptance.

## The Power of Visibility and Education

Visibility and education play significant roles in challenging stereotypes, fostering acceptance, and creating change in the Middle East. Openly gay individuals who are willing to share their stories and experiences can have a profound impact on shifting societal attitudes and dispelling misconceptions about homosexuality.

**Example:** Ahmad Danny Ramadan, a gay Syrian-Canadian author, has used his platform to raise awareness about the challenges faced by LGBTQ individuals in the Middle East. Through his powerful storytelling, he aims to humanize the LGBTQ experience and inspire empathy and understanding.

## Embracing Intersectionality

Recognizing the intersectionality of various identities and experiences is crucial when addressing the challenges faced by openly gay individuals in the Middle East. LGBTQ individuals may also face additional forms of discrimination based on their gender, socioeconomic status, or religious background.

**Example:** The LGBTQ community in the Middle East is incredibly diverse, encompassing individuals from various cultural, religious, and ethnic backgrounds. Embracing intersectionality means acknowledging the unique challenges faced by different individuals within the LGBTQ community and working towards inclusive solutions.

## International Solidarity and Collaboration

Building alliances and fostering connections with global LGBTQ movements can provide critical support to LGBTQ individuals in the Middle East. International solidarity and collaboration can amplify their voices, increase visibility, and put pressure on governments to address the challenges faced by the LGBTQ community.

**Example:** The collaboration between Middle Eastern LGBTQ organizations and global advocacy groups like Human Rights Watch and Amnesty International has helped shine a spotlight on the challenges faced by LGBTQ individuals in the region. It has also drawn attention to the urgent need for policy reform and cultural change.

In conclusion, being openly gay in the Middle East comes with a multitude of challenges, including oppression, discrimination, social isolation, and limited access to resources and support. However, through advocacy, education, and international collaboration, there is hope for a more inclusive and accepting future for LGBTQ individuals in the Middle East.

## Breaking Cultural Norms through Advocacy

In this section, we will explore how Omar Sharif Jr. has been breaking cultural norms through his advocacy work. He has been pushing boundaries and challenging long-held beliefs in order to create a more inclusive society for LGBTQ individuals in the Middle East.

## Understanding Cultural Norms

Cultural norms refer to the behaviors and beliefs that are considered acceptable and expected within a particular society or culture. In the Middle East, traditional values and religious beliefs often shape cultural norms, and these norms can be particularly restrictive when it comes to LGBTQ rights and acceptance.

Breaking cultural norms requires courage, determination, and a deep understanding of the cultural context. Omar Sharif Jr. recognizes the importance of respecting cultural traditions while advocating for change. He navigates the fine line between challenging cultural norms and alienating communities by promoting dialogue and understanding.

## Promoting Dialogue and Education

One of the key strategies Omar Sharif Jr. employs to break cultural norms is promoting dialogue and education. By engaging in conversations about LGBTQ issues, he aims to challenge misconceptions and stereotypes that exist within Middle Eastern societies.

Through his advocacy work, Omar Sharif Jr. encourages open discussions about sexual orientation and gender identity, providing a platform for individuals to ask questions, share their concerns, and learn from one another. This approach fosters empathy and understanding, helping to bridge the gap between traditional values and LGBTQ acceptance.

## Collaborations with Traditional Institutions

Another way Omar Sharif Jr. breaks cultural norms is through collaborations with traditional institutions. By partnering with religious leaders, community organizations, and educational institutions, he aims to initiate conversations about LGBTQ rights from within established structures.

These collaborations allow him to challenge traditional beliefs in a respectful and inclusive manner. By presenting evidence-based arguments and sharing personal stories, he aims to create a space for dialogue and reflection, encouraging gradual change rather than confrontation.

## Storytelling and Personal Narratives

Storytelling is a powerful tool for challenging cultural norms and changing hearts and minds. Omar Sharif Jr. understands the impact of personal narratives and uses his voice to share his own story. By telling his story, he humanizes the LGBTQ experience and breaks down stereotypes.

Through interviews, articles, and public speaking engagements, Omar Sharif Jr. shares his journey, highlighting the struggles and triumphs of being LGBTQ in the Middle East. His personal narrative serves as a catalyst for empathy, encouraging others to question their preconceived notions and reconsider their stance on LGBTQ issues.

## Cultural Sensitivity and Contextualization

Breaking cultural norms requires a nuanced understanding of the cultural, religious, and social context in which change is sought. Omar Sharif Jr. emphasizes the importance of cultural sensitivity in his advocacy efforts.

He recognizes that change cannot be imposed from the outside but rather must arise from within the community. By contextualizing the struggle for LGBTQ acceptance within the framework of existing cultural values, he creates a space for dialogue and understanding.

## Challenges and Considerations

Breaking cultural norms through advocacy is not without its challenges. Omar Sharif Jr. has faced criticism, backlash, and even threats due to his outspoken stance on LGBTQ rights. However, he remains committed to his cause, understanding that change takes time and perseverance.

It is important to note that breaking cultural norms should always be approached with respect and sensitivity. Each culture has its own unique set of values and beliefs, and progress towards LGBTQ acceptance must take into account these complexities.

## Conclusion

Through his work, Omar Sharif Jr. has been at the forefront of breaking cultural norms in the Middle East. By promoting dialogue, collaborating with traditional institutions, sharing personal narratives, and maintaining cultural sensitivity, he has made significant strides in creating a more inclusive society.

His advocacy serves as an inspiration for LGBTQ individuals and allies around the world, demonstrating the power of challenging cultural norms in the pursuit of equality and acceptance.

## Balancing His Public and Private Life

Finding and maintaining a balance between one's public and private life can be a challenging task for anyone, but for someone like Omar Sharif Jr. who is a prominent LGBTQ activist, it can be even more complex. In this section, we will delve into the strategies and challenges faced by Omar Sharif Jr. in balancing his personal and public life, and the lessons we can learn from his experiences.

### Navigating Public Scrutiny

As an LGBTQ activist, Omar Sharif Jr. has chosen to live his life openly and authentically, advocating for equality and acceptance for all individuals, regardless of their sexual orientation. However, this decision comes with its fair share of challenges, particularly in regards to privacy.

Being in the public eye means that every aspect of Sharif's life is subject to scrutiny and judgment. Balancing the need to remain true to oneself while maintaining a level of privacy can be a delicate dance. Omar has often had to weigh the importance of his personal life against the greater mission of his activism.

### Setting Boundaries

To navigate the challenges of a public and private life, Omar has had to establish clear boundaries for himself and those around him. This includes carefully selecting what aspects of his personal life he chooses to share with the public and what he keeps private. By setting boundaries, he is able to maintain a sense of control and protect his own well-being.

For example, Omar makes a conscious effort to separate his personal relationships from his public persona. He understands the importance of keeping certain aspects of his personal life private, which allows him to maintain healthy relationships and protect the privacy of his loved ones.

### Prioritizing Self-Care

As an advocate for LGBTQ rights, it can be easy to become consumed by the cause and neglect one's own well-being. However, Omar recognizes that taking care of oneself is essential in order to continue the fight for equality.

Sharif prioritizes self-care by engaging in activities that bring him joy and provide a sense of balance. Whether it's spending quality time with loved ones, engaging in hobbies, or practicing mindfulness, he understands the importance of finding moments of peace and fulfillment in order to thrive as an individual and as an activist.

### Surrounding Himself with a Supportive Network

A strong support system is crucial when balancing a public and private life. Omar has cultivated a network of friends, family, and fellow activists who provide emotional support, guidance, and understanding.

These individuals not only offer unconditional support but also help him navigate the challenges that come with his activism. Whether it's providing a listening ear, offering insights, or brainstorming solutions, having a supportive network allows Omar to balance his public and private life more effectively.

### Finding Time for Reflection and Recharge

In the midst of a demanding advocacy career, it can be easy to become overwhelmed and lose sight of one's personal goals and values. Omar Sharif Jr. understands the importance of regularly taking time for reflection and recharge.

He carves out moments for introspection, allowing himself the opportunity to evaluate his experiences and reconnect with his purpose. This time for reflection allows him to recalibrate, gain new perspectives, and make adjustments as needed in order to maintain a healthy balance between his public and private life.

### The Unconventional Solution: Embracing Vulnerability

In his journey of balancing his public and private life, Omar Sharif Jr. has found an unconventional yet powerful solution: embracing vulnerability. By openly sharing his personal experiences, struggles, and triumphs, he has created a genuine connection with his audience and supporters.

Being vulnerable not only humanizes him but also inspires others to do the same. Through his vulnerability, Omar has fostered a sense of community and fostered a belief that we are all in this together. This has allowed him to maintain a better balance between his public and private life by reminding himself and others that it's okay to be both an activist and a person with private struggles.

### Conclusion

Balancing a public and private life is a constant juggling act, demanding careful navigation and thoughtful decision making. Omar Sharif Jr. has successfully managed to find harmony between his personal and activist pursuits by establishing boundaries, prioritizing self-care, surrounding himself with support, finding time for reflection and recharge, and embracing vulnerability.

This section has explored the challenges and triumphs faced by Omar in balancing his public and private life. By following his example, future activists can learn valuable lessons on maintaining a healthy and fulfilling balance between their personal lives and their commitment to advocating for meaningful change.

# The Road to Activism

## The Catalyst for Change

Change is often sparked by a defining moment, an event that propels an individual towards a greater purpose. For Omar Sharif Jr., the catalyst for his journey of activism and advocacy was a profound realization that ignited a desire for social change.

1. Coming Face-to-Face with Injustice

Growing up in a traditional Middle Eastern family, Omar Sharif Jr. witnessed firsthand the discrimination and stifling of voices within the LGBTQ community. He observed the immense courage of those who lived in secrecy, concealing their true identities for fear of persecution and harm. It was during his formative years that he began to question the deep-rooted prejudice that existed within his own culture.

2. A Transformative Personal Experience

The catalyst for change came when Omar had an epiphany of self-discovery. It was a moment of profound realization when he recognized his own sexual orientation, and with it, the burden of living in authenticity. This personal journey of self-acceptance propelled him towards a greater purpose - to raise awareness and fight for the rights of the LGBTQ community, not only within his own community but on a global scale.

3. Facing the Battle Head-On

With a newfound sense of purpose, Omar found himself facing a battle of immense proportions. He recognized that the fight for LGBTQ rights and acceptance was not an easy one, especially within the conservative landscape of the Middle East. However, this only ignited his determination to bring about change, regardless of the obstacles that lay ahead.

4. Transforming Personal Struggles into a Catalyst

Omar's personal struggles with his identity served as a catalyst for empathy and understanding. He knew that he needed to use his own experiences to connect with others who may be going through similar challenges. By openly discussing his journey, he hoped to provide solace and support to those who felt trapped or isolated because of their sexual orientation.

5. Spreading Awareness and Education

The catalyst for change also lay in the power of education and awareness. Omar recognized the need to debunk myths and misconceptions about the LGBTQ community, particularly within the conservative Middle Eastern society. He made it his mission to provide accurate information, addressing the fears and misconceptions that hindered progress towards acceptance and equality.

6. Building Bridges Between Communities

In his quest for change, Omar Sharif Jr. understood the importance of bridging LGBTQ advocacy with Middle Eastern advocacy. He aimed to create a space where both communities could come together to challenge societal norms and promote understanding. Through his work, he sought to build connections and engage in dialogue, encouraging collaboration and intersectionality in the fight for equality.

7. Inspiring Others to Join the Movement

The catalyst for change also involved inspiring others to join the movement. Omar recognized that change could not be brought about by one individual alone. He utilized his platform to encourage others to embrace their identities and become advocates for change. By sharing his story and speaking openly about his struggles, he hoped to empower and motivate others to take action.

In conclusion, the catalyst for change in Omar Sharif Jr.'s journey towards activism and advocacy was a profound realization of his own identity and the injustices faced by the LGBTQ community. With unwavering determination and a commitment to education and awareness, he set out to spark change, bridging the gap between LGBTQ and Middle Eastern activism, inspiring others to join the movement and lay the groundwork for a more inclusive future. The journey was not without its challenges, but Omar's resilience and passion continue to pave the way for a better, more accepting world.

## Connecting with LGBTQ Communities

Connecting with LGBTQ communities is a vital aspect of Omar Sharif Jr.'s advocacy work. By actively engaging with and supporting these communities, he has been able to amplify their voices and work towards creating a more inclusive and accepting world. In this section, we will explore how Omar Sharif Jr. connects with LGBTQ communities, the importance of community involvement, and the impact it has on his activism.

## Understanding the Importance of LGBTQ Communities

To effectively advocate for LGBTQ rights, it is crucial to understand the experiences, struggles, and aspirations of the LGBTQ community. Omar Sharif Jr. recognizes the diverse and intersectional nature of this community, which includes individuals from different racial, ethnic, and socio-economic backgrounds, as well as varying gender identities and sexual orientations.

By actively engaging with LGBTQ communities, Omar Sharif Jr. gains firsthand knowledge of their unique challenges and needs. This understanding allows him to tailor his advocacy efforts and provide support in a way that is both meaningful and impactful.

## Creating Safe and Supportive Spaces

Omar Sharif Jr. recognizes the importance of creating safe and supportive spaces for LGBTQ individuals. These spaces serve as a refuge where they can freely express themselves, seek guidance, and connect with others who share their experiences.

One way Omar Sharif Jr. fosters these spaces is through his involvement and support of LGBTQ organizations and community centers. These organizations not only provide essential resources and services but also empower LGBTQ individuals to become agents of change within their own communities.

## Collaborating with LGBTQ Organizations

Collaborating with LGBTQ organizations is an important aspect of Omar Sharif Jr.'s advocacy work. By partnering with these organizations, he leverages their expertise, resources, and networks to amplify his impact.

Through partnerships, Omar Sharif Jr. has been able to organize events, workshops, and campaigns that address the specific needs of LGBTQ communities. By pooling together their knowledge and resources, these collaborations create a powerful force for change.

## Engaging with LGBTQ Youth

Engaging with LGBTQ youth is a particular focus of Omar Sharif Jr.'s advocacy efforts. He understands the unique challenges faced by young LGBTQ individuals, such as bullying, discrimination, and isolation. By reaching out to them, he offers support, guidance, and mentorship.

A key approach Omar Sharif Jr. uses to connect with LGBTQ youth is through educational initiatives. He participates in school visits, workshops, and seminars to raise awareness, educate, and inspire young individuals to embrace their identities and stand up against discrimination.

## Providing Resources and Support

Omar Sharif Jr. recognizes the importance of providing resources and support to LGBTQ communities. By hosting events, creating online platforms, and developing informative materials, he ensures that individuals have access to the tools and information they need to navigate their personal journeys.

Moreover, he collaborates with mental health professionals, counselors, and support groups to offer guidance and assistance to LGBTQ individuals who may be facing challenges related to their identities.

## Empowering LGBTQ Voices

One of the fundamental principles of Omar Sharif Jr.'s advocacy work is to uplift and amplify LGBTQ voices. He recognizes that it is not his place to speak for the community but rather to create platforms and opportunities for their voices to be heard.

Through interviews, panel discussions, and public speaking engagements, Omar Sharif Jr. ensures that LGBTQ individuals are at the forefront of the conversation. By showcasing their stories and experiences, he challenges stereotypes and promotes understanding and acceptance.

## The Unconventional Approach: LGBTQ Storytelling

In addition to traditional advocacy methods, Omar Sharif Jr. employs an unconventional approach to connect with LGBTQ communities: storytelling. By sharing his personal journey and experiences, he not only humanizes the struggles faced by LGBTQ individuals but also inspires others to embrace their authentic selves.

Through various mediums such as books, documentaries, and social media, Omar Sharif Jr. utilizes the power of storytelling to evoke empathy, spark conversations, and foster a sense of community.

## Example: LGBTQ Youth Empowerment Workshop

To further illustrate how Omar Sharif Jr. connects with LGBTQ communities, let's dive into an example of a workshop he organizes specifically for LGBTQ youth empowerment.

In collaboration with local LGBTQ organizations and community centers, Omar Sharif Jr. hosts a full-day workshop aimed at empowering and supporting LGBTQ youth. The workshop covers a range of topics, including self-acceptance, mental health, legal rights, and community involvement.

The workshop starts with an icebreaker activity that allows participants to get to know each other and establish a safe and inclusive space. This is followed by interactive sessions on self-acceptance and embracing one's identity. Mental health professionals provide guidance on coping strategies, dealing with discrimination, and building resilience.

Legal experts then educate participants on their rights and highlight the importance of advocating for LGBTQ-inclusive policies and legislation. This segment emphasizes the power of collective action and the role youth can play in effecting change.

The workshop also includes panel discussions featuring LGBTQ individuals who have excelled in various fields, such as arts, sports, and activism. These panelists share their experiences, challenges, and successes, inspiring participants to pursue their passions and dreams without limiting themselves based on their sexual orientation or gender identity.

Throughout the day, participants have access to a resource fair, where they can learn about local LGBTQ organizations, support groups, and online platforms that provide additional resources and support.

By the end of the workshop, LGBTQ youth walk away feeling empowered, connected, and armed with the knowledge and tools to navigate their personal journeys with confidence. They are encouraged to join ongoing community initiatives, engage with LGBTQ organizations, and become advocates for change within their own communities.

## Summary

In this section, we explored how Omar Sharif Jr. connects with LGBTQ communities as part of his advocacy work. We discussed the importance of understanding LGBTQ experiences, creating safe spaces, collaborating with organizations, engaging with LGBTQ youth, providing resources and support, and empowering LGBTQ voices.

Omar Sharif Jr.'s approach to connecting with LGBTQ communities showcases the power of community involvement in driving change. By actively engaging with LGBTQ individuals, he ensures that his advocacy efforts are informed, impactful, and aligned with their needs. Through his continuous connection with LGBTQ communities, Omar Sharif Jr. strives to create a more inclusive and accepting world for all.

## The Power of Visibility and Representation

Visibility and representation are fundamental pillars of LGBTQ activism, and Omar Sharif Jr. has harnessed their power to bring about meaningful change. In this section, we will delve into the importance of visibility, explore the impact of representation, and discuss how Omar Sharif Jr. has utilized these forces to advance LGBTQ and Middle Eastern advocacy.

## Visibility: Shining a Light on LGBTQ Lives

Visibility refers to the act of openly and authentically sharing one's LGBTQ identity with the public. It is the act of shining a light on the lives and experiences of LGBTQ individuals, challenging societal norms, and breaking down stigmas. Visibility creates opportunities for connection, understanding, and empathy among individuals of different backgrounds.

One of the main reasons visibility is crucial is that it counters stereotypes and misconceptions about LGBTQ individuals. By being visible, LGBTQ people can educate others about the diversity within their community and debunk harmful myths. This helps to foster acceptance and create a more inclusive environment for all.

Sharif Jr. understands the power of visibility and has fearlessly lived his life authentically. By openly discussing his own journey of self-discovery and coming to terms with his sexuality, he has become a beacon of hope and inspiration for others struggling with their own identities. His decision to be visible has shown countless LGBTQ individuals that they are not alone and that it is possible to lead fulfilling lives true to their authentic selves.

## Representation: Amplifying LGBTQ Voices

Representation goes hand in hand with visibility. It is the act of ensuring that LGBTQ individuals are portrayed accurately and authentically in the media, entertainment industry, and other public platforms. Representation matters because it allows LGBTQ individuals to see themselves reflected positively in society, thus validating their experiences and identities.

Omar Sharif Jr. recognizes the significance of representation, particularly for marginalized communities such as LGBTQ people in the Middle East. By leveraging his platform as a public figure, he has actively sought out opportunities to amplify LGBTQ voices and stories. Whether through interviews, media appearances, or collaborations with artists and filmmakers, he has worked tirelessly to ensure that the narratives of LGBTQ individuals are heard and respected.

Representation also plays a vital role in challenging cultural norms and prejudices. By showcasing diverse representations of LGBTQ individuals, including those from Middle Eastern backgrounds, Sharif Jr. is dismantling harmful stereotypes and fostering greater understanding and acceptance within both LGBTQ and Middle Eastern communities.

## The Impact of Visibility and Representation

The power of visibility and representation cannot be overstated. They have the potential to spark social change, inspire others, and create a more inclusive world. By being visible and advocating for representation, Omar Sharif Jr. has opened doors for dialogue, empathy, and progress.

Visibility and representation help combat the isolation and discrimination that many LGBTQ individuals face. When LGBTQ people see others who share their experiences and identities, it instills a sense of belonging and hope. It shows them that they can embrace their true selves without fear or shame.

Moreover, visibility and representation empower LGBTQ individuals to share their stories and contribute to a broader social dialogue. By sharing their experiences, they humanize the LGBTQ community, breaking down barriers of ignorance and prejudice. This can lead to greater acceptance, policy changes, and a shift in societal attitudes towards LGBTQ rights.

In conclusion, visibility and representation are powerful tools in the fight for LGBTQ equality and Middle Eastern advocacy. Omar Sharif Jr., through his own visibility and commitment to representation, has demonstrated the transformative impact of sharing one's story authentically. It is through these efforts that we can support and uplift marginalized communities, creating a more inclusive future for all.

## Building Bridges between LGBTQ and Middle Eastern Advocacy

In this section, we delve into the complex task of bridging LGBTQ and Middle Eastern advocacy, exploring the challenges, opportunities, and strategies required to bridge these two important movements. Omar Sharif Jr. has been at the forefront of this effort, using his platform to create dialogue and understanding between these seemingly disparate worlds. Let's embark on this journey together as we explore the intricacies of building bridges between LGBTQ and Middle Eastern advocacy.

## Understanding the Context

To effectively bridge LGBTQ and Middle Eastern advocacy, it is crucial to understand the unique cultural, social, and historical contexts of both movements. Middle Eastern societies, steeped in tradition and sometimes influenced by conservative religious beliefs, have often been challenging environments for LGBTQ individuals.

Cultural sensitivities and deeply ingrained beliefs about gender roles and sexuality can create significant barriers to acceptance and understanding. However, it is essential to recognize that the Middle East is not a monolith; there is incredible diversity within the region, with varying levels of acceptance and legal protections for LGBTQ individuals.

At the same time, the LGBTQ movement has made significant strides globally, championing for equal rights, societal acceptance, and the recognition of LGBTQ rights as human rights. By understanding the progress made in the LGBTQ movement and respecting the cultural nuances of the Middle East, we can begin the work of building bridges.

## Creating Dialogue and Understanding

Building bridges between LGBTQ and Middle Eastern advocacy requires fostering dialogue and understanding. This starts with creating safe spaces for open and honest conversations about LGBTQ rights and Middle Eastern cultural norms. These spaces can be physical locations or virtual platforms where individuals from both communities can share their experiences and perspectives.

As activists, it is important to approach these conversations with empathy and respect, acknowledging the lived experiences of LGBTQ individuals in the Middle East while also advocating for their rights. By actively listening and engaging in constructive dialogue, we can build trust and lay the groundwork for collaboration and change.

## Cultural Sensitivity and Collaboration

To bridge LGBTQ and Middle Eastern advocacy successfully, it is vital to approach the work with cultural sensitivity. This means understanding and respecting the unique cultural, religious, and social dynamics of the Middle East while advocating for LGBTQ rights.

Collaboration between LGBTQ activists and Middle Eastern organizations is key to creating effective change. By partnering with local LGBTQ groups, human rights organizations, and community leaders, we can align goals and build relationships based on understanding and mutual respect. This collaboration allows for the development of tailored strategies that consider the specific needs and challenges faced by LGBTQ individuals in the Middle East.

**Education and Awareness**

Education plays a central role in building bridges between LGBTQ and Middle Eastern advocacy. By challenging misconceptions and stereotypes, we can foster greater understanding and empathy within both communities.

Educational initiatives that highlight the shared values and experiences between LGBTQ individuals and Middle Eastern communities can help bridge cultural divides. This includes promoting LGBTQ-inclusive curriculum, organizing workshops and seminars, and leveraging social media and other platforms to raise awareness and share diverse narratives.

**Advocating for Legal Protections and Policy Changes**

Advocacy for legal protections and policy changes is paramount for building bridges between LGBTQ and Middle Eastern advocacy. Understanding the legal landscape and working within its framework is crucial for effecting change while respecting the rights and sovereignty of each nation.

By engaging with policymakers, local governments, and international organizations, LGBTQ activists can advocate for reforms that protect the rights of LGBTQ individuals while addressing the concerns of Middle Eastern societies. This approach ensures that the advocacy efforts are grounded in local cultural contexts, making them more effective and sustainable.

**Personal Stories and Representation**

Personal stories have the power to humanize the LGBTQ experience, making it relatable and fostering empathy. By sharing personal stories of LGBTQ individuals in the Middle East, we can challenge stereotypes and create a deeper understanding of the struggles they face.

Representation in media and popular culture is another essential aspect of building bridges. By amplifying the voices and experiences of LGBTQ individuals from the Middle East, we can broaden societal perspectives and challenge negative narratives.

## Challenges and Future Outlook

Building bridges between LGBTQ and Middle Eastern advocacy is not without its challenges. Balancing the desire for equality and acceptance with cultural sensitivities can be a delicate task. It requires navigating a complex web of social, political, and religious factors while ensuring the safety and well-being of LGBTQ individuals.

However, the increasingly interconnected nature of our world presents opportunities for collaboration and change. By embracing diversity, fostering understanding, and leveraging the power of collective action, we can continue to build bridges and create a more inclusive and accepting society.

As we look to the future, it is crucial to keep pushing the boundaries of LGBTQ and Middle Eastern advocacy. This requires continued efforts to challenge existing norms, advocate for legal protections, and provide support and resources for LGBTQ individuals in the Middle East.

Omar Sharif Jr.'s trailblazing journey serves as an inspiration and reminder that change is possible, even in the face of daunting challenges. By following in his footsteps and building upon the foundation he has laid, we can create a world where LGBTQ individuals in the Middle East are valued, respected, and fully embraced for who they are.

In conclusion, building bridges between LGBTQ and Middle Eastern advocacy is a complex but necessary undertaking. It requires understanding the cultural context, fostering dialogue, and collaboration, advocating for legal protections, and challenging stereotypes. By working together, we can create a world that champions equality, respect, and acceptance for all individuals, regardless of their sexual orientation or gender identity.

# Impactful Influences

## Trailblazers of LGBTQ Activism

In the fight for LGBTQ rights, there have been numerous trailblazers whose tireless efforts and groundbreaking work have paved the way for future generations. These individuals have fearlessly advocated for equality, challenged societal norms, and shattered barriers. Their stories and accomplishments serve as a reminder of the progress made and the work that still lies ahead. In this section, we will explore some of these remarkable trailblazers and the impact they have had on LGBTQ activism.

### Harvey Milk: The Mayor of Castro Street

No discussion of LGBTQ activism would be complete without mentioning Harvey Milk, an American politician and the first openly gay elected official in California. Milk's courageous fight for LGBTQ rights and his commitment to serving the community made him a true hero and a trailblazer.

Milk became involved in politics in the 1970s, advocating for the rights of the LGBTQ community and other marginalized groups. In 1977, he was elected to the San Francisco Board of Supervisors, becoming the first openly gay person to hold public office in a major U.S. city. During his short time in office, Milk worked tirelessly to pass legislation promoting LGBTQ rights, fighting against discrimination, and advocating for the rights of all marginalized communities.

Tragically, Milk's life was cut short when he was assassinated in 1978. However, his legacy lives on, and his impact on LGBTQ activism cannot be overstated. Milk's unwavering dedication and his message of hope and unity continue to inspire activists around the world.

### Marsha P. Johnson: A Pioneer of the LGBTQ Rights Movement

Marsha P. Johnson, a transgender woman of color, was a prominent figure in the LGBTQ rights movement and a key participant in the Stonewall uprising in 1969. Johnson's activism and advocacy played a crucial role in advancing the rights of transgender individuals and the overall LGBTQ community.

As a founding member of the Gay Liberation Front and the Street Transvestite Action Revolutionaries (STAR), Johnson fought tirelessly for the rights of transgender individuals, sex workers, and other marginalized communities. She was known for her activism, her vibrant personality, and her unwavering commitment to social justice.

Johnson's influence extended far beyond her own community. Her advocacy and visibility helped to raise awareness of the struggles faced by transgender individuals, challenging societal prejudices and paving the way for future generations.

### Audre Lorde: The Intersectional Champion

Audre Lorde, a black lesbian poet, writer, and feminist, made significant contributions to both feminist and LGBTQ activism. Lorde's work focused on the intersections of race, gender, and sexuality, highlighting the importance of embracing and celebrating one's multiple identities.

Throughout her career, Lorde fearlessly confronted systems of oppression and encouraged others to do the same. She challenged traditional feminist movements to be more inclusive of the experiences and struggles faced by women of color and LGBTQ individuals.

Lorde's writings, including her groundbreaking collection of essays titled "Sister Outsider," continue to be regarded as influential works within feminist and LGBTQ literature. Her emphasis on intersectionality provides a framework for understanding the interconnections between various forms of oppression and the importance of solidarity and inclusion.

### Sylvia Rivera: A Transgender Trailblazer

Sylvia Rivera, a transgender activist and self-identified drag queen, was another key figure in the Stonewall uprising and a steadfast advocate for transgender rights. Rivera's activism focused on the needs of transgender individuals, especially those who faced homelessness, poverty, and discrimination.

Through her involvement in STAR, alongside Marsha P. Johnson, Rivera provided support and resources for transgender youth and individuals living on the streets. She fought for transgender rights within the LGBTQ rights movement itself, challenging the exclusion and marginalization of transgender voices.

Rivera's activism spanned decades, and she continued to fight for transgender rights until her passing in 2002. Her courage and resilience in the face of adversity continue to inspire activists working for the rights and inclusion of transgender individuals.

## Conclusion

The trailblazers of LGBTQ activism showcased in this section have left an indelible mark on the fight for equality. They have shattered barriers, challenged societal norms, and paved the way for the progress we have seen in LGBTQ rights today. These individuals embody the strength and resilience of the LGBTQ community, and their relentless activism serves as a beacon of hope for future generations. As we honor their legacy, we must also recognize the ongoing struggle for full equality and commit ourselves to continuing their fight. The journey towards a more inclusive world is far from over, but with the inspiring examples set by these pioneers, we can move forward with determination and hope.

## Lessons from Historical LGBTQ Figures

In the journey of LGBTQ activism, it is important to look back and draw inspiration from historical figures who have paved the way. These individuals have not only made significant contributions to the LGBTQ community but have also left behind valuable lessons that can guide us in our fight for equality and acceptance. Let's explore some of these influential figures and the lessons we can learn from their experiences.

1. **Harvey Milk:** Harvey Milk was a pioneering LGBTQ activist and the first openly gay elected official in California. His life and tragic assassination have become emblematic of the struggle for LGBTQ rights. Milk believed in the power of visibility and representation. He taught us that by openly expressing our authentic selves, we can challenge societal norms and inspire change. Milk's famous quote, "Hope will never be silent," reminds us to continue speaking up and advocating for our rights, even in the face of opposition.

2. **Marsha P. Johnson:** Marsha P. Johnson was a transgender woman and prominent figure in the Stonewall uprising of 1969, one of the catalysts for the LGBTQ rights movement. She fought tirelessly for the rights of transgender individuals and those most marginalized within the LGBTQ community. Johnson's activism teaches us the importance of intersectionality and inclusivity. She showed us that fighting for LGBTQ rights means fighting for the rights of all individuals, regardless of their gender identity, race, or socioeconomic background.

3. **Audre Lorde:** Audre Lorde was a Black lesbian poet, writer, and civil rights activist. She emphasized intersectional feminism and encouraged the LGBTQ community to understand the links between various forms of oppression. Lorde taught us the significance of self-care and self-love as tools for activism. She believed that by embracing our identities and practicing self-acceptance, we can become stronger advocates for change.

4. **Bayard Rustin:** Bayard Rustin was a gay African American civil rights leader and strategist. He played a crucial role in organizing the March on Washington for Jobs and Freedom in 1963. Rustin's activism taught us the importance of coalition-building and solidarity. He recognized that progress can only be achieved through collective action and alliances with other social justice movements.

5. **Sylvia Rivera:** Sylvia Rivera was a transgender activist and advocate for LGBTQ rights, particularly within the transgender and gender non-conforming communities. She co-founded Street Transvestite Action Revolutionaries (STAR), an organization that provided support and shelter for LGBTQ youth. Rivera's legacy teaches us the need for inclusivity within the LGBTQ community itself. She fought against the erasure of transgender experiences and reminded us of the importance of uplifting all voices within the movement.

These historical LGBTQ figures have left us with a rich tapestry of experiences and lessons. By studying their stories, we gain insight into the challenges they faced, the strategies they employed, and the resilience they displayed. Their legacies remind us that progress is not linear and that the fight for LGBTQ rights is ongoing. We must continue to learn from their lessons and apply them to our advocacy work, always striving to create a more inclusive and accepting world for all.

## The Role of Family in Supporting His Activism

The unconditional love and support of family can be a powerful driving force for individuals pursuing their passions and making a difference in the world. In Omar Sharif Jr.'s journey as an LGBTQ activist, his family played a crucial role in supporting his activism and empowering him to create change.

From an early age, Omar Sharif Jr. was surrounded by a family that nurtured his curiosity and instilled in him the values of compassion, understanding, and acceptance. Growing up in a traditional Middle Eastern family, he was exposed to the richness of his cultural heritage and the importance of family bonds. However, he also faced the challenge of reconciling his identity as a member of the LGBTQ community with the cultural expectations of his background.

1. Family as an Anchor of Love and Understanding: Family acts as a safe haven where one can truly be themselves without fear of judgment or rejection. In Omar's case, his family provided him with a supportive environment where he could freely explore and express his true identity. They listened to his concerns, validated his emotions, and reassured him that he was loved unconditionally. This unwavering support bolstered his confidence and gave him the courage to embrace his LGBTQ identity openly.

2. Strength in Diversity: Omar Sharif Jr.'s family taught him the value of embracing diversity and respecting different perspectives. They encouraged open discussions about LGBTQ issues and Middle Eastern culture, fostering a safe space for dialogue and understanding. This nurturing environment allowed Omar to navigate the complexities of his identity and advocate for change without feeling isolated or disconnected from his heritage.

3. Challenging Stereotypes and Promoting Change: Omar's family recognized the power of his voice and encouraged him to challenge stereotypes and misconceptions surrounding the LGBTQ community. They instilled in him a sense of responsibility to create change and make a positive impact on society. By supporting his activism, they reinforced the belief that change begins at home and within communities, and that it is essential to bridge the gap between LGBTQ and Middle Eastern advocacy.

4. Role Models and Inspiration: Family serves as a source of inspiration and motivation. In Omar's case, his family provided him with role models, including his famous grandfather, Omar Sharif. Seeing his grandfather's success and how he used

his platform to advocate for causes close to his heart, Omar Jr. felt inspired to follow in his footsteps and make a difference in his own right. The support he received from his family fueled his determination to push boundaries and challenge societal norms.

5. Balancing Family Values and Activism: Navigating activism while honoring family values can be a delicate balancing act, especially in cultures where certain topics are considered taboo. Omar's family taught him the importance of respect and open communication, allowing him to bridge the gap between his activism and cultural sensitivities. They helped him find compromise and navigate difficult conversations with respect and understanding.

In conclusion, the role of family in supporting Omar Sharif Jr.'s activism cannot be overstated. They provided him with a solid foundation of love and acceptance, empowering him to embrace his LGBTQ identity and create positive change. Through their support, they demonstrated the power of love, understanding, and open dialogue in breaking down barriers and transforming lives. Family can truly be a driving force behind an individual's activism, nurturing their passions and enabling them to leave a lasting impact on the world.

## Collaborations with Other Advocates

Collaboration is at the heart of any successful advocacy movement, and Omar Sharif Jr. has been a shining example of this principle throughout his career. His ability to build bridges between different communities and work with fellow activists has played a significant role in advancing LGBTQ rights and Middle Eastern advocacy. In this section, we will explore some of Omar Sharif Jr.'s notable collaborations and the impact they have had on his advocacy work.

### The Power of Unity

Omar Sharif Jr. understands that meaningful change happens when people come together. He has actively sought out opportunities to collaborate with other advocates, recognizing the strength in shared goals and collective action. By joining forces with like-minded individuals and organizations, he has been able to amplify his voice and realize greater impact.

### Global Alliances

One of the pillars of Omar Sharif Jr.'s advocacy work has been to establish global alliances with organizations and activists working towards LGBTQ rights and Middle Eastern advocacy. Through these alliances, he has been able to leverage international support and resources to tackle issues on a larger scale. By joining forces with organizations such as Human Rights Campaign, Amnesty International, and GLAAD, Omar has been able to draw attention to the challenges faced by LGBTQ individuals in the Middle East and advocate for change.

## Collaborations within the Middle East

Recognizing the unique cultural context of the Middle East, Omar Sharif Jr. has also actively collaborated with local organizations and activists in the region. These collaborations have been crucial in challenging societal norms and working towards greater acceptance of LGBTQ individuals. By partnering with organizations like the Arab Foundation for Freedoms and Equality, Helem, and Bedayaa, Omar has been able to foster dialogue and create safe spaces for LGBTQ individuals in the Middle East.

## Intersectional Collaborations

Omar Sharif Jr. understands that the fight for LGBTQ rights intersects with various other social justice movements. He has actively sought collaborations with advocates from diverse backgrounds, recognizing the importance of building coalitions to bring about lasting change. By working alongside activists fighting for racial justice, gender equality, and immigrant rights, Omar has been able to promote a more holistic approach to advocacy, addressing the intersecting issues faced by marginalized communities.

## Creative Collaborations

In addition to working with fellow activists, Omar Sharif Jr. has also embraced collaborations within the creative space. He has partnered with artists, filmmakers, and writers to use their platforms to raise awareness and challenge stereotypes. Through collaborations with filmmakers and production companies, he has contributed to the creation of LGBTQ-inclusive media content and provided representation for queer individuals.

## Lessons Learned from Collaborations

Collaborating with other advocates has taught Omar Sharif Jr. important lessons about the power of unity and dialogue. Through these collaborations, he has learned the importance of active listening, empathy, and understanding different perspectives. He has recognized the value of building relationships based on trust and respect, working towards shared goals while acknowledging each individual's unique strengths and contributions.

## Unconventional Approach

One unconventional approach Omar Sharif Jr. has employed is collaborating with religious leaders and communities. Recognizing the impact of religion on society in the Middle East, he has reached out to religious leaders to engage in conversations about LGBTQ rights and acceptance. By opening dialogues and building bridges, he has been able to challenge misconceptions and foster more inclusive interpretations of religious teachings.

## Life Stories and Collaborations

One powerful way Omar Sharif Jr. has collaborated with other advocates is through sharing personal life stories. By openly discussing his coming out journey and the challenges he has faced, he has inspired others to embrace their own identities and become advocates for change. Through collaborations with LGBTQ storytellers, writers, and journalists, Omar has been able to amplify the voices and experiences of LGBTQ individuals, breaking down barriers and fostering understanding.

In conclusion, collaborations with other advocates have played a crucial role in Omar Sharif Jr.'s journey as an LGBTQ activist and Middle Eastern advocate. From establishing global alliances to working with local organizations and embracing intersectional collaborations, Omar has shown that collective action is essential for driving meaningful change. Through these collaborations, he has learned valuable lessons, challenged societal norms, and built bridges between communities. By continuing to collaborate and inspire others, Omar Sharif Jr. is leaving a lasting impact on LGBTQ rights and Middle Eastern advocacy.

# Chapter 2: The Rise of a LGBTQ Icon

## Chapter 2: The Rise of a LGBTQ Icon

### Chapter 2: The Rise of a LGBTQ Icon

In this chapter, we explore the incredible journey of Omar Sharif Jr., as he rises to become a LGBTQ icon. From the challenges he faced in his personal life to the impact he made on a global scale, Sharif's story is one of resilience, authenticity, and empowerment.

### The Coming Out Journey

Amidst the glitz and glamour of Hollywood, coming out as LGBTQ is never an easy decision. The pressure to conform to societal norms often leaves individuals feeling isolated and afraid. In this section, we delve into Sharif's internal struggle and the pivotal moment when he decided to publicly come out.

Sharif's journey to self-discovery was a difficult and emotional one. He grappled with societal expectations and the fear of being rejected by his loved ones. However, he found the courage to embrace his authentic self and reveal his true identity to the world. This decision was not only freeing for Sharif, but it also served as an inspiration for countless others struggling with their own sexual orientation.

### Dealing with Reactions and Backlash

Coming out is a deeply personal and vulnerable experience, and it often elicits a variety of reactions from those around you. In this section, we explore how Sharif navigated through the sometimes difficult and challenging responses to his public coming out.

While Sharif received an outpouring of love and support, he also faced backlash and prejudice from individuals who were less accepting. This section highlights the resilience and strength displayed by Sharif as he tackled this adversity head-on. His unwavering commitment to authenticity and his unyielding belief in the power of love and acceptance have made him a beacon of hope for LGBTQ individuals worldwide.

### Inspiring Others to Embrace Their Identities

Once Sharif publicly embraced his LGBTQ identity, he transformed into a powerful advocate for others who were still struggling to do the same. In this section, we explore the ways in which Sharif used his platform to inspire and uplift others.

Through his activism and advocacy work, Sharif became a voice for the voiceless. He shared his personal story, spoke about the challenges he faced, and encouraged others to embrace their own identities and live authentically. By sharing his journey, Sharif helped countless individuals feel seen, understood, and empowered.

### The Power of Authenticity in Activism

In the world of activism, authenticity is a powerful tool for change. It allows individuals to connect with others on a deeper level and fosters a sense of trust and understanding. This section explores how Sharif harnessed the power of his authentic self to create impactful change.

Sharif's unwavering commitment to living his truth has allowed him to break down barriers and challenge the norms of society. By embracing his LGBTQ identity with pride and dignity, he has opened the hearts and minds of people from all walks of life. This section delves into the ways in which Sharif's authenticity has served as a catalyst for social change and paved the way for a more inclusive and accepting world.

## Conclusion

The rise of Omar Sharif Jr. as a LGBTQ icon has been nothing short of remarkable. From his personal journey of self-discovery to his global impact as an advocate, Sharif's story is one of hope, resilience, and empowerment.

In this chapter, we explored the challenges and triumphs Sharif faced as he navigated his own journey of coming out. We witnessed his strength in the face of adversity and his unwavering commitment to living an authentic life. Through his activism, Sharif has inspired countless individuals to embrace their own identities and fight for a more inclusive world.

As we move forward, we will continue to follow Sharif's legacy and explore the lasting impact of his advocacy work. In the next chapters, we will dive deeper into the specific initiatives and campaigns he undertook to bridge LGBTQ and Middle Eastern advocacy, further positioning him as an influential figure in the fight for equality.

## The Coming Out Journey

### The Decision to Publicly Come Out

In this pivotal chapter of Omar Sharif Jr.'s extraordinary journey, we delve into the personal and emotional struggle he faced when deciding to publicly come out as a gay man. It is a decision that would not only shape his life but also ignite a powerful flame of advocacy and inspire countless others to embrace their own identities.

### The Weight of Secrecy

Omar Sharif Jr., the grandson of the legendary actor Omar Sharif, grew up in a traditional Middle Eastern family where expectations of conformity and adherence to strict cultural norms loomed large. For years, he bore the weight of secrecy, hiding a fundamental aspect of his identity from his loved ones and the world.

> **Problem**
>
> Can you imagine the anxiety and emotional toll of hiding an integral part of who you are? Reflect on a time when you felt the need to hide or suppress a part of yourself. How did it make you feel? How did it impact your relationships and well-being? Share your thoughts in the comments below.

### Torn Between Fear and Authenticity

As Omar Sharif Jr. wrestled with his sexuality, fear and uncertainty became constant companions. The prospect of rejection and isolation loomed large in his mind, as he grappled with the potential consequences of coming out in a society where being LGBTQ was not widely accepted.

> **Problem**
>
> Imagine facing the decision to reveal your true self to the world, knowing that it might come at a high personal cost. Reflect on the fears and doubts you might have in such a situation. What obstacles would you anticipate facing? How would you find the strength and courage to navigate these challenges? Share your thoughts in the comments below.

## Finding Support and Encouragement

In the midst of his internal struggle, Omar Sharif Jr. found unexpected sources of support and encouragement. While he had initially anticipated rejection from his family, he discovered that love and acceptance can transcend cultural boundaries. His mother, in particular, played a crucial role in offering unconditional support during this pivotal time.

> **Problem**
>
> Think about the people in your life who have shown you unwavering support during challenging times. Who has been there for you when you needed it the most? How has their support influenced your decisions and outcomes? Take a moment to reach out and express your gratitude to them.

## Embracing the Power of Authenticity

With support from loved ones, Omar Sharif Jr. made the courageous decision to embrace his true self and step into the spotlight. He recognized that living authentically was not just a personal victory but a powerful act of resistance and empowerment. By coming out publicly, he hoped to shatter stereotypes, challenge cultural norms, and inspire a new generation of LGBTQ individuals to embrace their own identities.

> **Problem**
>
> Consider the power of authenticity in your own life. How does living authentically enhance your well-being, relationships, and overall sense of fulfillment? Reflect on moments when you have chosen authenticity over conformity. What positive outcomes have emerged as a result? Share your own experiences in the comments below.

## Breaking the Chains of Secrecy

In this section, we explored the pivotal decision Omar Sharif Jr. made to publicly come out as a gay man. We witnessed his journey from the burden of secrecy to the freedom of authenticity and discovered the transformative power of embracing one's true self. In the next chapter, we will delve into how Omar Sharif Jr. took the stage as an LGBTQ icon and became a fierce advocate for change.

## Dealing with Reactions and Backlash

In his journey towards living authentically as an openly gay man, Omar Sharif Jr. faced numerous challenges, including reactions and backlash from various individuals and communities. This section explores how he navigated through these obstacles, finding strength and resilience along the way.

## The Decision to Publicly Come Out

One of the most significant moments in Omar's life was the decision to publicly come out as gay. This was a deeply personal and courageous step for him, as he knew that it would inevitably attract attention and potentially face negative reactions from different quarters. Despite the potential risks, Omar believed that his visibility as a public figure could have a positive impact on the LGBTQ community, especially in the Middle East where homosexuality is still largely stigmatized.

## Dealing with Criticism and Hate

The decision to come out always carries with it the risk of facing criticism, hate, and backlash from individuals and broader societal structures. Omar Sharif Jr. experienced his fair share of negative reactions, ranging from social media trolls to attacks from conservative religious groups. However, he never let these reactions deter him from his mission. Omar understood that being a visible advocate for LGBTQ rights meant being a target for those who opposed his cause. He faced the hate head-on, responding with grace and resilience.

## Finding Support in the LGBTQ Community

Despite the backlash, Omar found immense support within the LGBTQ community, both locally and globally. This network of support provided him with the strength and encouragement to continue his advocacy work. Through LGBTQ organizations, support groups, and initiatives, Omar was able to connect with individuals who had similar experiences and understood the challenges he faced. These connections formed a vital support structure that helped him navigate through the difficult times.

## Engaging in Constructive Dialogue

As an advocate for LGBTQ rights, Omar recognized the importance of engaging in constructive dialogue with those who held opposing views. Rather than responding to hate with more hate, he chose to seek understanding and initiate conversations that challenged misconceptions and prejudices. By approaching individuals with empathy and respect, Omar was able to bridge the divide and foster dialogue that encouraged change and acceptance.

## Turning Negativity into Motivation

In the face of backlash, Omar Sharif Jr. saw an opportunity to turn negativity into motivation. Instead of allowing the hate to discourage him, he used it as fuel to further his advocacy work. The more resistance he encountered, the more determined he became to push for change and create spaces of acceptance. Omar's ability to channel negativity into productive action served as an inspiring example to others facing similar challenges.

## Building a Supportive Network

To overcome the backlash and continue his activism, Omar surrounded himself with a supportive network of friends, allies, and fellow advocates. He understood the importance of collaboration and creating alliances with like-minded individuals and organizations. Through these connections, Omar bolstered his resilience and established a strong foundation for his advocacy work.

## Educating and Raising Awareness

Omar Sharif Jr. recognized that many negative reactions and backlash stemmed from fear, ignorance, and misinformation. To counter this, he focused on educating and raising awareness about LGBTQ issues. Through public speaking engagements, media appearances, and community events, he shared his lived experiences and provided accurate information about sexual orientation and gender identity. By doing so, he sought to dispel misconceptions and foster empathy and understanding.

## Maintaining Self-Care and Resilience

In the face of significant backlash, self-care and resilience became crucial for Omar's well-being. He recognized the need to take breaks, engage in activities that brought him joy, and seek professional support when necessary. This commitment to self-care allowed him to navigate through difficult times and continue his advocacy work effectively.

## Focusing on the Positive Impact

Throughout his journey, Omar Sharif Jr. remained focused on the positive impact he was making on individuals and communities. By keeping his goals in mind and celebrating the small victories, he was able to overcome the negativity that came his way. Omar's ability to find strength in the positive impact of his work served as a reminder that perseverance and determination can bring about tangible change.

Dealing with reactions and backlash is an inevitable part of any advocacy journey, especially when challenging long-held beliefs and societal norms. However, by staying true to oneself, seeking support, engaging in constructive dialogue, and maintaining resilience, individuals like Omar Sharif Jr. can navigate through the challenges and make a profound and lasting impact on the world around them.

## Inspiring Others to Embrace Their Identities

In this section, we explore the inspiring journey of Omar Sharif Jr. as he navigates the challenging path of self-acceptance and shares his story of embracing his LGBTQ identity. His journey not only serves as a beacon of hope for those struggling with their own identities but also inspires others to embrace their true selves.

## The Power of Personal Narrative

One of the most impactful ways that Omar Sharif Jr. inspires others is through the power of his personal narrative. By openly sharing his own struggles and triumphs, he humanizes the LGBTQ experience and creates a safe space for others to do the same.

Through heartfelt speeches, interviews, and even his social media presence, Omar breaks down barriers and shows that it is possible to live authentically in the face of adversity. His honest and vulnerable storytelling resonates with people from all walks of life, fostering empathy and understanding.

## Empowering Authenticity

Omar empowers others to embrace their identities by shining a light on the strength and courage it takes to be true to oneself. He emphasizes that there is no shame in being LGBTQ and encourages individuals to celebrate their uniqueness.

Through his advocacy work and public appearances, Omar demonstrates that authenticity is not only liberating for oneself but also a powerful catalyst for change. By living his truth, he inspires others to do the same, fostering a sense of community and empowerment within the LGBTQ community.

## Promoting Self-Discovery and Self-Acceptance

Inspiring others to embrace their identities goes beyond just coming out as LGBTQ. Omar encourages individuals to embark on a journey of self-discovery and self-acceptance, urging them to explore their passions, dreams, and values.

Through his own personal transformation, Omar demonstrates that embracing one's identity is a lifelong process. He encourages self-reflection and questioning societal norms, empowering individuals to embrace their true selves and lead fulfilling lives.

## Challenging Societal Expectations

Omar challenges societal expectations by encouraging individuals to break free from the constraints imposed by society. He inspires others to challenge gender norms, stereotypes, and expectations surrounding sexuality.

By fostering conversations about LGBTQ issues and advocating for more inclusive and accepting societies, Omar creates space for others to challenge the status quo. His fearless approach to advocacy sparks meaningful discussions and brings about positive change.

## Providing Support and Resources

Understanding the difficulties faced by individuals struggling with their identities, Omar is dedicated to providing support and resources. Through his advocacy work, he strives to ensure that LGBTQ individuals have access to mental health resources, support networks, and inclusive educational opportunities.

Omar collaborates with organizations and institutions, both within and outside the LGBTQ community, to create safe spaces and avenues for support. By connecting people with the necessary resources, he helps individuals on their journey of self-discovery and self-acceptance.

## Unconventional Approach: The Power of Art

Beyond traditional avenues of advocacy, Omar also explores the power of art in inspiring others to embrace their identities. He uses various artistic mediums such as film, theater, and literature to tell stories that challenge societal norms and ignite conversations about LGBTQ experiences.

Through the power of storytelling, visual representation, and artistic expression, Omar reaches a broader audience and encourages individuals to examine their own identities and biases. His creative approach allows for a more nuanced understanding of LGBTQ experiences, inspiring empathy and fostering acceptance within society.

## Inclusive Education: A Vehicle for Inspiration

Omar recognizes the importance of inclusive education in inspiring others to embrace their identities. He advocates for LGBTQ-inclusive curricula that provide accurate information, dispel myths, and promote understanding.

By working with educational institutions and policymakers, Omar strives to ensure that LGBTQ experiences are acknowledged and respected within the education system. Inclusive education not only fosters acceptance but also empowers individuals to embrace their identities and celebrate the diversity that exists within society.

In conclusion, Omar Sharif Jr.'s journey of embracing his LGBTQ identity serves as a powerful inspiration to others. Through personal storytelling, empowerment, challenging societal expectations, and providing support and resources, he creates a pathway for individuals to discover and embrace their true selves. Through his advocacy work, he has a lasting impact on the LGBTQ community, encouraging others to live authentically and fostering a more inclusive and accepting world.

## The Power of Authenticity in Activism

Authenticity is a powerful force that drives activism, especially when it comes to advocating for LGBTQ rights. In this section, we will explore the significance of authenticity in activism and how it can inspire change, empower individuals, and foster a sense of belonging within the LGBTQ community.

## The Importance of Being True to Oneself

Authenticity in activism begins with being true to oneself. For many LGBTQ individuals, embracing their identity can be a challenging and transformative journey. It requires acknowledging and accepting one's own truth, regardless of societal expectations or norms.

In the case of Omar Sharif Jr., his decision to publicly come out as gay was a pivotal moment in his life. By embracing his authentic self, he not only found personal liberation but also became a beacon of hope for others struggling with their sexuality. Being true to oneself is a revolutionary act that challenges the status quo and inspires others to do the same.

## Inspiring Change through Personal Stories

One of the most powerful tools in activism is the ability to share personal stories. Authenticity in activism lies in the willingness to open up and speak vulnerably about one's experiences. By sharing personal stories, activists create connections, educate others, and challenge stereotypes.

Omar Sharif Jr.'s decision to publicly share his coming out journey resonated with countless individuals across the globe. His story humanized the struggles faced by LGBTQ individuals in the Middle East and shed light on the importance of acceptance and inclusion.

*Example*: In one of his powerful speeches, Omar described the emotional turmoil he experienced while navigating his sexuality within a traditional Middle Eastern family. He eloquently shared the pain of hiding his true self and the transformative power of living authentically. This personal story not only touched the hearts of those listening but also sparked conversations and pushed boundaries within the LGBTQ community and beyond.

## Breaking Down Barriers

Authenticity in activism has the power to break down barriers and challenge preconceived notions. By being true to oneself, activists challenge societal expectations, stereotypes, and stigmas associated with being LGBTQ.

Omar Sharif Jr.'s presence as an openly gay individual from the Middle East challenges the common misconception that homosexuality is incompatible with Middle Eastern culture. By authentically sharing his experiences and advocating for LGBTQ rights, he breaks down barriers, fosters understanding, and promotes acceptance.

## Empowering Others

Authenticity in activism is empowering, both for the individuals advocating for change and for those who find inspiration in their stories. By living authentically and speaking out, activists empower others to embrace their identities, take pride in who they are, and stand up for their rights.

Omar Sharif Jr.'s authentic activism sends a powerful message to LGBTQ individuals, especially those from conservative backgrounds. By showcasing his authenticity, he inspires others to find their voice, defy societal expectations, and live their truth.

*Example*: Through his advocacy, Omar has worked with LGBTQ youth support organizations in the Middle East, empowering young individuals to embrace their identities and providing them with resources and support. By offering a safe space and encouraging authenticity, he helps create a generation of empowered LGBTQ youth who will continue to advocate for change.

## The Need for Intersectionality

Authenticity in activism must also recognize the importance of intersectionality. The LGBTQ community is diverse, and different individuals face unique challenges based on their race, ethnicity, gender identity, and socioeconomic background. To create meaningful change, activists must authentically engage with these intersecting identities and work towards a more inclusive society.

As Omar Sharif Jr. demonstrates, authentic activism includes amplifying the voices of marginalized LGBTQ individuals within the community. By recognizing and addressing the layered experiences of individuals, activism becomes more effective in advocating for equal rights and dismantling systems of oppression.

## Building Bridges through Authenticity

Authenticity in activism has the power to build bridges between different communities. By sharing personal stories and fostering genuine connections, activists can promote understanding and empathy.

Omar Sharif Jr.'s work in bridging LGBTQ and Middle Eastern advocacy is a testament to the power of authenticity. By fearlessly sharing his journey and engaging in dialogue with different communities, he creates opportunities for mutual understanding and promotes collaboration towards a shared goal of equality and acceptance.

## Conclusion

The power of authenticity in activism cannot be understated. By embracing and sharing personal stories, breaking down barriers, empowering others, and recognizing intersectionality, activists like Omar Sharif Jr. inspire change, challenge norms, and build bridges. Authenticity brings humanity, empathy, and connection to the forefront, fueling the momentum towards a more inclusive world. Let us continue to harness the power of authenticity in our own activism, making a lasting impact for generations to come.

# Omar Sharif Jr Takes the Stage

## Becoming a Voice for the Voiceless

In this chapter, we delve into the pivotal moment in Omar Sharif Jr.'s journey when he decided to become a voice for the voiceless within the LGBTQ community. It was a brave and selfless choice that would propel him into the forefront of the fight for equality and acceptance.

## The Birth of Activism

For Omar Sharif Jr., activism was not something that happened overnight. It was a gradual awakening fueled by his own personal experiences and the struggles he witnessed within the LGBTQ community. As a member of this community, he recognized the need for a voice that could represent the countless individuals who felt silenced and marginalized.

## Unveiling the Power of Visibility

One of the most powerful tools in Omar Sharif Jr.'s advocacy arsenal has been the power of visibility. By stepping into the spotlight and openly embracing his LGBTQ identity, he shattered stereotypes and challenged societal norms. He became a symbol of hope and inspiration for others who were still hiding in the shadows, afraid to be their authentic selves.

## Harnessing the Media for Change

Omar Sharif Jr. quickly realized that one of the most effective ways to reach a wide audience and effect change was through the media. He utilized his background in the entertainment industry to engage with journalists, participate in interviews, and share his story on various platforms. By doing so, he pushed boundaries and confronted uncomfortable conversations head-on, sparking much-needed dialogue around LGBTQ issues.

## Turning Adversity into Motivation

As an openly gay activist from the Middle East, Omar Sharif Jr. faced his fair share of opposition and criticism. However, instead of succumbing to these challenges, he turned them into motivation. Each negative encounter fueled his determination to push for greater LGBTQ visibility and acceptance, inspiring others to do the same.

## Collaborating with Like-minded Advocates

Omar Sharif Jr. recognized the power of collaboration and actively sought out partnerships with like-minded advocates. By joining forces with individuals and organizations that shared his vision of a more inclusive world, he amplified his voice and broadened his reach. Together, they organized events, campaigns, and initiatives that aimed to break down barriers and dismantle prejudices.

## Going Beyond Borders

Omar Sharif Jr.'s advocacy extended far beyond the borders of his home country. As a global citizen, he recognized that the fight for LGBTQ rights and acceptance was universal. He utilized his platform to connect with LGBTQ communities around the world, speaking at conferences, engaging with activists, and forming lasting partnerships. By sharing his experiences and listening to the stories of others, he fostered a sense of unity and solidarity among LGBTQ individuals worldwide.

## The Power of Personal Narratives

Throughout his journey, Omar Sharif Jr. discovered the immense power of personal narratives. By sharing his own story and encouraging others to do the same, he humanized the LGBTQ experience, challenging stereotypes and misconceptions. He recognized that by putting a face and a voice to the struggle, it became harder to ignore the injustices faced by the community.

## Embracing Vulnerability

Key to Omar Sharif Jr.'s success as an advocate has been his willingness to be vulnerable. By exposing his own fears, doubts, and insecurities, he created a safe space for others to do the same. In embracing vulnerability, he inspired empathy, understanding, and ultimately drove the movement for LGBTQ rights forward.

## Paving the Way for Change

Omar Sharif Jr.'s journey as a voice for the voiceless has left an indelible mark on the LGBTQ community. Through his fearless advocacy, he has paved the way for change, challenging societal norms, and demanding equality. His impact will continue to reverberate for generations to come, inspiring future activists to stand up, speak out, and fight for the rights of all.

## Advocacy in the Media and Entertainment Industry

The power of media and entertainment cannot be underestimated when it comes to advocating for LGBTQ rights. In this section, we will explore how Omar Sharif Jr. utilized the media and entertainment industry to amplify his message of inclusivity, challenge stereotypes, and promote understanding and acceptance.

## The Influence of Pop Culture

Pop culture has a significant impact on society, shaping attitudes and perceptions. Omar recognized this and saw it as an opportunity to challenge existing narratives and stereotypes surrounding LGBTQ individuals. By appearing in popular TV shows, movies, and magazines, he was able to reach a broad audience and promote LGBTQ visibility and representation.

One of the ways that Omar made waves in the media and entertainment industry was through his participation in high-profile interviews. These interviews allowed him to share his story, open up discussions about LGBTQ issues, and help normalize the LGBTQ experience. Through his appearances on talk shows, he offered personal insights, offered words of encouragement to LGBTQ individuals, and debunked common misconceptions.

## Creating Inclusive Content

Omar also recognized the importance of creating LGBTQ-inclusive content in the media and entertainment industry. He understood that representation matters and that seeing oneself reflected in mainstream media can have a powerful impact on individuals' self-acceptance and society's perception of the LGBTQ community.

As an advocate, Omar actively supported and participated in the creation of LGBTQ-inclusive TV shows, movies, and commercials. He worked closely with writers, producers, and directors to ensure authentic portrayals of LGBTQ characters and storylines. By doing so, he challenged harmful stereotypes and promoted understanding and empathy.

Omar's involvement in LGBTQ-inclusive projects not only contributed to a more inclusive media landscape but also showcased the talent and diversity within the LGBTQ community. His presence and visibility in these projects helped break down barriers and further normalize LGBTQ experiences.

## Using Social Media as a Platform

In addition to traditional media, Omar made effective use of social media platforms to advocate for LGBTQ rights. Social media provided him with a direct and immediate connection to his audience, allowing him to share stories, experiences, and resources.

Through his social media accounts, Omar shared personal stories, triumphs, and struggles, inviting his followers into his journey. He also used these platforms to educate and raise awareness on LGBTQ issues, sharing resources, news articles, and impactful stories from around the world. His engaging and relatable content helped spark conversations and inspire others to get involved in advocating for LGBTQ rights.

## Shaping Public Opinion

Advocacy in the media and entertainment industry goes beyond personal appearances and content creation. Omar recognized the importance of engaging with different audiences and shaping public opinion through various media channels.

He actively participated in panel discussions, debates, and public speaking engagements to address the misconceptions and prejudices that exist about LGBTQ individuals. By sharing personal anecdotes, research-based evidence, and logical arguments, he challenged homophobia, transphobia, and discrimination in all their forms. His persuasive and charismatic style of speaking played a crucial role in changing hearts and minds.

## Capitalizing on Influence

Omar understood that having a platform in the media and entertainment industry comes with immense influence, which he harnessed to further LGBTQ advocacy. He collaborated with fellow celebrities and influencers to amplify their collective voices and reach wider audiences.

Through partnerships and collaborations, Omar leveraged his relationships with other advocates to promote inclusivity and equality. By joining forces with like-minded individuals, he created a united front against discrimination and pushed for policy changes that protected the rights of LGBTQ individuals.

## Unconventional Yet Relevant Approach

To break down barriers, Omar employed an unconventional yet relevant approach in advocating for LGBTQ rights in the media and entertainment industry. He utilized humor and wit to engage his audience, making challenging conversations more approachable and relatable.

Omar actively participated in comedy sketches, stand-up performances, and satirical content that centered around LGBTQ experiences. By using humor as a tool, he was able to address serious issues with a touch of levity, opening the door for fruitful discussions and dispelling myths surrounding the LGBTQ community.

## Resources and Support

To support LGBTQ individuals in the media and entertainment industry, Omar Sharif Jr. established a resource center that provides guidance, mentorship, and networking opportunities. This center serves as a hub for LGBTQ professionals, including actors, writers, directors, and producers, to connect, share experiences, and collaborate on projects that break barriers and promote LGBTQ inclusion.

Additionally, Omar actively supports LGBTQ organizations and initiatives within the industry, providing financial assistance and raising awareness through fundraising events and campaigns. By nurturing the LGBTQ talent within the media and entertainment industry, he ensures a sustainable and ongoing legacy of LGBTQ advocacy.

## Conclusion

Advocacy in the media and entertainment industry is a powerful tool that Omar Sharif Jr. utilized to challenge stereotypes, promote LGBTQ visibility, and shape public opinion. Through personal appearances, the creation of inclusive content, and leveraging social media, he was able to amplify his message and inspire change. His unconventional yet relevant approach and commitment to supporting LGBTQ professionals within the industry lay a foundation for a more inclusive and accepting future.

## Challenging Stereotypes and Misconceptions

Stereotypes and misconceptions often plague the LGBTQ community, reinforcing harmful biases and discrimination. In this section, we explore how Omar Sharif Jr. has challenged these stereotypes and fought against the misconceptions that hinder progress towards LGBTQ acceptance and equality. By using his platform and influence, Omar has effectively debunked myths, shattered preconceived notions, and paved the way for a more inclusive society.

### Breaking Down Stereotypes

Stereotypes surrounding the LGBTQ community are deeply ingrained in society and can perpetuate harmful beliefs. One common stereotype is that LGBTQ individuals are inherently promiscuous or deviant. Omar has been instrumental in debunking this stereotype by openly sharing his personal experiences and showcasing the diversity within the community.

By highlighting the complexity of LGBTQ lives, Omar has shown that love, commitment, and healthy relationships are just as important to LGBTQ individuals as they are to anyone else. His engagement with the media, including interviews and public appearances, has allowed him to challenge these stereotypes head-on, shedding light on the fact that sexuality does not dictate one's moral character.

### Dispelling Myths

Misconceptions about the LGBTQ community often arise from a lack of understanding or misinformation. Omar Sharif Jr. has taken it upon himself to dispel these myths by providing factual information and personal anecdotes that humanize the LGBTQ experience.

One common myth is that homosexuality is a choice or a result of external influences. Omar has shared his journey of self-discovery, emphasizing that sexual orientation is an inherent aspect of one's identity. He has emphasized the importance of acceptance and understanding, urging society to move beyond narrow-minded assumptions and embrace the truth that sexual orientation is not a choice.

Another myth Omar has tackled is the notion that being LGBTQ is incompatible with faith or religious beliefs. As a voice for LGBTQ Muslims, he has shown that it is possible to be both religious and queer, challenging the misconception that one's sexual orientation is antithetical to their spirituality. By sharing his personal connection to Islam and his LGBTQ identity, Omar has opened up discussions about the intersection of religion and queerness, encouraging dialogue and understanding.

## Case Studies and Real-Life Examples

To further challenge stereotypes and misconceptions, Omar has used real-life examples and case studies to humanize the LGBTQ community. By sharing stories of individuals from diverse backgrounds and cultures, he has demonstrated that queer experiences are not limited to a single narrative.

One such example is Muna. With Omar's help, her story reached a global audience. Muna is a transgender woman from Saudi Arabia who faced immense challenges in her journey towards self-acceptance and gender affirmation. By highlighting Muna's story, Omar shed light on the struggles faced by transgender individuals in the Middle East and the importance of supporting and celebrating their identities.

Through these case studies, Omar has effectively dismantled stereotypes by showing the complexity, resilience, and humanity of LGBTQ individuals. By amplifying their voices and sharing their stories, he has fostered empathy and understanding, challenging the misconceptions that often persist in society.

## Educational Initiatives

Education is a key tool in challenging stereotypes and misconceptions. Omar recognized the importance of inclusive education and has worked towards creating LGBTQ-inclusive curricula and resources. By collaborating with educators and organizations, he has helped develop educational materials that promote understanding and acceptance.

Omar's initiatives have aimed to address the knowledge gap that fuels stereotypes and misunderstandings. By providing accurate information about LGBTQ identities, experiences, and history, he has equipped individuals with the tools to challenge existing biases and foster a more inclusive society.

## Promoting Intersectionality

Intersectionality, the recognition of overlapping forms of discrimination and privilege, is a crucial aspect of challenging stereotypes and misconceptions. Omar has consistently advocated for the intersectional experiences of LGBTQ individuals, emphasizing the need to consider the impact of multiple identities.

By embracing intersectionality, Omar has broadened the conversation around LGBTQ rights to include discussions on race, gender, religion, and socioeconomic status. He has highlighted the unique challenges faced by LGBTQ individuals from marginalized communities and advocated for inclusive policies and practices that address these intersecting oppressions.

## Unconventional Approach: Empathy Exercises

In his efforts to challenge stereotypes and misconceptions, Omar has adopted an unconventional approach to promote empathy and understanding. He has developed empathy exercises that encourage individuals to put themselves in the shoes of LGBTQ individuals, fostering a deeper sense of compassion and connection.

One such exercise involves participants reflecting on their own experiences of feeling excluded or misunderstood, drawing parallels between their own emotions and the experiences of LGBTQ individuals. By engaging people emotionally, Omar has facilitated meaningful conversations that humanize the LGBTQ community and bridge the divide between different identities.

## Summary

In challenging stereotypes and misconceptions, Omar Sharif Jr. has played a pivotal role in debunking myths, dispelling misinformation, and promoting understanding. Through his courageous advocacy and educational initiatives, he has fostered empathy, encouraged dialogue, and paved the way for a more inclusive society. By challenging these stereotypes head-on, Omar has left an indelible mark on the fight for LGBTQ acceptance and equality.

## Making a Global Impact

In this section, we explore how Omar Sharif Jr. has made a significant global impact through his activism and advocacy work. His efforts have not only brought attention to the LGBTQ community in the Middle East but have also helped bridge the gap between LGBTQ rights and Middle Eastern advocacy on a global scale. By leveraging his platform and utilizing various strategies, he has successfully influenced public opinion, changed societal perceptions, and contributed to policy changes worldwide.

## The International Stage

Omar Sharif Jr.'s international presence has been instrumental in raising awareness about LGBTQ issues beyond the Middle East. Through his compelling speeches and appearances at global LGBTQ conferences, he has brought attention to the challenges faced by LGBTQ individuals in the region and emphasized the need for inclusivity and equality. His eloquent and passionate delivery has captivated audiences and inspired individuals to take action in their own communities.

Furthermore, Sharif Jr. has actively collaborated with queer activists worldwide, amplifying their voices and creating solidarity among LGBTQ communities across borders. By sharing their stories and experiences, he has shed light on the diverse struggles faced by LGBTQ individuals globally, fostering a sense of shared humanity and encouraging cross-cultural understanding.

### Harnessing the Power of Media

One of the most effective platforms Sharif Jr. has utilized to make a global impact is social media. Through his active engagement on platforms such as Twitter, Instagram, and YouTube, he has reached millions of individuals from different corners of the world. By sharing his own journey, advocating for LGBTQ rights, and challenging prejudice and discrimination, he has effectively challenged societal norms and encouraged conversations about equality and acceptance.

In addition, Sharif Jr. has been a catalyst for change in the media and entertainment industry. He has pushed for LGBTQ-inclusive content, both in the Middle East and globally, challenging stereotypes and providing representation for queer individuals. By partnering with filmmakers, producers, and content creators, he has advocated for authentic portrayals of LGBTQ characters, encouraging empathy and understanding among viewers.

### Creating Safe Spaces

Recognizing the need for safe spaces for LGBTQ individuals, Sharif Jr. has been actively involved in establishing LGBTQ centers and support networks on a global scale. These spaces provide resources, counseling, and support for LGBTQ individuals, serving as a refuge from the discrimination and prejudice they may face in their daily lives. Through his efforts, he has worked towards fostering acceptance and understanding within local communities, empowering individuals to live authentically.

Furthermore, these safe spaces have played a crucial role in advocating for LGBTQ rights and educating the wider community. By organizing workshops, seminars, and educational programs, they aim to break down barriers and challenge misconceptions about the LGBTQ community. The exchange of knowledge and experiences within these spaces plays a vital role in inspiring change and fostering a more inclusive society.

## Public Speaking Engagements

Omar Sharif Jr.'s powerful public speaking has been a driving force in creating a global impact. He has engaged with diverse audiences, including universities, NGOs, and corporate organizations, spreading his message of equality and acceptance. His ability to connect with people from different backgrounds, cultures, and beliefs has been key in engaging individuals who may not have been previously exposed to LGBTQ issues.

Sharif Jr. motivates others to take action by highlighting the importance of allyship and solidarity, encouraging individuals to stand up against discrimination and actively work towards creating a more tolerant and inclusive world. With his dynamic and charismatic speaking style, he weaves personal stories, statistical evidence, and calls to action into his speeches, leaving a lasting impact on his audience.

## Inspiring Grassroots Movements

Beyond his individual efforts, Sharif Jr.'s work has inspired grassroots movements around the world. By openly sharing his experiences and struggles, he has given a voice to countless individuals who have faced similar challenges. This shared sense of resilience and defiance has fostered a global community of activists, advocating for LGBTQ rights in their own societies.

These grassroots movements have been successful in effecting change at the local level, challenging discriminatory policies, and pushing for LGBTQ-inclusive legislations. These efforts, when combined, create a ripple effect that contributes to the overall global shift towards acceptance and equality.

## The Importance of Intersectionality

Sharif Jr. recognizes the importance of intersectionality in advocating for LGBTQ rights globally. He understands that the fight for equality cannot be separated from other forms of discrimination, such as racism, sexism, and ableism. By acknowledging and addressing the interconnectedness of various forms of oppression, he has advocated for a more inclusive approach to activism.

Intersectional approaches to activism acknowledge that queer individuals are part of diverse communities and should not be reduced to a single identity. Through collaborations with organizations and individuals fighting for racial and gender equality, Sharif Jr. has emphasized the importance of solidarity and collective action, working towards an inclusive world for all.

## Conclusion

In this section, we have explored how Omar Sharif Jr. has made a significant global impact through his activism and advocacy work. Through his international presence, media engagement, creation of safe spaces, public speaking engagements, and inspiration of grassroots movements, he has effectively influenced public opinion, changed societal perceptions, and contributed to policy changes worldwide.

Moreover, by recognizing the importance of intersectionality, Sharif Jr. has demonstrated a holistic approach to activism, understanding the interconnectedness of various forms of discrimination and the need for collaboration between marginalized communities.

Omar Sharif Jr.'s ongoing journey as an advocate and his commitment to creating a more inclusive world serve as an inspiration for future generations. His legacy will continue to shape the future of LGBTQ activism, bridging the gap between LGBTQ rights and Middle Eastern advocacy, and fostering a more accepting and equal society globally.

# Bridging Cultures

## The Importance of Cultural Sensitivity

In the journey of LGBTQ activism, one aspect that is often overlooked is the importance of cultural sensitivity. Recognizing and respecting the various cultural norms, values, and traditions of different regions and communities is crucial for effective advocacy and creating lasting change. In this section, we will explore the significance of cultural sensitivity in the context of Omar Sharif Jr.'s work, as well as provide insights and strategies for navigating cultural differences in LGBTQ activism.

Cultural sensitivity is the ability to understand, appreciate, and interact effectively with individuals from diverse cultural backgrounds. In the case of LGBTQ activism, it involves recognizing the unique challenges faced by LGBTQ individuals and communities within specific cultural, social, and religious contexts. By acknowledging and respecting these differences, activists can approach their work more effectively and foster meaningful change.

One of the key reasons why cultural sensitivity is important in LGBTQ activism is the need to build bridges and form alliances with local communities. In many parts of the world, LGBTQ rights are often seen as conflicting with traditional values and beliefs. Without cultural sensitivity, activists risk alienating potential allies and hindering progress. By taking the time to understand and respect cultural nuances, activists can find common ground, challenge stereotypes, and work towards greater acceptance and understanding.

However, cultural sensitivity does not mean compromising on the principles of LGBTQ activism. It means finding the most effective ways to communicate the importance of LGBTQ rights while considering the cultural context. This requires a delicate balance between respecting cultural values and challenging discriminatory practices. Omar Sharif Jr.'s approach of engaging in open dialogue, educating, and raising awareness about LGBTQ issues within the Middle Eastern context is a testament to the power of cultural sensitivity.

An important aspect of cultural sensitivity is the inclusion of local voices and perspectives. It is essential to involve LGBTQ individuals and allies from the specific cultural context in the advocacy process. This ensures that the narrative is not dominated by outsiders but is driven by the people who are directly affected by the issues at hand. By amplifying local voices, activists can challenge stereotypes and misconceptions from within the community itself, ultimately leading to greater acceptance and understanding.

Another element of cultural sensitivity is the recognition of the intersectionality of identities. LGBTQ individuals come from diverse backgrounds and may face additional forms of discrimination based on race, ethnicity, religion, or socioeconomic status. Understanding and addressing these intersecting identities is essential for effective advocacy. By considering and addressing the unique challenges faced by LGBTQ individuals within different cultural contexts, activists can create more comprehensive and inclusive solutions.

In the era of globalization and the internet, cultural sensitivity is not only relevant within local communities but also in the global LGBTQ movement. Activists must be aware of the cultural differences within the broader movement and adapt their advocacy strategies accordingly. This means acknowledging the diverse approaches to LGBTQ rights across different regions, learning from the successes and challenges faced by activists worldwide, and collaborating with global partners to foster a more inclusive world.

It is worth noting that cultural sensitivity is not without its challenges. It requires ongoing self-reflection, a willingness to learn, and the ability to navigate complex cultural dynamics. Mistakes may be made along the way, but a genuine commitment to understanding and respecting cultural differences can help overcome these challenges. By prioritizing cultural sensitivity in LGBTQ activism, we can create a more inclusive and equitable world for all.

## Case Study: LGBTQ Advocacy in the Middle East

To illustrate the importance of cultural sensitivity in LGBTQ activism, let's look at the case of LGBTQ advocacy in the Middle East. This region is characterized by a mix of cultural, religious, and social norms that shape attitudes towards LGBTQ individuals.

In countries where homosexuality is criminalized or highly stigmatized, advocating for LGBTQ rights requires a nuanced and culturally sensitive approach. Activists like Omar Sharif Jr. have been at the forefront of this movement, navigating the complexities of the cultural landscape in the Middle East.

One of the strategies employed by activists in the Middle East is to focus on raising awareness about LGBTQ issues through storytelling and personal narratives. By sharing stories of LGBTQ individuals within a cultural context, activists can challenge stereotypes and foster empathy and understanding.

Cultural sensitivity also involves engaging with religious leaders and communities. Religion plays a significant role in the lives of many individuals in the Middle East, and addressing LGBTQ issues within a religious framework can help bridge cultural divides. By highlighting the progressive interpretations of religious texts and engaging in interfaith dialogue, activists can foster a more inclusive understanding of LGBTQ identities.

Collaboration with local LGBTQ organizations is another important aspect of cultural sensitivity in the Middle East. These organizations are often at the forefront of creating safe spaces, providing support services, and advocating for policy change. By working together with these organizations, activists can ensure that their efforts are aligned with the needs and priorities of the local LGBTQ community.

Ultimately, cultural sensitivity in LGBTQ activism in the Middle East is about recognizing and respecting the diversity of cultures, religions, and traditions within the region. It is about finding common ground, challenging stereotypes, and advocating for LGBTQ rights in a way that resonates with local communities.

## Challenges and Strategies for Cultural Sensitivity

While cultural sensitivity is essential in LGBTQ activism, it is not without its challenges. Activists must navigate complex cultural dynamics, address deep-rooted prejudices, and overcome resistance to change. Here are some common challenges and strategies for practicing cultural sensitivity in LGBTQ activism.

**Challenge 1: Balancing cultural respect with the need for change.** One challenge in cultural sensitivity is striking a balance between respecting cultural values and challenging discriminatory practices. Activists must navigate this delicate balance, ensuring that their advocacy promotes inclusivity without alienating local communities.

A strategy for addressing this challenge is to emphasize shared values and focus on the universal principles of human dignity, equality, and justice. By framing LGBTQ rights within a broader framework of human rights, activists can appeal to universal values that can resonate with people across different cultural contexts.

**Challenge 2: Engaging with religious communities.** Religion often plays a significant role in shaping attitudes towards LGBTQ individuals. Engaging with religious leaders and communities is essential in fostering acceptance and understanding.

A strategy for engaging with religious communities is to find common ground and highlight progressive interpretations of religious texts that support LGBTQ inclusion. This can involve partnering with progressive religious leaders, engaging in interfaith dialogue, and promoting theological arguments for LGBTQ inclusivity.

**Challenge 3: Addressing multiple intersecting identities.** LGBTQ individuals face discrimination not only based on their sexual orientation or gender identity but also due to other intersecting identities such as race, ethnicity, religion, or socioeconomic status. Cultural sensitivity requires acknowledging and addressing these intersecting identities.

A strategy for addressing this challenge is to adopt an intersectional approach in LGBTQ activism. This involves recognizing and advocating for the rights of individuals who experience compounded forms of discrimination. By promoting inclusive policies and programs that address intersecting identities, activists can create more equitable and inclusive spaces.

**Challenge 4: Collaborating with local LGBTQ organizations.** Cultural sensitivity involves collaborating with local LGBTQ organizations and amplifying local voices. However, building trust and strong partnerships can be challenging, particularly when activists are seen as outsiders.

A strategy for overcoming this challenge is to approach collaboration with humility, respect, and a willingness to listen and learn. Activists should aim to understand the local context, recognize and respect the expertise of local organizations, and work collaboratively towards shared goals. Building trust takes time, but the benefits of authentic partnerships are invaluable.

## Conclusion

Cultural sensitivity is essential in LGBTQ activism as it allows activists to navigate complex cultural dynamics, build bridges with local communities, and create lasting change. By recognizing and respecting cultural differences, activists can find common ground, challenge stereotypes, and foster greater acceptance and understanding.

Omar Sharif Jr.'s advocacy demonstrates the power of cultural sensitivity in advancing LGBTQ rights, particularly in the Middle Eastern context. Through engaging in open dialogue, raising awareness, and collaborating with local organizations, he has made significant strides in challenging prejudices and fostering a more inclusive society.

As the global LGBTQ movement continues to evolve, cultural sensitivity will remain a crucial aspect of effective activism. By acknowledging the diverse cultural contexts and intersecting identities of LGBTQ individuals, activists can create more comprehensive and inclusive strategies for change.

In the next section, we will explore the role of media in LGBTQ activism and how it can be harnessed to challenge prejudices, change perceptions, and create a more inclusive society.

## Working to Change Perceptions in the Middle East

In the journey of LGBTQ activism, changing perceptions is a critical step towards creating a more inclusive and accepting society. In the Middle East, where traditional beliefs and cultural norms often clash with LGBTQ rights, working to change these perceptions becomes even more challenging. However, Omar Sharif Jr. has faced this challenge head-on and has become a leading figure in bridging the gap between LGBTQ advocacy and the Middle Eastern culture.

## Understanding Cultural Sensitivity

One of the first steps in changing perceptions in the Middle East is recognizing the importance of cultural sensitivity. Cultural norms and religious beliefs play a significant role in shaping attitudes towards LGBTQ individuals. To effectively advocate for LGBTQ rights in this region, it is essential to understand and respect these cultural and religious values.

Omar Sharif Jr. has always emphasized the need for conversations that are rooted in empathy and understanding. By approaching discussions with respect and a willingness to listen, he has been able to create a dialogue with individuals who may initially hold negative views about the LGBTQ community.

## Education as a Tool for Change

Education is a powerful tool that can challenge misconceptions and break down barriers. Omar Sharif Jr. recognizes this and has been a staunch advocate for LGBTQ-inclusive education in the Middle East. By promoting education, he aims to provide accurate information about sexual orientation and gender identity, dispelling myths and stereotypes.

To change perceptions effectively, educational initiatives must be tailored to suit the cultural and religious context of the Middle East. Sensitivity to cultural norms while still promoting LGBTQ rights is essential. For example, workshops and awareness campaigns can be conducted in collaboration with religious leaders and scholars to address concerns and reconcile religious teachings with LGBTQ acceptance.

## Creating Safe Spaces

Creating safe spaces for LGBTQ individuals in the Middle East is crucial for both personal growth and societal change. Omar Sharif Jr. has been at the forefront of establishing LGBTQ centers and support networks in the region. These spaces provide a sense of community and support for individuals who may be facing isolation and discrimination.

In addition to physical safe spaces, online platforms can also serve as virtual safe havens for LGBTQ individuals in the Middle East. These platforms offer information, resources, and connections to a global community, providing much-needed support and guidance.

## Collaborations and Partnerships

Collaboration and partnership-building are vital strategies in the fight for LGBTQ rights in the Middle East. Omar Sharif Jr. has actively sought collaborations with Middle Eastern organizations, governments, and NGOs to create a unified front in advocating for change.

By collaborating with key stakeholders, including human rights organizations, government officials, and religious leaders, Omar Sharif Jr. aims to bridge the gap between LGBTQ advocacy and cultural acceptance. These partnerships allow for more effective communication, resource sharing, and the development of policies that reflect the needs and rights of LGBTQ individuals in the region.

## Art and Media as Agents of Change

Art and media have the power to challenge stereotypes and influence public opinion. Omar Sharif Jr. recognizes the importance of utilizing these mediums to drive social change in the Middle East. Through his work in the entertainment industry, he actively promotes LGBTQ visibility and representation.

By showcasing diverse LGBTQ narratives in films, TV shows, and other forms of media, Omar Sharif Jr. helps to humanize the LGBTQ experience and foster empathy among viewers. This representation plays a crucial role in changing perceptions and dismantling harmful stereotypes.

## Overcoming Challenges

Working to change perceptions in the Middle East is not without its challenges. Homophobia and transphobia are deeply ingrained in the culture, and there is often resistance to LGBTQ rights. Omar Sharif Jr. has faced personal and professional challenges, including threats and attacks, as a result of his activism.

However, he remains resilient and continues to push forward. By staying true to his beliefs and engaging in respectful dialogue, he has been able to make progress in changing perceptions and advocating for LGBTQ rights in the region.

### Unconventional Approach: Inspiring Change through Art

In his journey to change perceptions in the Middle East, Omar Sharif Jr. has embraced an unconventional approach: utilizing art as a medium for social change. Through his talent as an actor and his passion for storytelling, he has been able to reach audiences on an emotional level, sparking conversations and challenging deeply-held beliefs.

By combining the power of art and advocacy, he not only captures the hearts and minds of individuals but also inspires them to question their preconceived notions and consider alternative perspectives. This unique approach has allowed him to go beyond traditional methods of activism and create a lasting impact on the perception of LGBTQ rights in the Middle East.

## Conclusion

Changing perceptions in the Middle East is a complex but essential task in advancing LGBTQ rights. Omar Sharif Jr.'s commitment to cultural sensitivity, education, safe spaces, collaboration, art, and media has paved the way for progress in this region. His bold and unconventional approach, coupled with his resilience in the face of challenges, has made him a true advocate for change.

As Omar Sharif Jr. continues his journey, he leaves a lasting legacy in the fight for LGBTQ rights in the Middle East. His work serves as an inspiration for future activists, reminding us that changing perceptions is not only possible but crucial in creating a more inclusive and accepting world.

### Collaborations with Middle Eastern Organizations

Collaboration is essential in any endeavor, and the field of LGBTQ advocacy is no exception. In order to bring about meaningful change and promote acceptance and equality, it is crucial to work together with organizations that share the same goals and values. Omar Sharif Jr., with his passion for bridging LGBTQ and Middle Eastern advocacy, understands the importance of collaborating with Middle Eastern organizations to advance LGBTQ rights in the region.

### Building Trust and Partnerships

Building trust and establishing partnerships are the foundations of successful collaborations. Omar Sharif Jr. recognizes the significance of engaging with Middle Eastern organizations that are dedicated to promoting social justice and human rights. By fostering relationships based on mutual respect and understanding, he ensures that the shared mission of achieving LGBTQ equality can be effectively pursued.

One example of collaboration is Omar's work with Middle Eastern LGBTQ organizations such as the Arab Foundation for Freedoms and Equality (AFE) and Helem. These organizations play a vital role in advancing LGBTQ rights in the region and provide invaluable support to individuals struggling with discrimination and marginalization.

## Amplifying Local Voices

Collaborating with Middle Eastern organizations allows Omar Sharif Jr. to amplify and center the voices of LGBTQ individuals within their own communities. By working alongside local activists and organizations, he ensures that the experiences and needs of Middle Eastern LGBTQ individuals are heard and addressed.

This collaboration involves actively listening to the concerns and challenges faced by LGBTQ individuals in the Middle East. Omar actively seeks opportunities to engage in dialogue and develop strategies that are sensitive to the cultural, religious, and social contexts of the region. Through this collaboration, he strives to empower local LGBTQ activists and organizations, recognizing their unique insights and expertise.

## Advocacy and Policy Development

Collaborations with Middle Eastern organizations also contribute to the development of effective advocacy strategies and the formulation of inclusive policies. Omar Sharif Jr. works alongside these organizations to promote LGBTQ-friendly legislation and policy reforms that protect the rights of LGBTQ individuals in the Middle East.

One example of this collaboration is the joint efforts in promoting anti-discrimination laws and advocating for the decriminalization of same-sex relations. By combining resources, expertise, and networks, Omar and Middle Eastern organizations push for legal changes that challenge the oppressive legal frameworks still present in the region.

## Cultural Sensitivity and Education

Culture plays a crucial role in shaping attitudes towards the LGBTQ community. Collaborating with Middle Eastern organizations allows Omar Sharif Jr. to promote cultural sensitivity and education as key components of LGBTQ advocacy.

By working together, Omar and Middle Eastern organizations develop educational programs, workshops, and awareness campaigns that aim to challenge societal misconceptions and combat homophobia and transphobia. These initiatives are culturally tailored to resonate with Middle Eastern audiences while still promoting acceptance and understanding.

## Overcoming Challenges

Collaborating with Middle Eastern organizations in the pursuit of LGBTQ equality is not without its challenges. Omar Sharif Jr. and these organizations must navigate a complex social and political landscape that often lacks legal protections for LGBTQ individuals.

These collaborations require perseverance, strategic planning, and advocacy skills to overcome resistance and opposition. Omar and Middle Eastern organizations must navigate diplomatic channels and engage in dialogue with religious leaders, policymakers, and societal influencers to challenge prevailing norms and effect change from within.

## An Unconventional Approach: Arab Unity Initiative

As an advocate for bridging LGBTQ and Middle Eastern advocacy, Omar Sharif Jr. has launched the Arab Unity Initiative—an unconventional approach to collaboration. This initiative aims to create a safe and inclusive space for dialogue between LGBTQ communities and religious leaders, fostering understanding, and challenging prejudice.

The Arab Unity Initiative seeks to unite Middle Eastern organizations, LGBTQ activists, and religious leaders in a collective effort to promote LGBTQ acceptance within the region. By engaging in dialogue, fostering relationships, and finding common ground, this initiative challenges the narrative that LGBTQ rights and religious beliefs are incompatible.

## Conclusion

Collaborations with Middle Eastern organizations are essential in advancing LGBTQ rights in the region. Through trust-building, amplifying local voices, advocacy and policy development, cultural sensitivity, and education, Omar Sharif Jr. and these organizations work together to bring about meaningful change. Overcoming challenges and taking an unconventional approach through initiatives like the Arab Unity Initiative further strengthen these alliances.

By collaborating with Middle Eastern organizations, Omar Sharif Jr. demonstrates that bridging LGBTQ and Middle Eastern advocacy is not only possible but crucial for creating a more inclusive and accepting world. Through these partnerships, he leaves a lasting impact on the LGBTQ community in the Middle East and paves the way for a brighter future.

## Championing LGBTQ Rights on a Global Scale

Omar Sharif Jr. has made it his mission to champion LGBTQ rights on a global scale, working tirelessly to promote equality and acceptance for the LGBTQ community around the world. In this section, we will explore his efforts in different regions and his strategies for effecting change.

### Recognizing the Global Landscape

Before diving into the specifics of his advocacy work, it is important to acknowledge the global landscape of LGBTQ rights. While significant progress has been made in some parts of the world, many countries still have discriminatory laws and policies that target LGBTQ individuals. It is within this context that Omar Sharif Jr. operates, fully aware of the challenges and complexities of championing LGBTQ rights globally.

### International Alliances and Partnerships

One of the key strategies Omar Sharif Jr. employs in his global advocacy is forging alliances and partnerships with like-minded organizations and activists. He recognizes that collaboration and collective action are essential for creating meaningful change. By partnering with local LGBTQ organizations, he is able to amplify their voices and provide support for their initiatives.

These alliances extend beyond borders, as Omar Sharif Jr. actively seeks opportunities to collaborate with international organizations dedicated to LGBTQ rights. Through joint initiatives and shared resources, they work together to advocate for legal reform, combat discrimination, and promote acceptance.

### Diplomatic Engagement

Another powerful tool in Omar Sharif Jr.'s arsenal is diplomatic engagement. Drawing on his unique position as an advocate, he actively engages with governments and policymakers across the globe to push for LGBTQ-inclusive policies and legislation. By forging relationships with decision-makers and leveraging his influence, he works to effect change at the highest levels.

Through dialogue, negotiations, and lobbying efforts, Omar Sharif Jr. highlights the importance of LGBTQ rights in promoting diversity, inclusivity, and social progress. He emphasizes that protecting and promoting the rights of LGBTQ individuals is not only a matter of human rights but also crucial for a thriving and prosperous society.

## Raising Awareness through Media and Entertainment

As a prominent figure in the media and entertainment industry, Omar Sharif Jr. recognizes the power of storytelling and representation in shaping public opinion. He actively uses his platform to raise awareness about LGBTQ issues and foster dialogue. Through interviews, speeches, and media appearances, he shares his personal story and experiences to humanize the struggles and triumphs of the LGBTQ community.

Moreover, Omar Sharif Jr. actively advocates for increased LGBTQ representation in media and entertainment. He believes that seeing authentic and diverse LGBTQ characters and stories can challenge stereotypes and foster empathy. By working with filmmakers, producers, and writers, he aims to create inclusive content that not only entertains but also educates and inspires.

## Education and Empowerment

Omar Sharif Jr. understands the transformative power of education in promoting acceptance and understanding. He actively engages in efforts to promote LGBTQ-inclusive education, advocating for curriculum reforms that address LGBTQ issues and experiences. By working with educators, policymakers, and community leaders, he aims to create safe and supportive learning environments for all students.

Additionally, Omar Sharif Jr. actively supports organizations that provide resources and support for LGBTQ individuals, particularly youth. He recognizes the unique challenges faced by LGBTQ youth and works to empower them through mentorship programs, scholarships, and mental health support services. By investing in the next generation, he ensures that the fight for LGBTQ equality continues beyond his own advocacy.

### Transnational Activism

One of the most powerful aspects of Omar Sharif Jr.'s advocacy is his ability to transcend national boundaries and connect with LGBTQ communities around the world. Through social media platforms and online advocacy campaigns, he reaches a global audience, fostering a sense of solidarity and unity.

Omar Sharif Jr. actively uses these platforms to raise awareness about LGBTQ issues in different countries and regions. He sheds light on the unique challenges faced by LGBTQ individuals and initiates conversations about the need for change. By harnessing the power of technology and digital activism, he extends his reach and impact beyond physical borders.

### Legacy and Future Endeavors

Omar Sharif Jr.'s commitment to championing LGBTQ rights on a global scale is an ongoing journey. He acknowledges that there is still work to be done, and his advocacy will continue to adapt and evolve in response to shifting societal and political landscapes. His legacy lies in inspiring future generations to fight for equality and creating a more inclusive world for all.

As we conclude this section, it is important to remember that championing LGBTQ rights on a global scale requires collective action, empathy, and a deep commitment to justice. Omar Sharif Jr.'s tireless efforts serve as a reminder that change is possible, and by working together, we can create a world where LGBTQ individuals are embraced, celebrated, and afforded the same rights and opportunities as their heterosexual counterparts.

*Exercise: Reflect on the strategies discussed in this section and brainstorm ways in which you can promote LGBTQ rights in your own community. Consider different avenues for advocacy, such as education, media, and partnership-building, and develop an action plan to start effecting change. Remember, even small steps can make a big difference in creating a more inclusive and accepting society.*

# The Power of Education

### Education as a Tool for Change

Education has long been regarded as a powerful tool for societal change, and in the context of LGBTQ advocacy, it is no different. By providing individuals with knowledge, understanding, and critical thinking skills, education becomes a catalyst for embracing diversity, challenging stereotypes, and promoting acceptance.

## The Importance of LGBTQ-Inclusive Education

In many parts of the world, LGBTQ individuals face significant challenges in accessing education that is inclusive and supportive of their identities. This lack of representation and understanding can lead to feelings of isolation, low self-esteem, and even discrimination within educational settings.

To address this, it is essential to prioritize LGBTQ-inclusive education. This means developing curricula that acknowledge and respect the diverse experiences and identities within the LGBTQ community. By integrating LGBTQ history, literature, and role models into the educational framework, students gain a deeper understanding of the struggles and contributions of LGBTQ individuals throughout history.

## Breaking Down Barriers Through Knowledge

Education has the power to break down barriers by dispelling misconceptions and promoting empathy. Providing accurate information about sexuality, gender identity, and LGBTQ issues helps debunk stereotypes and challenge harmful prejudices. This knowledge equips students with the necessary tools to combat discrimination and create more inclusive communities.

To illustrate the impact of education, let's consider an example. In a high school health class, students are taught comprehensive and inclusive sex education that covers topics such as consent, sexual health, and LGBTQ identities. By debunking myths and providing accurate information, students develop a better understanding of diverse sexual orientations and gender identities. Armed with this knowledge, they can become allies and advocates, promoting acceptance both within and outside the classroom.

## Empowering LGBTQ Youth Through Education

Education plays a vital role in empowering LGBTQ youth to embrace their identities and navigate the challenges they may face. By fostering a safe and inclusive environment, educational institutions can help LGBTQ students develop a sense of belonging and increase their self-esteem.

Supportive school policies and programs, such as LGBTQ clubs, gender-neutral facilities, and trained staff, create spaces where students feel valued and accepted.

Additionally, educators must receive training on LGBTQ issues to ensure they can provide appropriate support and guidance.

An unconventional but effective approach to empowering LGBTQ youth through education is the use of storytelling. By incorporating LGBTQ narratives into the curriculum and highlighting positive role models, students can see themselves represented and find inspiration in the experiences of others. This approach not only provides validation but also encourages empathy and understanding among their peers.

## Resources and Partnerships

To effectively integrate LGBTQ-inclusive education, it is crucial to provide resources and establish partnerships. Educational materials, such as textbooks, should include accurate and age-appropriate information about LGBTQ identities and issues. Online platforms and websites can also offer valuable resources for both students and educators.

Additionally, partnerships with LGBTQ organizations and community leaders can enhance the impact of LGBTQ-inclusive education. These organizations can offer workshops, trainings, and mentorship opportunities for educators, ensuring they have the necessary tools and knowledge to support LGBTQ students effectively.

Together, education, resources, and partnerships form the foundation for creating a more inclusive and accepting society. By equipping individuals with the understanding and empathy needed to challenge discrimination, we pave the way for a future where LGBTQ individuals are celebrated for their contributions and fully embraced for who they are.

## Exercises

1. Reflect on your own educational experiences. Were LGBTQ issues and identities addressed in your schooling? How did this lack of representation impact your perception of LGBTQ individuals?

2. Research and identify existing LGBTQ-inclusive educational programs in your community or country. Evaluate their effectiveness in promoting acceptance and providing resources for LGBTQ students.

3. Develop a lesson plan that integrates LGBTQ history or literature into an existing subject in the curriculum (e.g., history, English). Consider how this inclusion can foster understanding and challenge stereotypes.

4. Conduct a survey within your educational institution to assess the level of knowledge and understanding regarding LGBTQ identities. Use the results to

identify areas for improvement and develop strategies for creating a more inclusive environment.

5. Engage in conversations with educators, administrators, and policymakers about the importance of LGBTQ-inclusive education. Advocate for policy changes or curriculum enhancements that promote acceptance and understanding.

# Bibliography

[1] GLSEN. 2019 National School Climate Survey. Retrieved from https://www.glsen.org/research/national-school-climate-survey-2019

[2] Human Rights Campaign. Welcoming Schools. Retrieved from https://www.welcomingschools.org/

[3] National LGBTQ Task Force. Safe Schools. Retrieved from https://www.thetaskforce.org/our-work/safe-schools/

## Advocating for LGBTQ-Inclusive Education

Education plays a crucial role in fostering acceptance and creating a more inclusive society. In this section, we explore the importance of advocating for LGBTQ-inclusive education and the impact it can have on the LGBTQ community and society as a whole.

## Understanding LGBTQ-Inclusive Education

LGBTQ-inclusive education encompasses a curriculum that promotes understanding, respect, and support for LGBTQ individuals. It goes beyond simply acknowledging their existence, but actively works to create an inclusive environment that celebrates diversity.

Inclusive education should address topics such as gender identity, sexual orientation, LGBTQ history, and the unique challenges faced by LGBTQ youth. By providing comprehensive and accurate information, it helps dispel myths, reduces stereotypes, and promotes empathy and understanding.

## The Benefits of LGBTQ-Inclusive Education

1. **Promoting acceptance and reducing discrimination:** LGBTQ-inclusive education helps break down barriers and promotes acceptance among students. It raises awareness about the challenges faced by LGBTQ individuals and fosters empathy and understanding. This, in turn, reduces discrimination and bullying in schools.

2. **Creating a safe and supportive environment:** LGBTQ-inclusive education creates a safe space for LGBTQ students to express their identity and provides them with the support they need. It helps dismantle the stigma surrounding LGBTQ issues and encourages a sense of belonging and acceptance.

3. **Improving mental health and well-being:** LGBTQ youth often face higher rates of mental health issues due to stigma, discrimination, and lack of support. LGBTQ-inclusive education can help address these concerns by promoting self-acceptance, educating students about mental health resources, and fostering a supportive community.

4. **Reducing health disparities:** LGBTQ individuals experience health disparities, including higher rates of HIV, substance abuse, and suicide. By including LGBTQ-specific health education, schools can provide vital information about sexual health, mental health support, and resources available to LGBTQ students.

## Implementing LGBTQ-Inclusive Education

Implementing LGBTQ-inclusive education can be a challenging task. Here are some strategies for effective implementation:

1. **Teacher education and training:** Educators need proper training and resources to create an LGBTQ-inclusive curriculum. Professional development programs should address LGBTQ issues, provide educators with accurate information, and equip them with skills to handle sensitive topics and create a safe environment.

2. **Incorporating LGBTQ perspectives across subjects:** LGBTQ-inclusive education should not be limited to a specific subject. It should be integrated across the curriculum, including history, literature, social studies, and health classes. This approach helps students understand the contributions and struggles of LGBTQ individuals throughout history and across various fields.

3. **Inclusive language and policies:** Schools should adopt inclusive language in their policies, codes of conduct, and anti-bullying measures. Creating a supportive

and inclusive environment goes beyond the curriculum and extends to the language used within the school community.

4. **Engaging with LGBTQ organizations and community resources:** Collaborating with LGBTQ organizations and community resources can provide valuable insights, guidance, and support in creating an inclusive education environment. These partnerships help ensure that the curriculum reflects the needs and realities of LGBTQ individuals.

## Challenges and Solutions

Implementing LGBTQ-inclusive education can face resistance and challenges. Here are some common challenges and potential solutions:

1. **Resistance from parents or community members:** Some parents or community members may hold conservative beliefs and resist LGBTQ-inclusive education. Transparent communication and education about the importance of inclusivity can help address concerns and build understanding.

2. **Limited resources and lack of curriculum guidelines:** Schools may struggle with limited resources and a lack of standardized curriculum guidelines. Engaging with LGBTQ organizations, sharing best practices, and seeking support from educational authorities can help overcome these challenges.

3. **Navigating legal and policy issues:** Schools need to navigate legal and policy frameworks to ensure compliance and protection for LGBTQ students and educators. Working closely with legal experts and staying up-to-date with legislation can help address these complexities.

4. **Providing ongoing support and training:** Ongoing support and training for educators are essential to ensure the effective implementation of LGBTQ-inclusive education. This includes professional development opportunities, access to resources, and spaces for dialogue and reflection.

## The Power of LGBTQ-Inclusive Education

LGBTQ-inclusive education serves as a catalyst for change, empowering LGBTQ youth, and promoting a more accepting society. By fostering empathy, understanding, and acceptance, it creates an environment where all students can thrive.

Through LGBTQ-inclusive education, we can challenge homophobia and transphobia, dismantle stereotypes, and ignite conversations that lead to social change. It is a powerful tool to shape a future where LGBTQ individuals are celebrated, respected, and provided with equal opportunities. Let us continue to advocate for LGBTQ-inclusive education, paving the way for a more inclusive and compassionate world.

## Breaking Down Barriers Through Knowledge

Omar Sharif Jr. understands the power of education as a tool for change and how it can break down barriers and promote inclusivity. In this section, we will explore the importance of LGBTQ-inclusive education and how it empowers individuals and communities. We will delve into the challenges faced in implementing inclusive education, provide strategies to overcome these obstacles, and highlight the impact this can have on the LGBTQ community.

## Education as a Tool for Change

Education has always been a powerful catalyst for societal transformation. It has the potential to challenge existing norms, dismantle stereotypes, and foster empathy and understanding. In the context of LGBTQ rights, inclusive education can play a crucial role in creating safer and more accepting environments for all individuals.

By integrating LGBTQ topics into curricula, schools cultivate an atmosphere that acknowledges and validates the diverse identities and experiences of students. LGBTQ-inclusive education equips young people with knowledge about sexual orientation, gender identity, and the history of LGBTQ rights movements. This knowledge empowers individuals to be more accepting, compassionate, and supportive allies and advocates.

## Advocating for LGBTQ-Inclusive Education

Achieving LGBTQ-inclusive education is not without its challenges. Many societies still face considerable resistance and opposition to LGBTQ visibility and acceptance. However, advocates like Omar Sharif Jr. recognize the importance of persistence and strategic efforts to overcome these barriers.

One effective strategy is engaging with educational policymakers, administrators, and teachers to emphasize the significance of inclusivity. By providing them with resources, workshops, and training, educators can develop the necessary skills and confidence to create LGBTQ-inclusive curricula. Additionally, collaborations between LGBTQ organizations, educators, and schools can help develop comprehensive guidelines and materials for implementing inclusive education.

Furthermore, partnering with parents and guardians to foster open dialogue and address any concerns they may have about inclusive education is crucial.

Sharing success stories and research-backed evidence that supports the positive impact LGBTQ-inclusive education has on student well-being and academic performance can help alleviate fears and misconceptions.

## Breaking Down Barriers Through Knowledge

Implementing LGBTQ-inclusive education goes beyond mere tokenism. It requires a fundamental shift in how education systems approach LGBTQ topics. Educators must aim to integrate these subjects seamlessly into existing curricula across disciplines, ensuring that LGBTQ perspectives are not relegated to a single lesson or theme.

One effective way to break down barriers is to highlight the contributions and achievements of LGBTQ individuals throughout history. By incorporating LGBTQ role models and their accomplishments into various subjects, educators can challenge norms and promote understanding. For example, in history classes, students can learn about influential LGBTQ activists, such as Harvey Milk or Marsha P. Johnson, who fought for equal rights.

Moreover, incorporating LGBTQ narratives into literature and English classes exposes students to diverse perspectives and experiences. By analyzing LGBTQ literature and storytelling, students can gain a deeper understanding of the challenges faced by these individuals and develop empathy.

## Empowering LGBTQ Youth Through Education

LGBTQ youth often face unique challenges within educational settings, such as bullying, harassment, and discrimination. Inclusive education provides a supportive environment that not only acknowledges their experiences but also equips them with the tools to navigate these challenges.

Educators must prioritize the mental health and well-being of LGBTQ students by creating safe spaces, establishing support networks, and offering counseling services. Additionally, integrating LGBTQ-inclusive sex education can provide vital information on healthy relationships, consent, and sexual health, which is often lacking for LGBTQ youth.

To further empower LGBTQ youth, it is crucial to involve them in decision-making processes related to education. This can include creating LGBTQ student organizations, organizing workshops and conferences, and providing platforms for their voices to be heard. By actively involving LGBTQ youth, their experiences can shape policies and curricula, ensuring that their needs are met while fostering a sense of ownership and empowerment.

## Conclusion

Breaking down barriers through knowledge is a fundamental aspect of promoting LGBTQ rights and fostering inclusivity. By incorporating LGBTQ topics and perspectives into education, we can create a more accepting and understanding society. Advocates like Omar Sharif Jr. continue to inspire change in education systems globally, empowering LGBTQ youth and ensuring a brighter, more inclusive future for generations to come.

Remember, education is not just about facts and figures; it is about cultivating empathy, understanding, and respect. Through LGBTQ-inclusive education, we can build a world where everyone's identity and experiences are acknowledged, valued, and celebrated. Let us embrace the power of knowledge to break down barriers and create an inclusive society for all.

## Empowering LGBTQ Youth Through Education

Education has always been recognized as a powerful tool for change and empowerment. When it comes to LGBTQ youth, education becomes even more crucial. By providing inclusive and supportive educational environments, we can empower LGBTQ youth to embrace their identities, overcome challenges, and thrive. In this section, we will explore the importance of LGBTQ-inclusive education, the barriers that exist, and strategies to empower LGBTQ youth through education.

### The Power of Inclusive Education

LGBTQ-inclusive education is essential because it fosters a sense of belonging and validation for LGBTQ youth. It goes beyond just teaching about LGBTQ issues; it encompasses creating a safe and accepting environment where students can fully be themselves. Inclusive education acknowledges and affirms diverse sexual orientations, gender identities, and gender expressions.

By incorporating LGBTQ-inclusive curricula in schools, educators can provide accurate information about LGBTQ history, identities, and experiences. This helps dispel harmful stereotypes and myths while promoting understanding and empathy among students. Inclusive education also helps to challenge heteronormative and cisnormative biases, encouraging critical thinking and promoting equality.

Moreover, inclusive education benefits not only LGBTQ youth but also their cisgender and heterosexual peers. It creates opportunities for all students to develop a broader understanding of diversity, foster respect, and build supportive relationships. Inclusive education has the power to create a more compassionate and inclusive society.

## Addressing Barriers to LGBTQ-Inclusive Education

Despite the importance of LGBTQ-inclusive education, there are various barriers that hinder its implementation and effectiveness. One of the major barriers is a lack of awareness and understanding among educators and administrators. Many schools still lack proper training and resources to address LGBTQ issues adequately.

Additionally, societal stigma and resistance can create obstacles to LGBTQ-inclusive education. Some communities may oppose the inclusion of LGBTQ topics in school curricula due to personal beliefs or cultural norms. This resistance can lead to a perpetuation of discrimination and erasure of LGBTQ experiences. Overcoming this barrier requires targeted efforts to engage with parents, community leaders, and policymakers to promote the value of inclusive education.

Another barrier is the absence of comprehensive anti-bullying and non-discrimination policies. LGBTQ students often face higher rates of bullying, harassment, and violence compared to their peers. To create a supportive educational environment, schools must establish and enforce policies that protect LGBTQ students from discrimination and provide appropriate resources for reporting incidents.

## Strategies for Empowering LGBTQ Youth Through Education

To empower LGBTQ youth through education, it is crucial to implement strategies that address the barriers and promote inclusivity. Here are a few strategies that can make a significant impact:

1. Professional Development: Providing comprehensive training and professional development opportunities for educators and school staff is essential. This training should focus on LGBTQ issues, cultural sensitivity, and inclusive curriculum design. By equipping educators with the knowledge and skills they need, schools can create supportive environments for LGBTQ youth.

2. LGBTQ-Inclusive Curriculum: Developing LGBTQ-inclusive curricula that cover diverse LGBTQ identities, history, and contributions is pivotal. This should be done across various subjects, not limited to health and sexuality education. Incorporating LGBTQ literature, arts, and achievements helps validate LGBTQ youth and promotes understanding among all students.

3. Safe Spaces: Creating designated safe spaces within schools, such as LGBTQ student clubs or support groups, can provide much-needed support for LGBTQ youth. These spaces foster a sense of community, reduce isolation, and provide resources for students to navigate their identities and experiences.

4. Community Engagement: Engaging with community organizations, LGBTQ advocates, and allies can help build a network of support for LGBTQ-inclusive education. Collaborations can lead to mentorship programs, guest speaker events, and resource sharing, empowering LGBTQ youth through diverse role models and opportunities.

## A Real-Life Example: The Genders & Sexualities Alliance Club

To illustrate the impact of LGBTQ-inclusive education, let's look at the example of the Genders & Sexualities Alliance (GSA) Club at Maple High School. The GSA Club is a student-led organization that promotes LGBTQ-inclusive education, support, and advocacy within the school community.

The GSA Club organizes regular workshops and presentations for students and staff, covering topics such as LGBTQ history, gender identities, and fostering inclusivity. Through these workshops, students learn about the importance of respect, allyship, and combating discrimination.

Furthermore, the GSA Club works closely with the school administration to ensure LGBTQ-inclusive policies are enforced and followed. They collaborate with teachers to incorporate LGBTQ themes into existing curriculum units, promoting inclusive education across various subjects.

The GSA Club also serves as a safe and supportive space for LGBTQ students, offering peer mentorship, social events, and access to resources. By providing this network of support, the GSA Club empowers LGBTQ youth to navigate their identities and build confidence.

Through their efforts, the GSA Club has created a more inclusive school environment where LGBTQ youth feel valued, supported, and empowered. Their work serves as a shining example of the transformative power of LGBTQ-inclusive education.

## Putting Knowledge into Action: Exercise

Exercise 1: Imagine you are an educator tasked with creating an LGBTQ-inclusive curriculum for a high school history class. Design a lesson plan that highlights the contributions of LGBTQ individuals throughout history. How would you present this information to ensure inclusivity and foster understanding among all students?

Exercise 2: As a member of a school's administration, you have received a request from a group of students to establish an LGBTQ-inclusive policy. Develop a draft of the policy, including guidelines for addressing bullying and discrimination, supporting LGBTQ students, and promoting LGBTQ-inclusive education. How would you ensure the policy is both comprehensive and enforceable?

Exercise 3: Create a social media campaign to raise awareness about LGBTQ-inclusive education. Design a series of posts and hashtags that emphasize the benefits of LGBTQ-inclusive education, challenge stereotypes, and encourage support from students, parents, and the wider community.

Remember, it is our collective responsibility to ensure the education of LGBTQ youth is inclusive, empowering, and transformative. By embracing LGBTQ-inclusive education, we can nurture a future generation that respects diversity, advocates for equality, and creates a more inclusive world.

# Building a Legacy

## Creating a Sustainable Movement

In the fight for LGBTQ rights and Middle Eastern advocacy, building a sustainable movement is crucial for long-term success. Omar Sharif Jr. has demonstrated exceptional leadership in creating a movement that thrives on the principles of inclusivity, equality, and empowerment. This section explores the key elements of creating a sustainable movement, including community engagement, strategic planning, collaboration, and legacy-building.

## Community Engagement: Building Strong Foundations

The foundation of any sustainable movement lies in the engagement and support of the community. Omar Sharif Jr. understands the importance of fostering connections and building relationships with LGBTQ individuals, allies, and organizations. Through community engagement initiatives, he has created safe spaces for dialogue, support, and education.

To ensure the movement's sustainability, it is vital to listen to the needs and concerns of the community. This can be achieved through town hall meetings, focus groups, and online surveys. By actively involving the community in decision-making processes, Omar Sharif Jr. has built a movement that responds to its constituents and promotes inclusivity.

## Strategic Planning: Setting Clear Goals

A sustainable movement requires clear goals and a well-defined roadmap. Strategic planning enables Omar Sharif Jr. and his team to outline their vision, identify key objectives, and develop actionable steps to achieve them. Through careful analysis of the political, social, and cultural landscape, they can navigate challenges and seize opportunities effectively.

Strategic planning also involves assessing available resources, both financial and human, and allocating them efficiently. By prioritizing initiatives that have the most significant impact, Omar Sharif Jr. ensures the movement's sustainability in the face of limited resources.

## Collaboration: Strength in Numbers

Collaboration is an essential element in any sustainable movement. Omar Sharif Jr. recognizes the power of partnership and has actively engaged with LGBTQ organizations, activists, and allies worldwide. By collaborating with diverse stakeholders, he can pool resources, share knowledge, and leverage collective expertise.

Through strategic alliances, Omar Sharif Jr. has expanded the reach of his movement, creating a global network of advocates. This collaboration strengthens the movement's influence and ensures that the fight for LGBTQ rights and Middle Eastern advocacy remains a collective effort.

## Legacy-Building: Inspiring Future Generations

To create a sustainable movement, it is crucial to inspire and empower future generations of activists. Omar Sharif Jr. has taken on the role of an inspirational figure, sharing his personal journey and experiences to motivate others. By showcasing the impact of LGBTQ activism and Middle Eastern advocacy, he encourages young individuals to join the cause.

Legacy-building also involves documenting the movement's history, milestones, and achievements. This ensures that future generations can learn from the past and build upon the progress made. By preserving the legacy of LGBTQ rights and Middle Eastern advocacy, Omar Sharif Jr. paves the way for a more inclusive future.

### Example: Collaborative Education Programs

To exemplify the strategies discussed above, let's consider an example of a collaborative education program initiated by Omar Sharif Jr. and partnering organizations. The program aims to provide LGBTQ-inclusive education in Middle Eastern countries, where it is often lacking.

The first step is community engagement, where town hall meetings are held to gather input from LGBTQ individuals, educators, and parents. This ensures that the program addresses their specific needs and concerns.

Strategic planning involves setting clear goals for the program, such as developing LGBTQ-inclusive curriculum materials and training teachers on LGBTQ issues. A timeline is created, and the necessary resources, including funding and human capital, are secured.

Collaboration is key in this program. Omar Sharif Jr. partners with local LGBTQ organizations, educational institutions, and NGOs to share responsibilities and resources. This collaborative approach strengthens the program's impact and ensures sustainability beyond the involvement of a single individual.

Legacy-building is integrated into the program through the creation of educational resources that can be used in the future. These resources are designed to be easily updated and adapted by future generations of educators. Additionally, the program tracks and celebrates its achievements, leaving a lasting impact on LGBTQ-inclusive education in the Middle East.

By implementing a collaborative education program, Omar Sharif Jr. demonstrates how a sustainable movement can be created, focusing on the specific needs of a community while leveraging partnerships and building a legacy for future generations.

In conclusion, creating a sustainable movement requires community engagement, strategic planning, collaboration, and legacy-building. Omar Sharif Jr. has exemplified these principles in his advocacy for LGBTQ rights and Middle Eastern advocacy. By involving the community, setting clear goals, collaborating with diverse stakeholders, and inspiring future generations, he has built a movement that continues to make a lasting impact.

## Passing the Torch to the Next Generation

As Omar Sharif Jr. continues on his journey as a LGBTQ activist, he recognizes the importance of nurturing and inspiring the next generation of advocates. He firmly believes that the fight for equality and justice should not be carried by one individual alone, but rather passed on to a collective of passionate individuals who are invested in creating a more inclusive world. In this chapter, we explore how Omar Sharif Jr. aims to empower and guide the emerging activists who will carry the torch forward.

## The Importance of Mentorship

Mentorship plays a vital role in shaping the future of any movement. As Omar Sharif Jr. reflects on his own growth as an activist, he acknowledges the invaluable mentorship he received from seasoned advocates who shared their wisdom and experience. Understanding this, he is committed to serving as a mentor himself, offering guidance, support, and knowledge to young activists who seek to make a difference.

Mentorship is a reciprocal relationship, benefiting both mentor and mentee. Through sharing experiences and perspectives, mentors can help their mentees navigate challenges, identify opportunities, and develop critical skills necessary for effective advocacy. Likewise, mentees can bring fresh perspectives, innovative ideas, and youthful energy to the mentor-mentee relationship, revitalizing the movement and inspiring change.

## Creating Opportunities for Youth Involvement

To fast-track the development and engagement of future LGBTQ activists, Omar Sharif Jr. emphasizes the importance of creating opportunities for youth involvement. He believes that young voices should be heard, valued, and incorporated into decision-making processes to ensure that their perspectives are represented.

One way to foster youth involvement is through mentorship programs, connecting experienced activists with aspiring youth advocates. These programs can offer guidance, networking opportunities, and platforms for young activists to share their experiences and ideas. Additionally, youth-led initiatives and organizations provide spaces for young individuals to develop leadership skills, collaborate with peers, and implement their own projects aimed at advancing LGBTQ rights.

## Advocating for Comprehensive LGBTQ Education

Education is a powerful tool for change. Omar Sharif Jr. recognizes that it is crucial to ensure that future generations are educated about LGBTQ issues, history, and rights. By advocating for comprehensive LGBTQ education, he aims to equip young people with the knowledge and understanding necessary to challenge societal norms, combat prejudice, and promote inclusivity.

Comprehensive LGBTQ education goes beyond simply teaching tolerance; it involves integrating LGBTQ history, culture, and experiences into various disciplines, including social studies, literature, and health education. It also entails creating safe spaces for dialogue and discussion, fostering empathy, and cultivating an environment where individuals can authentically express their identities.

## Encouraging Intersectional Activism

As the torch is passed from one generation to the next, Omar Sharif Jr. emphasizes the importance of intersectional activism. Recognizing that identities and experiences intersect in complex ways, he encourages young activists to broaden their perspective and advocate for social justice beyond LGBTQ issues alone.

Intersectional activism acknowledges the interconnectedness of various forms of oppression, including racism, sexism, ableism, and classism. By embracing intersectionality, activists can build coalitions, collaborate with other movements, and address the root causes of injustice. This inclusive approach fosters solidarity, amplifies marginalized voices, and ultimately leads to a more equitable society.

## Preserving Personal Narratives

Each individual has a unique story to tell, and Omar Sharif Jr. recognizes the power of personal narratives in creating social change. He encourages young activists to preserve personal narratives, documenting their experiences, challenges, and triumphs. These narratives serve as a reminder of the progress that has been made and inspire future generations to continue the fight for equality.

Preserving personal narratives can take various forms, such as oral histories, written memoirs, or digital storytelling. These narratives humanize the struggle for LGBTQ rights, making it relatable and tangible for others. They provide a platform for marginalized individuals to share their truths and create a sense of community.

## Conclusion

In passing the torch to the next generation, Omar Sharif Jr. understands the importance of mentorship, youth involvement, comprehensive education, intersectional activism, and preserving personal narratives. By empowering and guiding young activists, he aims to create a lasting impact and pave the way for a more inclusive and equitable world. As he continues his own journey, Omar Sharif

## Leaving a Lasting Impact on LGBTQ Activism

Leaving a lasting impact on LGBTQ activism is at the core of Omar Sharif Jr.'s mission. Throughout his journey, he has demonstrated a profound commitment to creating a more inclusive and accepting world for all individuals, regardless of their sexual orientation or gender identity. In this section, we will explore the various ways in which Omar has made a significant impact and discuss the strategies he has employed to ensure the continued growth and success of the LGBTQ movement.

## Building Sustainable Movements

One of the key aspects of Omar Sharif Jr.'s advocacy is the emphasis on building sustainable movements. He understands that lasting change requires more than just a single individual's efforts but rather a collective effort that continues long after one person has stepped away from the forefront. To accomplish this, Omar has focused on empowering LGBTQ communities and encouraging them to take ownership of their rights.

Omar has initiated and supported the establishment of LGBTQ community centers and support networks in various regions. These safe spaces provide a platform for individuals to come together, share experiences, and find strength in unity. By nurturing local communities and organizations, Omar ensures that the work carries on even when he is not directly involved. Through these efforts, he leaves a lasting legacy that empowers future activists and ensures the sustainability of the LGBTQ movement.

## Passing the Torch to the Next Generation

Recognizing the importance of nurturing future generations, Omar Sharif Jr. actively engages with young LGBTQ individuals, providing them with the necessary tools and resources to continue the fight for equality. He has created mentorship programs that pair experienced activists with emerging leaders, fostering a strong support system for LGBTQ youth.

Moreover, Omar has been vocal about the need for LGBTQ-inclusive education. He advocates for comprehensive educational reforms that address the unique challenges faced by LGBTQ students. By expanding access to inclusive and supportive educational environments, Omar seeks to empower young individuals to become agents of change and carry the momentum of LGBTQ activism forward.

## Creating a Global Movement

Omar Sharif Jr. understands that progress in LGBTQ rights is a global endeavor. He has actively participated in international conferences and collaborated with queer activists from around the world to create a truly global movement. By amplifying the voices of queer activists worldwide, Omar ensures that the struggles and triumphs of LGBTQ communities are shared and heard on a global scale.

Using the power of social media, Omar has leveraged technology to bridge the geographical divide. He consistently creates LGBTQ-inclusive content that challenges prejudices and discrimination, reaching millions of people who may otherwise have limited exposure to diverse perspectives. This global outreach not only raises awareness but also fosters empathy and understanding, ultimately contributing to the lasting impact of LGBTQ activism.

## Advocating for Intersectionality and Inclusivity

Omar Sharif Jr. recognizes that LGBTQ activism must encompass the experiences and struggles of individuals who face multiple forms of marginalization. He advocates for intersectionality, a term that emphasizes the interconnected nature of different identities, such as race, gender, and socioeconomic status.

By centering the experiences of LGBTQ individuals from marginalized communities, Omar strives to create a more inclusive and equitable movement. He collaborates with organizations that address the specific needs of these communities and works to ensure that their voices are represented in LGBTQ activism.

## Continuing the Journey

Leaving a lasting impact on LGBTQ activism is an evolving process. Omar Sharif Jr. remains committed to the cause and recognizes that there are always new challenges to overcome and causes to champion. As he continues his journey, he remains open to adapting his strategies, leveraging new technologies, and collaborating with diverse stakeholders.

Omar invites individuals from all backgrounds to join the ongoing fight for LGBTQ rights and encourages them to find their own unique ways to contribute. By doing so, he ensures that the impact of his activism extends far beyond his individual efforts, leaving an indelible mark on the LGBTQ movement.

As we conclude this section, we celebrate Omar Sharif Jr.'s unwavering commitment, resilience, and remarkable contributions to LGBTQ activism. His journey serves as an inspiration for us all, reminding us of the power of collective action and the potential for creating a more inclusive and accepting world.

Remember, progress is not achieved overnight, and the fight for LGBTQ rights is ongoing. Let us carry forward the invaluable lessons learned from Omar's journey and continue to advocate for equal rights, respect, and dignity for all individuals, regardless of their sexual orientation or gender identity.

## The Future of Omar Sharif Jr.'s Advocacy

As Omar Sharif Jr.'s journey continues, his future in advocacy holds great promise and potential. His unwavering dedication to LGBTQ and Middle Eastern advocacy has already made a significant impact, but there is still much work to be done. In this section, we will explore the goals, strategies, and challenges that lie ahead for Omar Sharif Jr.'s advocacy.

### Setting New Goals

With each milestone achieved, Omar Sharif Jr. continues to set his sights on new goals and aspirations for his advocacy work. One of his primary objectives is to further dismantle the stereotypes, prejudices, and discrimination faced by the LGBTQ community in the Middle East. He aims to create a world where LGBTQ individuals are embraced and celebrated for their authenticity, without fear of persecution.

Additionally, Omar Sharif Jr. intends to expand his reach globally, forging partnerships with like-minded advocates and organizations, to tackle LGBTQ rights issues on a larger scale. By leveraging his platform, he can amplify the voices of those who are often unheard, ensuring their stories and experiences are at the forefront of the fight for equality.

### Developing Innovative Strategies

To achieve these goals, Omar Sharif Jr. recognizes the need for innovative strategies in advocacy. He understands that traditional approaches may not always be effective in tackling deeply ingrained cultural and societal norms. As such, he continues to explore new avenues for creating change.

One such strategy is utilizing the power of digital media and technology. By leveraging social media platforms, Omar Sharif Jr. aims to connect with a broader audience, disseminate information, and challenge misconceptions about LGBTQ individuals and the Middle East. Through engaging content, he can spark conversations, inspire empathy, and foster a sense of community across geographical boundaries.

Furthermore, Omar Sharif Jr. believes in the importance of collaboration and coalition-building. By partnering with other influential advocates, organizations, and governments, he can leverage collective strength and influence to drive systemic change. This strategic approach allows for a more unified front in the fight for LGBTQ rights and greater impact on policies and legislation.

## Addressing Emerging Challenges

As the landscape of LGBTQ advocacy continues to evolve, new challenges emerge that demand innovative solutions. Omar Sharif Jr. remains committed to navigating these obstacles with resilience and determination.

One such challenge is the rise of online hate speech and cyberbullying. As the advocacy work extends to digital platforms, Omar Sharif Jr. understands the importance of promoting a safe and inclusive online environment. He intends to collaborate with tech giants, governments, and non-profit organizations to address these issues and implement measures that protect LGBTQ individuals from online harassment and discrimination.

Moreover, as LGBTQ rights make significant progress in some regions, complacency can become a hurdle. Omar Sharif Jr. recognizes the importance of continued activism and advocacy, even in places where significant strides have been made. He aims to inspire others to join in the fight, emphasizing that equality is not a destination but an ongoing journey that requires sustained commitment.

## Embracing Change and Adaptation

The future of Omar Sharif Jr.'s advocacy lies in embracing change and adaptation. He understands that the fight for LGBTQ rights will evolve over time, and the strategies that worked in the past may not be effective in the future. With an open mind and a willingness to learn, he remains poised to adapt to new circumstances, emerging issues, and shifting public opinions.

Omar Sharif Jr. also recognizes the power of storytelling. By sharing personal narratives and lived experiences, he can humanize the struggle for LGBTQ rights and foster empathy and understanding. Through his own journey, he hopes to inspire others to embrace authenticity, advocate for change, and create a world that is more accepting and inclusive for future generations.

## Conclusion: A Hero for Our Times

Omar Sharif Jr.'s advocacy has transcended boundaries, challenged norms, and inspired countless individuals around the world. His dedication to bridging LGBTQ and Middle Eastern advocacy has made a lasting impact and will continue to shape the future of both movements.

As he looks towards the future, Omar Sharif Jr. remains steadfast in his commitment to amplifying marginalized voices, dismantling barriers, and fighting for the rights and equality of LGBTQ individuals, not only in the Middle East but on a global scale. Through his innovative strategies, collaborative spirit, and unwavering determination, he has become a hero for our times, leaving an indelible mark on the world of activism.

The future of Omar Sharif Jr.'s advocacy holds great promise, and with the continued support and collaboration of allies and advocates, his impact will only grow stronger. Together, we can strive for a world where love, acceptance, and equality are the foundation upon which we build a brighter future for all.

# Chapter 3: Challenges and Triumphs

## Chapter 3: Challenges and Triumphs

### Chapter 3: Challenges and Triumphs

In this chapter, we delve into the incredible challenges and triumphs that Omar Sharif Jr. faced throughout his journey as an LGBTQ activist. From personal and professional obstacles to groundbreaking victories, Sharif Jr.'s story is a testament to the power of resilience, determination, and unwavering commitment to creating a more inclusive world.

**The Price of Activism**

Being an LGBTQ activist comes with its own set of unique challenges. For Omar Sharif Jr., these challenges were further amplified by his Middle Eastern background and the cultural norms that clashed with his advocacy work. In this section, we explore the personal and professional difficulties he encountered on his path to creating change.

**Facing Personal and Professional Challenges:** As an openly gay man in the Middle East, Sharif Jr. faced significant personal and emotional challenges. Coming to terms with his own identity was not easy, and it took immense courage to embrace his true self. The pressure to conform to societal expectations and the fear of rejection added additional layers of complexity to his journey.

On a professional level, Sharif Jr. encountered resistance and opposition from individuals and organizations who were not prepared to accept the LGBTQ movement. He faced discrimination, threats, and even attacks on his character and credibility. However, instead of letting these challenges deter him, Sharif Jr. used them as fuel to drive his activism forward.

**Dealing with Threats and Attacks:** Standing up for LGBTQ rights in a region where they are often suppressed came with its own set of risks. Sharif Jr. faced threats to his personal safety, as well as the safety of his loved ones. However, he refused to be silenced or intimidated. Instead, he continued to speak out, using his platform to shed light on the injustices faced by the LGBTQ community.

**Overcoming Obstacles on the Path of Advocacy:** Advocacy work is rarely a linear journey. It is marked by highs and lows, victories and setbacks. Sharif Jr. experienced pushback from those who resisted change and clung to outdated beliefs. However, he remained undeterred, always finding new ways to push the boundaries and create positive change.

**Finding Strength in the Face of Adversity:** Through it all, Omar Sharif Jr. found strength within himself and the support of his allies. He drew inspiration from the countless LGBTQ individuals who faced persecution and stood up for their rights, often with little recognition or support. Their resilience and courage fueled his own determination to make a difference.

## Celebrating Victories

While the path of an LGBTQ activist is filled with challenges, it is also marked by incredible victories. In this section, we celebrate the milestones and successes that Omar Sharif Jr. achieved throughout his activism career.

**Milestones in LGBTQ Rights:** Sharif Jr. witnessed significant milestones in LGBTQ rights both globally and within the Middle East. From the legalization of same-sex marriage in several countries to the decriminalization of homosexuality in certain regions, these victories represented important steps towards a more inclusive society. Sharif Jr. actively participated in these movements, campaigning for change and amplifying the voices of those who fought for equality.

**Conquering Homophobia and Transphobia:** One of the greatest triumphs of Sharif Jr.'s activism was the progress made in combating homophobia and transphobia. Through his advocacy work, he initiated conversations and challenged societal norms, leading to greater acceptance and understanding of the LGBTQ community. He worked tirelessly to break down stereotypes and dismantle discriminatory attitudes, creating spaces for dialogue and education.

**Making Strides in Middle Eastern Advocacy:** While LGBTQ rights still face significant challenges in the Middle East, Omar Sharif Jr.'s activism contributed to progress within the region. He played a pivotal role in elevating the voices of LGBTQ individuals and organizations, highlighting their stories, and advocating for change at both the grassroots and institutional levels. His unwavering commitment to creating a more accepting Middle East has paved the way for future generations of activists.

**The Power of Collective Action:** Sharif Jr. understood the importance of collective action in driving social change. He actively collaborated with other LGBTQ activists and advocacy groups, recognizing the power of unity in the face of adversity. By joining forces and standing strong in solidarity, they were able to achieve remarkable victories, challenging oppressive systems and policies.

As we celebrate the victories achieved by Omar Sharif Jr., we are reminded of the incredible impact that one person's determination can have on an entire movement. His resilience and unwavering commitment to LGBTQ rights serve as an inspiration to activists around the world. In the face of immense challenges, Sharif Jr. continues to forge ahead, creating a lasting legacy of change.

# The Price of Activism

## Facing Personal and Professional Challenges

Life as an LGBTQ activist is not without its challenges. In this section, we will explore the personal and professional obstacles that Omar Sharif Jr. has faced throughout his journey. From dealing with personal struggles to navigating the complexities of the advocacy landscape, Omar has shown resilience and determination in overcoming these challenges.

### The Struggle for Self-Acceptance

Like many people in the LGBTQ community, Omar faced a long and difficult journey towards self-acceptance. While growing up in a traditional Middle Eastern family, he grappled with his own sexuality and the fear of not being accepted by his loved ones. This internal conflict took a toll on his mental well-being and hindered his ability to live authentically.

**The Pressure to Conform** As a member of a prominent Middle Eastern family, Omar felt immense pressure to conform to societal expectations. The fear of disappointing his family and risking their love and acceptance added an extra layer of complexity to his struggle. This internal battle between his true self and the expectation placed upon him caused immense internal turmoil.

**Navigating Cultural Norms** In many Middle Eastern societies, LGBTQ identities are often stigmatized and even criminalized. Omar faced the challenge of reconciling his own desires and identity with the cultural norms of his community. This created a constant tension between his personal freedom and the need to maintain a positive relationship with his family and society.

**The Courage to Be Authentic**  Overcoming these challenges required immense courage and self-acceptance. Omar had to confront his own fears and make the difficult decision to live authentically. This involved embracing his LGBTQ identity and finding the strength to challenge societal expectations and cultural norms.

## Professional Challenges

As an outspoken LGBTQ activist, Omar Sharif Jr. has also faced numerous professional challenges along the way. From dealing with backlash and attacks to navigating the complexities of advocacy work, Omar's journey has not been without its obstacles.

**Criticism and Backlash**  As a public figure, Omar has faced criticism, backlash, and even personal attacks for his LGBTQ advocacy. His decision to come out and publicly embrace his identity was met with both support and hostility. However, instead of allowing the negativity to deter him, Omar used it as fuel to continue his fight for LGBTQ rights.

**Balancing Personal and Professional Life**  Being an activist requires commitment, time, and emotional energy. Balancing his personal life and advocacy work has been a constant challenge for Omar. With a demanding schedule and the need to be constantly on the frontlines of activism, he had to find ways to maintain boundaries and prioritize self-care.

**Navigating Public Image**  As a visible LGBTQ activist, Omar had to navigate the complexities of public image. Balancing authenticity with the expectations of being a role model and spokesperson for the LGBTQ community was no easy task. He had to constantly evaluate and refine his messaging and communication to ensure he was effectively representing the diverse experiences of the community.

**Effecting Change in Conservative Environments**  Advocacy work in conservative societies poses unique challenges. Omar's Middle Eastern background meant that he had to navigate the complexities of promoting LGBTQ rights in countries with strict cultural norms and legal frameworks that are hostile to LGBTQ individuals. This required strategic thinking, creative approaches, and collaboration with local activists to effect change.

## Overcoming Challenges: Lessons Learned

Despite the personal and professional challenges he has faced, Omar Sharif Jr. has emerged as a resilient and inspiring advocate. His journey offers valuable lessons for aspiring activists:

**Self-Acceptance Is a Journey**   Omar's story reminds us that self-acceptance is a journey with its ups and downs. It takes time to embrace one's true identity fully. The path to self-acceptance requires patience, self-reflection, and the willingness to confront internal biases and societal expectations.

**Authenticity Is Empowering**   Living authentically is a powerful act of liberation. By embracing his LGBTQ identity, Omar found the strength and courage to advocate for the rights of others. His authenticity not only inspires others but also challenges societal norms and promotes inclusivity.

**Resilience is Key**   Navigating the challenges of activism requires resilience. Omar's ability to bounce back from setbacks, criticism, and personal attacks is a testament to his resilience. It is a reminder that setbacks should not deter us from pursuing our passions and fighting for what we believe in.

**Collaboration and Community Support**   Omar's journey highlights the importance of collaboration and community support. He has built alliances with other activists, NGOs, and grassroots movements, recognizing that collective action is key to effecting change. By leveraging the power of collaboration, activists can amplify their impact and create lasting change.

In conclusion, facing personal and professional challenges is an inherent part of being an LGBTQ activist. By overcoming these obstacles, Omar Sharif Jr. has demonstrated the power of resilience, authenticity, and collaboration. His journey teaches us valuable lessons about the importance of self-acceptance, embracing one's true identity, and fighting for equality in the face of adversity.

## Dealing with Threats and Attacks

In Omar Sharif Jr.'s journey as an LGBTQ activist, he has faced numerous threats and attacks from individuals who oppose his advocacy. These challenges have required him to develop strategies for both personal safety and continued activism. In this section, we will explore the different types of threats and attacks that Omar has encountered, as well as the ways in which he has dealt with them.

### Types of Threats and Attacks

As an openly gay LGBTQ activist, Omar Sharif Jr. has been subjected to various forms of threats and attacks throughout his career. These can take different shapes, ranging from online harassment to physical violence. Here are some common types of threats and attacks that Omar has experienced:

1. **Online Harassment:** In the digital age, social media platforms and online forums have become breeding grounds for hate speech and harassment. Omar has encountered trolls and cyberbullies who use derogatory language, make threats, and launch smear campaigns against him.

2. **Physical Assault:** Sadly, physical violence against LGBTQ individuals is still prevalent in many parts of the world. Omar has faced the risk of physical assault due to his advocacy work, especially when participating in public events or demonstrations.

3. **Threats to Personal Safety:** Activists like Omar often receive threats that aim to instill fear and silence their voices. These threats can come in the form of anonymous messages, intimidating phone calls, or even direct confrontations.

4. **Defamation and Stigmatization:** Some individuals or groups may attempt to tarnish Omar's reputation by spreading false information, rumors, or engaging in character assassination. This can negatively impact his credibility and effectiveness as an activist.

### Strategies for Dealing with Threats and Attacks

To navigate the challenges posed by threats and attacks, Omar Sharif Jr. has developed several strategies to protect himself and continue his advocacy work. These strategies focus on personal safety, psychological well-being, and maintaining a strong public presence. Let's explore some of these strategies:

1. **Secure Online Platforms:** In the face of online harassment, Omar takes steps to ensure his online presence is secure. He maintains strong privacy settings on social media platforms and employs strategies to minimize the impact of trolls and cyberbullies. This includes blocking or reporting abusive accounts and engaging with positive supporters while avoiding unnecessary interactions with detractors.

2. **Physical Security Measures:** Omar prioritizes his personal safety by implementing physical security measures. This includes hiring personal security when attending public events, working with event organizers to ensure adequate safety measures are in place, and avoiding potentially unsafe situations whenever possible. He also collaborates with local law enforcement agencies and organizations to mitigate risks during public appearances.

3. **Emotional and Mental Well-being:** Dealing with threats and attacks can take a toll on an activist's mental health. Omar practices self-care to maintain emotional well-being, seeking support from friends, family, and mental health professionals. He also engages in activities that bring him joy and relaxation, such as yoga, meditation, and spending time in nature.

4. **Community Support:** Omar finds strength in his community of supporters. He actively engages with LGBTQ organizations, activists, and allies who offer solidarity and protection. Building a strong network of support helps mitigate the negative impact of threats and attacks and provides a sense of belonging and resilience.

5. **Legal Protection and Advocacy:** Omar is well-versed in the legal frameworks that protect his rights as an LGBTQ activist. He collaborates with legal experts and human rights organizations to understand and utilize applicable laws and regulations. When necessary, he takes legal action against individuals or groups that engage in hate speech or physical violence.

## Navigating Fear and Adversity

Dealing with threats and attacks can be a daunting and challenging experience. However, Omar Sharif Jr. has found ways to navigate fear and adversity, turning these negative experiences into opportunities for growth and empowerment. Here are some key principles and guidance that Omar follows:

1. **Keeping the Focus on the Cause:** Omar reminds himself of the importance of his advocacy work and the positive impact it has on countless individuals. By shifting his focus from personal attacks to the broader goal of creating change, he finds renewed motivation and determination to continue his activism.

2. **Utilizing Nonviolent Resistance:** Omar strongly believes in the power of nonviolence as a form of resistance. Rather than responding to hate with hate, he advocates for peaceful dialogue, education, and understanding. By prioritizing empathy and compassion, he aims to break down barriers and create opportunities for meaningful conversations.

3. **Turning Struggles into Opportunities:** Omar sees each threat or attack as an opportunity for growth. By sharing his own experiences of adversity, he aims to inspire others facing similar challenges. By transforming personal struggles into sources of resilience and empowerment, he empowers others to embrace their identities and fight for their rights.

4. **Education and Awareness:** Omar recognizes the importance of education in combating ignorance and prejudice. He actively engages in public speaking, media interviews, and educational initiatives to raise awareness about LGBTQ rights and foster inclusivity. Through these efforts, he hopes to challenge societal norms and bridge gaps of understanding.

Dealing with threats and attacks is an unfortunate reality for many LGBTQ activists. Still, individuals like Omar Sharif Jr. have shown incredible resilience in the face of adversity. By adopting strategies for personal safety, emotional well-being, and community support, Omar continues to make a significant difference in the lives of LGBTQ individuals globally.

## Overcoming Obstacles on the Path of Advocacy

Advocacy is a powerful tool for creating change and promoting equality. However, it is not without its challenges. In the journey of LGBTQ activism, Omar Sharif Jr. has faced numerous obstacles that have tested his resilience and determination. This section explores some of the key hurdles he has encountered and how he has successfully overcome them, inspiring others along the way.

### The Cultural Barrier

One of the most significant obstacles on the path of LGBTQ advocacy is the deep-rooted cultural norms and beliefs that exist in many societies, particularly in the Middle East. These norms often perpetuate homophobia, making it difficult for individuals to express their true selves and advocate for LGBTQ rights openly.

Omar Sharif Jr. has confronted this cultural barrier head-on. By being open and honest about his sexuality, he strives to challenge the stereotypes and misconceptions surrounding LGBTQ individuals in the Middle East. His courage and authenticity have played a vital role in shifting perceptions and promoting acceptance within these conservative societies.

*Example:* One powerful way Omar Sharif Jr. overcame the cultural barrier is through his participation in Middle Eastern talk shows and interviews. By sharing his personal journey and engaging in thought-provoking discussions, he has been able to raise awareness and foster understanding among audiences who may have had limited exposure to LGBTQ issues. Through these platforms, he continues to break down barriers and change hearts and minds.

## Navigating Legal Constraints

Another significant obstacle faced by LGBTQ activists, including Omar Sharif Jr., is navigating legal constraints that limit or deny basic rights to the community. In many Middle Eastern countries, homosexuality is criminalized, making it dangerous and challenging for LGBTQ individuals to openly advocate for their rights.

In the face of such hurdles, Omar Sharif Jr. has worked tirelessly with local and international organizations to challenge discriminatory laws and policies. His determination and strategic approach have resulted in significant progress. By mobilizing public support and engaging with governments and NGOs, he has successfully influenced policy changes and legal reforms, paving the way for a more inclusive society.

*Example:* Omar Sharif Jr.'s collaboration with human rights organizations, such as Human Rights Watch and Amnesty International, has been instrumental in advocating for the decriminalization of homosexuality in the Middle East. Through their joint efforts, they have successfully pressured governments to reassess discriminatory laws and create a safer environment for LGBTQ individuals to live authentically.

## Countering Backlash and Threats

Public figures often face backlash and threats when advocating for controversial issues such as LGBTQ rights. Omar Sharif Jr. has not been immune to this challenging aspect of activism. However, he has shown remarkable resilience in the face of adversity, refusing to be silenced by threats and standing firm in his commitment to creating a more inclusive world.

To overcome this obstacle, Omar Sharif Jr. has employed a multi-faceted approach. He has increased his personal security measures while actively engaging with law enforcement agencies to address potential threats. Additionally, he continues to build a strong support system within the LGBTQ community and beyond, ensuring that he has a network of allies who can provide assistance and guidance in times of distress.

*Example:* One notable example of Omar Sharif Jr.'s resilience in the face of threats is his social media campaign, which aims to raise awareness about the challenges faced by LGBTQ individuals in restrictive societies. By sharing stories and experiences, he emphasizes the importance of solidarity and garners public support to combat discrimination and hatred.

## Embracing Intersectionality

Intersectionality is a critical aspect of LGBTQ activism, as it recognizes that individuals face multiple forms of discrimination based on their intersecting identities such as race, gender, religion, and socioeconomic status. Overcoming these intersecting barriers requires a nuanced approach that addresses the unique challenges faced by different communities.

Omar Sharif Jr. has been a vocal advocate for intersectionality, recognizing the importance of collaboration and inclusivity in the fight for equality. He actively engages in partnerships and alliances with organizations and individuals representing diverse backgrounds. By doing so, he ensures that the advocacy efforts are comprehensive and representative, leaving no one behind.

*Example:* In collaboration with grassroots LGBTQ organizations and social justice groups, Omar Sharif Jr. has initiated intersectional campaigns that highlight the importance of recognizing and addressing the unique challenges faced by LGBTQ individuals with intersecting identities. These campaigns create a space for dialogue, education, and empowerment, ultimately fostering a stronger and more united movement.

## Unconventional Strategies

In addition to navigating well-known obstacles, Omar Sharif Jr. has often employed unconventional strategies to overcome unique challenges. His innovative approach to advocacy has allowed him to reach new audiences, challenge existing norms, and amplify the voices of marginalized communities.

*Example:* One unconventional strategy that Omar Sharif Jr. has utilized is leveraging the power of the entertainment industry. By collaborating with filmmakers, writers, and artists, he has incorporated LGBTQ narratives into mainstream media, effectively humanizing and normalizing queer experiences. Through these collaborations, he has been able to influence public opinion and create a platform for dialogue on LGBTQ rights.

In conclusion, Omar Sharif Jr. has overcome numerous obstacles on his advocacy journey. From challenging cultural barriers to navigating legal constraints, countering backlash, embracing intersectionality, and employing unconventional strategies, he has demonstrated resilience, determination, and innovation. By sharing his story and fighting for LGBTQ rights, he continues to inspire others and create a lasting impact on the path to a more inclusive and equal world.

## Finding Strength in the Face of Adversity

In the journey of activism, one of the most challenging aspects is facing adversity. Omar Sharif Jr. has encountered numerous obstacles throughout his career, but he has always found the strength to overcome them. In this section, we will explore the various forms of adversity he has faced and the strategies he has employed to find strength in the midst of it all.

### Personal and Professional Challenges

Activism often comes with personal and professional challenges that can deeply affect an individual. Omar Sharif Jr. has had to navigate through these challenges and develop resilience in the face of adversity. Personal challenges may include dealing with mental health issues, stress, and burnout. Professional challenges may involve facing backlash from conservative communities, threats, and attacks on social media platforms.

To address these challenges, Omar emphasizes the importance of self-care and mental health. He acknowledges that it is vital to take breaks, seek support from loved ones, and engage in activities that bring joy and relaxation. Additionally, he advocates for therapy and counseling as valuable resources in maintaining emotional well-being and building resilience.

### Dealing with Threats and Attacks

As a high-profile LGBTQ advocate, Omar Sharif Jr. has faced threats and attacks from individuals who oppose his activism. These attacks can range from online harassment to physical dangers. In such situations, finding strength requires courage, resilience, and the support of a community.

Omar emphasizes the importance of surrounding oneself with a strong network of allies and friends who can provide emotional support during challenging times. This network helps to counterbalance the negativity and reminds individuals of their worth and the significance of their work.

Furthermore, advocacy organizations and legal resources play a crucial role in ensuring the safety of activists facing threats and attacks. Omar encourages individuals to report instances of harassment or violence to the appropriate authorities and seek legal support whenever necessary.

## Overcoming Obstacles on the Path of Advocacy

The path of advocacy is not without its fair share of obstacles. Omar Sharif Jr. has experienced roadblocks in his journey, but he has learned to navigate them with resilience and determination. Whether it is facing resistance from conservative communities, challenging cultural norms, or dealing with bureaucracy, overcoming these obstacles requires strategic thinking and perseverance.

One effective strategy Omar has employed is education and awareness-raising. By actively engaging with different communities and offering resources that debunk stereotypes and misconceptions, he has been able to foster understanding and create space for dialogue.

Additionally, building bridges and collaborations with organizations and individuals holding diverse perspectives can help overcome obstacles. Finding common ground and shared goals can lead to fruitful partnerships that result in tangible progress.

## Finding Strength in Community

Omar Sharif Jr. firmly believes in the power of community in finding strength during adversity. LGBTQ individuals, particularly those residing in conservative environments, can often feel isolated and unsupported. In such instances, building a strong support system becomes essential.

Omar encourages individuals to seek out LGBTQ support networks, both online and offline, where they can connect with like-minded individuals going through similar challenges. These support networks provide a safe space for sharing experiences, seeking guidance, and finding solidarity.

Furthermore, allies and advocates outside the LGBTQ community also play a significant role in providing support. By being allies, individuals can uplift LGBTQ voices, challenge prejudice, and create more inclusive spaces. Omar emphasizes the importance of forming alliances with individuals and organizations that share the values and goals of the LGBTQ movement.

### The Power of Resilience and Hope

Resilience and hope are two crucial components that enable individuals to find strength in the face of adversity. Omar Sharif Jr. believes that even in the most challenging circumstances, it is possible to create positive change and make a difference.

By staying focused on their goals and persevering through difficult times, activists can continue their advocacy work and inspire others to join the cause. Omar believes that every small step towards progress, no matter how incremental, matters and contributes to a larger movement for equality and social justice.

In conclusion, finding strength in the face of adversity is a vital aspect of activism, and Omar Sharif Jr.'s journey serves as an inspiration. By emphasizing self-care, building supportive networks, overcoming obstacles, and fostering resilience and hope, individuals can navigate through the challenges of advocacy and make a lasting impact on the world.

# Celebrating Victories

## Milestones in LGBTQ Rights

The journey towards LGBTQ rights has been marked by significant milestones, each representing a step forward in the fight for equality and acceptance. Let's explore some of the key achievements that have shaped the landscape of LGBTQ rights around the world.

## Decriminalization of Homosexuality

One of the earliest milestones in LGBTQ rights was the decriminalization of homosexuality in various parts of the world. In 1791, France became the first country to decriminalize same-sex sexual acts. Since then, many countries have followed suit, gradually repealing laws that criminalized homosexuality.

In 1969, the Stonewall riots in New York City marked a turning point in the LGBTQ rights movement. The uprising against police harassment and discrimination sparked a wave of activism and advocacy, leading to the modern LGBTQ rights movement.

## Recognition of Same-Sex Relationships

Another significant milestone in the fight for LGBTQ rights has been the recognition of same-sex relationships. The legalization of same-sex marriage has been a major step forward in achieving equality for LGBTQ individuals and couples.

In 2001, the Netherlands became the first country to legalize same-sex marriage. Since then, more than 30 countries, including Canada, the United States, and several European nations, have followed suit. This recognition has granted same-sex couples the same legal rights and protections enjoyed by heterosexual couples.

## Adoption and Parental Rights

The recognition of adoption and parental rights for same-sex couples has been a crucial milestone in LGBTQ rights. In many parts of the world, same-sex couples have faced legal barriers when trying to adopt children or establish legal parent-child relationships.

However, progress has been made in this area. In 2010, Iceland became the first country to grant same-sex couples the same rights as heterosexual couples when it comes to adoption. Since then, more countries have followed suit, ensuring that LGBTQ individuals and couples have the opportunity to become parents and provide loving homes for children.

## Protection Against Discrimination

The protection against discrimination based on sexual orientation and gender identity is another significant milestone in LGBTQ rights. Laws and policies that safeguard LGBTQ individuals from discrimination in areas such as employment, housing, and public accommodations play a crucial role in achieving equality.

In 1994, Sweden became the first country to introduce laws protecting LGBTQ individuals from discrimination. In the United States, the Civil Rights Act of 1964 has been interpreted to include protections against discrimination based on sexual orientation and gender identity by the Supreme Court.

## Transgender Rights

Transgender rights have also advanced significantly in recent years, although there is still work to be done. The recognition of transgender individuals and their rights has become an important aspect of the overall LGBTQ rights movement.

In 2004, Spain became the first country to allow individuals to legally change their gender without undergoing surgery or sterilization. Since then, many countries have introduced similar legislation, recognizing transgender individuals' rights to self-identification.

## Visibility and Representation

The increase in visibility and representation of LGBTQ individuals in media, politics, and society at large has been a powerful milestone in the fight for LGBTQ rights. Positive and accurate portrayals in media and the presence of openly LGBTQ politicians and public figures contribute to greater acceptance and understanding.

Award-winning films like "Brokeback Mountain" and "Moonlight" and television shows like "RuPaul's Drag Race" have helped raise awareness and foster empathy for the LGBTQ community. Additionally, the election of openly LGBTQ politicians, such as Harvey Milk and Tammy Baldwin, has paved the way for further LGBTQ representation and political advocacy.

## Global Impact

The milestones in LGBTQ rights have had a global impact, inspiring movements and advocacy efforts in countries where LGBTQ individuals still face significant challenges. Through cultural exchanges, collaborations, and support networks, activists and allies worldwide are working together to promote LGBTQ rights and create more inclusive societies.

The ongoing fight for LGBTQ rights requires continued activism, advocacy, and education. By celebrating these milestones and acknowledging the challenges that remain, we can work towards a future where all LGBTQ individuals are treated with dignity, respect, and equality.

## Exercises:

1. Research and discuss a landmark LGBTQ rights case in your country. 2. Identify and analyze a movie or TV show that had a significant impact on LGBTQ visibility and representation. 3. Investigate the current status of LGBTQ rights in a country where homosexuality is criminalized. Discuss potential strategies for change. 4. Create a social media campaign to raise awareness about an LGBTQ rights issue in your community. 5. Reflect on how the milestones in LGBTQ rights have influenced your own understanding and support for LGBTQ equality.

## Conquering Homophobia and Transphobia

In this section, we explore the tremendous progress made in conquering homophobia and transphobia, two major barriers to LGBTQ rights. Homophobia and transphobia are deeply rooted in societal attitudes and prejudices, and overcoming them requires a multifaceted approach that includes education, advocacy, and policy change. Omar Sharif Jr. has been at the forefront of this fight, using his platform to challenge these harmful beliefs and promote acceptance and understanding.

## Understanding the Impact

Homophobia and transphobia have far-reaching consequences for individuals and communities. They perpetuate discrimination, prejudice, and violence against LGBTQ individuals, leading to social exclusion, mental health issues, and limited access to basic human rights. It is essential to recognize the harmful effects of these attitudes in order to address them effectively.

**Example:** Consider a transgender individual who faces daily hostility and discrimination due to their gender identity. This person may experience challenges in finding employment, accessing healthcare, and securing safe housing. These barriers not only impact their personal well-being but also restrict their ability to fully participate in society.

## Education and Awareness

One of the most critical strategies in conquering homophobia and transphobia is through education and awareness campaigns. By challenging stereotypes, providing accurate information, and promoting empathy, we can create a more inclusive and accepting society. Education plays a crucial role in dispelling misconceptions and fostering understanding.

**Example:** Educational initiatives can include workshops and seminars in schools, universities, and workplaces that address LGBTQ issues, gender identity, and sexual orientation. These sessions provide a platform for open dialogue, allowing individuals to ask questions, challenge biases, and gain knowledge about diverse identities.

## Laws and Policies

Legislation and policies play a vital role in dismantling systemic discrimination and promoting equality. By enacting comprehensive anti-discrimination laws, protecting LGBTQ rights, and recognizing same-sex relationships, governments can send a powerful message of inclusivity. It is essential to advocate for legal protections that ensure equal rights and opportunities for all individuals, regardless of their sexual orientation or gender identity.

**Example:** Marriage equality laws have a significant impact on conquering homophobia and transphobia. They recognize same-sex relationships as equal and challenge the societal belief that LGBTQ individuals are somehow inferior or undeserving of love and commitment.

## Challenging Stereotypes

Another critical aspect of conquering homophobia and transphobia is challenging stereotypes and misconceptions. By showcasing the diversity within the LGBTQ community and highlighting positive representations, we can counter harmful narratives and foster acceptance.

**Example:** Media representation plays a crucial role in challenging stereotypes. Television shows, movies, and literature that feature LGBTQ characters as multidimensional, relatable individuals help break down prejudices and humanize the LGBTQ experience.

## Community Support

Building strong, supportive communities is instrumental in conquering homophobia and transphobia. Through LGBTQ organizations, support groups, and community centers, individuals can find a sense of belonging, support, and solidarity. These spaces provide resources, safe environments, and a platform for advocacy.

**Example:** Pride festivals and LGBTQ parades create opportunities for celebration, visibility, and raising awareness. These events serve as powerful displays of resilience and unity, challenging homophobia and transphobia with joy and pride.

## Intersecting Struggles

It is crucial to recognize that the fight against homophobia and transphobia intersects with other struggles for social justice. LGBTQ individuals of color, those with disabilities, and those from marginalized communities often face compounded discrimination. It is essential to address these intersecting oppressions collectively.

**Example:** Recognizing the unique challenges faced by LGBTQ refugees can help build a more inclusive and intersectional movement. By amplifying the voices of LGBTQ refugees and advocating for their rights, we can challenge the systemic barriers they face.

## Ongoing Work

While significant strides have been made in conquering homophobia and transphobia, the work is far from over. It requires continued dedication, activism, and collaboration to create lasting change. The journey towards equality must be ongoing and adaptive to address new challenges that arise.

**Unconventional Approach:** One innovative approach to conquering homophobia and transphobia is through art and creative expression. Using mediums such as theater, visual arts, and music, artists can challenge societal norms, provoke thought, and inspire change. Art has a unique ability to tap into emotions and create empathy, making it a powerful tool in the fight against discrimination.

In conclusion, conquering homophobia and transphobia requires a multifaceted approach that includes education, policy change, challenging stereotypes, fostering community support, and recognizing intersecting struggles. By working collectively, we can overcome these barriers and create a more inclusive and accepting world for all LGBTQ individuals. Omar Sharif Jr.'s advocacy and activism exemplify the power of resilience and determination in the face of adversity.

## Making Strides in Middle Eastern Advocacy

In the journey of LGBTQ activism, Omar Sharif Jr. has not only been a trailblazer for the community but has also made significant strides in Middle Eastern advocacy. This section explores his efforts to challenge societal norms, foster understanding, and promote equality in the Middle East.

## Understanding the Cultural Context

Advocacy in the Middle East presents unique challenges due to the conservative cultural and religious beliefs prevalent in the region. Omar understood the importance of respecting and understanding these cultural nuances in his advocacy work. He recognized the need to approach Middle Eastern advocacy with sensitivity, acknowledging that progress would be achieved through dialogue and education rather than confrontation.

## Promoting Acceptance and Tolerance

One of the key aspects of Omar's Middle Eastern advocacy was to promote acceptance and tolerance towards the LGBTQ community. He recognized that change needed to come from within, and actively engaged in conversations with religious leaders, community organizations, and influential figures to challenge stigma and misconceptions surrounding homosexuality.

Omar was instrumental in creating safe spaces for LGBTQ individuals in the Middle East. He collaborated with local organizations to establish LGBTQ community centers that offered support, resources, and a sense of belonging. These centers focused on providing educational programs, counseling services, and promoting dialogue between LGBTQ individuals, their families, and the wider community.

## Engaging with Government and Institutions

Advocacy for LGBTQ rights in the Middle East not only requires engaging with individuals and communities but also working alongside government bodies and institutions to effect change. Omar worked tirelessly to build bridges and establish partnerships with these entities.

He collaborated with government officials, NGOs, and human rights organizations to advocate for the decriminalization of same-sex relationships and the implementation of laws protecting LGBTQ individuals from discrimination. Through his work, Omar aimed to influence policy and legislation that would lead to greater acceptance and equality for the LGBTQ community.

## Creating Positive Media Representation

One of the most impactful ways to challenge stereotypes and promote understanding is through media representation. Omar utilized his platform in the media and entertainment industry to create positive and authentic portrayals of LGBTQ individuals in the Middle East.

He actively sought opportunities to share his personal story, experiences, and struggles, humanizing the LGBTQ community and providing a voice for those who had been silenced. By reaching a wide audience, Omar aimed to break down prejudices and challenge societal norms surrounding LGBTQ identities.

## Collaborating with Middle Eastern Organizations

Omar recognized the importance of collaboration and collective action in Middle Eastern advocacy. He actively sought partnerships with local LGBTQ organizations and human rights groups to amplify their voices and work together towards shared goals.

By collaborating with these organizations, Omar was able to leverage his platform to raise awareness and provide support in regions where LGBTQ rights are often repressed. Together, they organized workshops, conferences, and grassroots campaigns to challenge discrimination, promote inclusivity, and advocate for legal protections for the LGBTQ community.

## Educating the Next Generation

One of the key drivers of lasting change is education. Omar understood the power of knowledge in challenging prejudices and fostering acceptance. He dedicated significant efforts to advocate for LGBTQ-inclusive education in Middle Eastern schools and universities.

Omar worked with educators, administrators, and policymakers to develop LGBTQ-inclusive curriculum that promotes understanding, empathy, and respect for all individuals, regardless of their sexual orientation or gender identity. He believed that by teaching acceptance from an early age, future generations would grow up to be more open-minded and supportive of LGBTQ rights.

## Challenges and Future Outlook

Advocacy for LGBTQ rights in the Middle East is not without its challenges. Omar faced backlash, threats, and personal hardships in his journey. However, he remained steadfast in his commitment to effect change and inspire hope.

Looking ahead, the future of Middle Eastern advocacy lies in continued dialogue, collaboration, and education. The perseverance and dedication of individuals like Omar Sharif Jr. pave the way for a more inclusive and accepting society, where everyone, regardless of their sexual orientation or gender identity, is treated with dignity and equality.

As Omar continues his activism, he is also aware that change may take time. However, he remains hopeful that through the collective efforts of LGBTQ advocates, Middle Eastern societies will evolve and embrace diversity, ensuring a brighter future for all.

## The Power of Collective Action

In the fight for LGBTQ rights and Middle Eastern advocacy, one of the most powerful tools at our disposal is collective action. When individuals come together with a common purpose, they can create a force that is much greater than the sum of its parts. It is through collective action that lasting change can be achieved.

Collective action refers to the organized efforts of individuals or groups who work together to pursue a common goal. Whether it is organizing protests, lobbying for policy changes, or advocating for the rights of marginalized communities, collective action is an essential strategy in creating a more inclusive and equitable society.

One of the key principles of collective action is solidarity. When like-minded individuals or groups unite, they can amplify their voices and demand the attention of those in power. Solidarity creates a sense of community and belonging, providing a support network for individuals who may have previously felt isolated or unheard.

In the context of LGBTQ rights and Middle Eastern advocacy, collective action has played a crucial role in advancing the cause. LGBTQ activists have formed organizations and alliances to fight for equality, using their collective power to challenge discriminatory laws and policies.

For example, in 2003, a group of LGBTQ activists in Lebanon formed Helem, the first LGBTQ rights organization in the Arab world. Through their collective efforts, Helem has been able to provide support and resources to LGBTQ individuals, challenge discrimination, and advocate for legal reform.

Collective action also extends beyond national borders, with activists collaborating on a global scale. International organizations such as Human Rights Watch and Amnesty International work to promote LGBTQ rights and advocate for the rights of Middle Eastern communities. Through partnerships and collaborations, these organizations are able to leverage their collective resources and expertise to bring about change.

One powerful example of collective action is the global Pride movement. Each year, Pride events are held around the world, bringing together LGBTQ individuals and allies to celebrate diversity and demand equality. These events not only provide a space for expression and celebration but also serve as a platform for advocacy and awareness-raising.

Collective action is not without its challenges. Activists often face resistance, backlash, and even violence as they challenge deeply ingrained social norms and prejudices. However, it is through collective action that marginalized communities can assert their rights and demand change.

To effectively harness the power of collective action, it is important to build broad-based alliances and coalitions. By bringing together people from diverse backgrounds and communities, we can create a unified front that is difficult to ignore. This collaboration allows for the sharing of resources, strategies, and knowledge, strengthening the overall movement for change.

In addition to building alliances, collective action requires strategic planning and coordination. Activists must identify their goals, develop action plans, and mobilize resources to achieve their objectives. This may involve organizing protests, conducting advocacy campaigns, or engaging in policymaking processes.

Furthermore, collective action should aim not only for short-term victories but also long-term systemic change. By addressing the root causes of discrimination and inequality, activists can create a lasting impact on society. This may involve challenging discriminatory laws, pushing for comprehensive policy reforms, and promoting education and awareness.

In conclusion, the power of collective action cannot be underestimated in the fight for LGBTQ rights and Middle Eastern advocacy. When individuals come together with a shared purpose, they can create a force that challenges prejudice, discrimination, and injustice. By building alliances, developing strategic plans, and advocating for systemic change, activists can create a more inclusive and equitable society for all. It is through collective action that the voices of marginalized communities can be amplified and their rights can be protected.

# Impacting Policy and Legislation

## Lobbying for LGBTQ Equality

Lobbying for LGBTQ equality is a crucial aspect of Omar Sharif Jr.'s activism. Through his advocacy, he has worked tirelessly to challenge discriminatory laws and policies, promote inclusivity, and fight for equal rights for LGBTQ individuals. In this section, we will explore the strategies and methods employed by Omar Sharif Jr. in his lobbying efforts, as well as the impact of his work in advancing LGBTQ equality.

## Understanding the Importance of Lobbying

Lobbying plays a crucial role in influencing policy and legislation. It involves advocating for specific causes, such as LGBTQ equality, by engaging with lawmakers, government officials, and other decision-makers. Lobbying efforts aim to shape public opinion, generate support, and ultimately bring about legal and social change.

Omar Sharif Jr. recognized that in order to effect meaningful change, it is vital to engage directly with those in positions of power. By lobbying for LGBTQ equality, he seeks to address the systemic barriers and discrimination faced by LGBTQ individuals and push for comprehensive legal protections.

## Building Alliances and Forming Coalitions

One of the key strategies employed by Omar Sharif Jr. in his lobbying efforts is building alliances and forming coalitions with other LGBTQ activists, organizations, and allies. By joining forces with like-minded individuals and groups, he is able to amplify the LGBTQ community's collective voice and increase the impact of their advocacy.

Through these partnerships, Omar Sharif Jr. has been able to create a united front, which is essential in lobbying for LGBTQ equality. By pooling resources, expertise, and networks, these coalitions can strategically plan and execute effective lobbying campaigns.

## Engaging Lawmakers and Government Officials

Central to lobbying for LGBTQ equality is the engagement of lawmakers and government officials. Omar Sharif Jr. actively seeks opportunities to meet with politicians and policymakers to discuss the importance of LGBTQ rights and the need for comprehensive legal protections.

By engaging in constructive dialogue, sharing personal stories and experiences, and providing evidence-based arguments, Omar Sharif Jr. effectively highlights the urgency and significance of LGBTQ equality. These interactions aim to educate lawmakers, dispel misconceptions, and garner support for legislative changes.

## Strategic Advocacy Campaigns

Omar Sharif Jr. understands that lobbying efforts must be accompanied by well-planned and strategic advocacy campaigns. Such campaigns can help raise awareness, mobilize public support, and create a sense of urgency around the need for LGBTQ equality.

Utilizing various communication channels, such as social media, traditional media outlets, and public speaking engagements, Omar Sharif Jr. effectively reaches a wide audience to advocate for LGBTQ rights. These campaigns often involve sharing personal stories, hosting community events, organizing rallies, and mobilizing grassroots support.

## Partnering with NGOs and Advocacy Organizations

Collaboration with non-governmental organizations (NGOs) and advocacy organizations is another critical aspect of Omar Sharif Jr.'s lobbying efforts. By partnering with these organizations, he is able to leverage their expertise, resources, and established networks.

NGOs and advocacy organizations focusing on LGBTQ rights have extensive knowledge of legislative processes and possess deep insights into the challenges faced by the community. Omar Sharif Jr.'s collaborations with these entities enable the development of comprehensive lobbying strategies and facilitate effective advocacy at local, national, and international levels.

## Working towards Policy Reforms

To achieve LGBTQ equality, Omar Sharif Jr. actively works towards policy reforms. This involves advocating for the repeal or amendment of discriminatory laws and the introduction of legislation that provides comprehensive legal protections for LGBTQ individuals.

Through his lobbying efforts, Omar Sharif Jr. seeks to influence public opinion and garner support from lawmakers to champion policy changes. This includes offering expertise, conducting research, and presenting compelling arguments, emphasizing the positive impact such reforms can have on LGBTQ individuals and society as a whole.

## Lobbying Challenges and Strategies

Lobbying for LGBTQ equality faces numerous challenges, including opposition from conservative groups, religious institutions, and societal prejudices. Omar Sharif Jr. acknowledges these challenges and employs several strategies to overcome them.

One such strategy is engaging in constructive dialogue with opponents of LGBTQ rights. By fostering understanding, addressing concerns, and highlighting the importance of inclusivity, Omar Sharif Jr. strives to change hearts and minds, gradually eroding resistance to LGBTQ equality.

Additionally, Omar Sharif Jr. utilizes education and awareness campaigns to dispel misconceptions and stereotypes about LGBTQ individuals. By sharing stories and experiences that humanize the LGBTQ community, he aims to create empathy and a deeper understanding of the struggles they face.

**Example: Advocating for Same-Sex Marriage**

One of the prominent areas in which Omar Sharif Jr. has lobbied for LGBTQ equality is advocating for same-sex marriage. Recognizing marriage equality as a fundamental human right, he has worked tirelessly to influence public opinion and lobby for legal reforms.

Through engaging with lawmakers, sharing personal stories of the importance of marriage equality, and emphasizing the economic and social benefits, Omar Sharif Jr. advocates for the recognition of same-sex marriage. He collaborates with NGOs, legal experts, and grassroots organizations to develop comprehensive strategies and mobilize support for this cause.

**Conclusion**

Lobbying for LGBTQ equality is a crucial aspect of Omar Sharif Jr.'s advocacy work. By engaging with lawmakers, forming coalitions, and utilizing strategic advocacy campaigns, he aims to bring about comprehensive legal protections and societal acceptance for the LGBTQ community. Through his lobbying efforts, Omar Sharif Jr. plays a significant role in driving positive change and creating a more inclusive world for all.

## Collaborations with Governments and NGOs

Collaborating with governments and non-governmental organizations (NGOs) is a crucial aspect of Omar Sharif Jr.'s advocacy work. By joining forces with these influential entities, he has been able to amplify his message, effect policy changes, and bring about greater equality for LGBTQ individuals. In this section, we will explore the significance of these collaborations and how they have contributed to the progress of LGBTQ rights.

## The Power of Partnership

Partnerships between LGBTQ activists like Omar Sharif Jr. and governments or NGOs serve as a powerful catalyst for change. By working together, they can combine their respective expertise, resources, and networks to address the challenges faced by the LGBTQ community.

Governments play a vital role in creating and enforcing laws that protect LGBTQ rights. By collaborating with national and local governments, Omar Sharif Jr. can advocate for legislative changes that guarantee equal rights and opportunities for LGBTQ individuals. Through meetings, consultations, and lobbying efforts, he can influence decision-makers to prioritize LGBTQ issues and implement inclusive policies.

On the other hand, NGOs are instrumental in mobilizing grassroots movements, providing essential support services, and raising awareness about LGBTQ rights. By partnering with these organizations, Omar Sharif Jr. can tap into their extensive networks, access their valuable resources, and collaborate on initiatives that promote inclusivity and acceptance.

## Addressing Legal Barriers

Collaborations with governments and NGOs are particularly crucial in overcoming legal barriers faced by LGBTQ individuals. Many countries still have laws that criminalize same-sex relationships or discriminate against LGBTQ individuals in areas such as employment, healthcare, and housing. Through partnerships with governments, advocates like Omar Sharif Jr. can work towards the repeal or amendment of these discriminatory laws.

One example of such a collaboration is advocating for the decriminalization of homosexuality. In some countries, same-sex relationships are still considered illegal and can lead to severe punishments, including imprisonment or even death. By partnering with governments and human rights organizations, Omar Sharif Jr. can advocate for the repeal of these laws and promote a more inclusive legal framework.

Additionally, collaborations with NGOs focused on legal aid and human rights can provide invaluable support to LGBTQ individuals facing discrimination. By partnering with these organizations, Omar Sharif Jr. can ensure that affected individuals have access to legal representation, resources, and the necessary support to navigate the legal system.

## Promoting Inclusive Policies

Collaborations with governments and NGOs also play a crucial role in promoting inclusive policies that protect the rights of LGBTQ individuals. This involves advocating for policies that address issues such as anti-discrimination, hate crime legislation, gender-affirming healthcare, and inclusive education.

Through partnerships with government bodies responsible for policy-making, Omar Sharif Jr. can contribute his expertise and lived experiences to shape policies that promote equality and inclusivity. By participating in policy development consultations, he can ensure that the voices and concerns of the LGBTQ community are heard and addressed.

Collaborations with NGOs focused on advocacy and policy change can also provide a platform to amplify the voices of LGBTQ individuals. Through joint campaigns, lobbying efforts, and public awareness initiatives, Omar Sharif Jr. can help influence public opinion and put pressure on governments to adopt policies that protect and empower the LGBTQ community.

## Overcoming Challenges and Building Trust

Collaborating with governments and NGOs is not without its challenges. Differences in ideologies, bureaucratic processes, and resistance to change can hinder progress. Therefore, building trust and fostering strong relationships are essential components of successful collaborations.

Omar Sharif Jr. understands the importance of engaging in open and transparent dialogue with government representatives and members of NGOs. By establishing meaningful relationships, he can bridge the gap between the LGBTQ community and these influential entities. Regular communication and constructive engagement can lead to a better understanding of the issues faced by LGBTQ individuals and facilitate the implementation of effective solutions.

It is also crucial to address any misconceptions or biases that exist within government institutions and NGOs. Through dialogue and education, Omar Sharif Jr. can challenge stereotypes, provide accurate information, and advocate for a more inclusive and accepting society.

## Unconventional Strategy: Leveraging Celebrity Influence

Omar Sharif Jr.'s celebrity status adds a unique dimension to his collaborations with governments and NGOs. His visibility and influence in the media and entertainment industry enable him to reach a wider audience and garner attention for LGBTQ rights.

By leveraging his celebrity status, Omar Sharif Jr. can draw attention to LGBTQ issues and engage the public in important conversations. Governments and NGOs can benefit from his platform and utilize his voice to promote their initiatives, increase public support, and mobilize resources.

Moreover, Omar Sharif Jr.'s connections within the entertainment industry can facilitate collaborations with influential figures who share his commitment to LGBTQ rights. Together, they can leverage their collective power to generate social and cultural change, challenging harmful narratives and promoting inclusivity.

## Conclusion

Collaborations with governments and NGOs are indispensable in advancing LGBTQ rights and creating a more inclusive society. By partnering with these influential entities, Omar Sharif Jr. can leverage their resources, pool expertise, and amplify his message. Through joint efforts, they can tackle legal barriers, promote inclusive policies, and build a more accepting world for LGBTQ individuals.

## Pushing for Change at the Institutional Level

In order to achieve full equality for the LGBTQ community, it is essential to push for change at the institutional level. This involves engaging with governments, NGOs, and other organizations to advocate for the rights and well-being of LGBTQ individuals. In this section, we will explore the various strategies and approaches that Omar Sharif Jr. has employed in his quest to effect institutional change.

### Understanding the Power of Institutions

Institutions play a crucial role in shaping societal norms and policies. They have the power to either perpetuate discrimination and inequality or promote inclusivity and acceptance. Recognizing this, Omar Sharif Jr. has focused his efforts on engaging with institutions to drive positive change for the LGBTQ community.

### Policy Advocacy

One of the most effective ways to bring about institutional change is through policy advocacy. Omar Sharif Jr. has worked tirelessly to influence governments and legislative bodies to enact laws that protect LGBTQ rights. This involves lobbying lawmakers, participating in policy discussions, and providing expert input on issues related to LGBTQ equality.

For example, in his collaborations with NGOs and LGBTQ rights organizations, Omar Sharif Jr. has advocated for the decriminalization of homosexuality and the implementation of comprehensive anti-discrimination laws. By leveraging his platform and visibility, he has been able to raise awareness about the importance of LGBTQ-inclusive policies and push for their adoption.

## Collaborating with Governments and NGOs

To effectively push for change at the institutional level, Omar Sharif Jr. has recognized the importance of building alliances with governments and NGOs. By establishing partnerships with these entities, he has been able to amplify the voices of the LGBTQ community and garner support for policy reforms.

For instance, Omar Sharif Jr. has collaborated with government officials to organize LGBTQ-focused conferences and seminars, where he has shared his experiences and insights. These initiatives provide a platform for dialogue and create opportunities for policymakers to better understand the challenges faced by the LGBTQ community.

Additionally, partnerships with NGOs have been instrumental in driving institutional change. Together with these organizations, Omar Sharif Jr. has advocated for the establishment of LGBTQ support centers, the development of LGBTQ-inclusive educational curricula, and the implementation of non-discrimination policies in various institutional settings.

## Promoting LGBTQ Representation

Representation is a powerful tool in effecting institutional change. By promoting LGBTQ representation in institutions, Omar Sharif Jr. has worked towards breaking down barriers and changing perceptions.

One strategy employed by Omar Sharif Jr. is encouraging LGBTQ individuals to pursue careers in government and other influential institutions. By increasing LGBTQ representation in decision-making bodies, he aims to ensure that the needs and rights of the community are adequately represented and considered.

In addition, Omar Sharif Jr. has collaborated with media organizations to amplify the voices of LGBTQ individuals and shed light on their experiences. Through interviews, articles, and other media platforms, he has shared his own story, as well as those of other LGBTQ individuals, with the goal of challenging stereotypes and prejudices.

### Changing Institutional Culture

Institutional change also involves shifting the culture within institutions to be more inclusive and accepting of LGBTQ individuals. Omar Sharif Jr. recognizes the importance of creating safe and welcoming spaces within institutions, where LGBTQ individuals can fully participate and thrive.

To achieve this, Omar Sharif Jr. has advocated for the implementation of LGBTQ-inclusive policies, such as non-discrimination and anti-harassment policies, within institutions. He has also worked with organizations to provide sensitivity training and education to staff members, promoting understanding and respect for LGBTQ individuals.

### Utilizing International Platforms

In order to promote change at the institutional level, Omar Sharif Jr. has utilized international platforms and collaborations. He has spoken at global LGBTQ conferences, participated in international advocacy campaigns, and engaged with global institutions to highlight the challenges faced by the LGBTQ community.

By leveraging international partnerships, Omar Sharif Jr. has been able to generate global awareness and support for the cause of LGBTQ rights. He recognizes the interconnectedness of LGBTQ issues and the importance of working collaboratively across borders to effect meaningful change.

### The Role of Intersectionality

In pushing for change at the institutional level, Omar Sharif Jr. emphasizes the importance of intersectionality. He recognizes that LGBTQ individuals experience discrimination and marginalization not only based on their sexual orientation or gender identity but also due to other intersecting factors such as race, religion, and socioeconomic status.

Omar Sharif Jr. advocates for an inclusive approach that takes into consideration the intersectional experiences of LGBTQ individuals. By highlighting the unique challenges faced by LGBTQ individuals from diverse backgrounds, he ensures that institutional change efforts are comprehensive and truly address the needs of the entire community.

In conclusion, pushing for change at the institutional level is a fundamental aspect of LGBTQ activism. Through policy advocacy, collaborations with governments and NGOs, promoting LGBTQ representation, changing institutional culture, utilizing international platforms, and embracing intersectionality, Omar Sharif Jr. has made significant strides in effecting institutional change. His efforts serve as an inspiration for future activists and highlight the importance of engaging with institutions to create a more inclusive and accepting world for the LGBTQ community.

## The Road to Full Equality

The journey towards achieving full equality for the LGBTQ community is a challenging and complex one. It requires a multi-faceted approach that encompasses policy changes, public awareness campaigns, grassroots activism, and the support of allies from all walks of life. In this section, we will explore the key elements involved in the road to full equality and the steps necessary to overcome the obstacles along the way.

## Understanding the Current Landscape

Before we can map out the road to full equality, it is crucial to understand the existing landscape and the barriers that hinder progress. Discrimination and prejudice against LGBTQ individuals persist globally, with varying degrees of acceptance across different countries and cultures. Legal frameworks often lag behind societal attitudes, leaving many LGBTQ individuals vulnerable to discrimination in employment, housing, healthcare, and education.

To tackle these challenges head-on, advocates for full equality must work towards changing laws and policies, challenging societal norms, and fostering understanding and acceptance among the general population. This multidimensional approach is crucial to ensure lasting change and comprehensive protection for LGBTQ individuals.

## Policy Advocacy and Legislative Change

A significant aspect of the road to full equality is advocating for policy changes and legislative reforms that safeguard LGBTQ rights. Activists and organizations work to introduce inclusive laws that protect individuals from discrimination based on sexual orientation or gender identity. They lobby for comprehensive anti-discrimination laws, hate crime legislation, and the recognition of same-sex relationships.

Successful policy advocacy involves mobilizing support from lawmakers, building coalitions with other social justice movements, and engaging in strategic public education campaigns. It is essential to highlight the importance of inclusive policies for the overall well-being of society, emphasizing the economic, social, and cultural benefits of equality for all.

*Example:* One example of successful policy advocacy is the landmark Obergefell v. Hodges case in the United States. This Supreme Court ruling in 2015 legalized same-sex marriage nationwide. It was the result of years of tireless advocacy by LGBTQ activists, legal experts, and supportive allies. The case highlighted the need for full legal recognition of same-sex relationships and set a precedent for equality in other countries.

## Community Engagement and Grassroots Activism

While policy advocacy is crucial, grassroots activism plays an equally vital role in paving the road to full equality. Local communities are the heartbeat of social change, and empowering LGBTQ individuals and their allies to create change at the grassroots level is essential. Grassroots activism involves community organizing, awareness campaigns, and direct action to bring about change within local communities.

Engaging LGBTQ individuals in activism and providing them with the tools and resources to advocate for their rights cultivates a sense of ownership and empowerment. It also creates a network of support and solidarity, ensuring that the voices and experiences of the community are at the forefront of the advocacy movement.

*Example:* The Stonewall Riots of 1969, where LGBTQ individuals fought back against police harassment at the Stonewall Inn in New York City, marked a turning point in the LGBTQ rights movement. The riots sparked a wave of grassroots activism and community engagement, leading to the formation of organizations and the emergence of a collective voice demanding equal rights. This example illustrates the power of grassroots activism in igniting change.

## Education and Awareness

Education plays a pivotal role in dismantling stereotypes, challenging prejudices, and fostering acceptance and understanding. As part of the road to full equality, advocates prioritize LGBTQ-inclusive education in schools and universities, as well as promoting awareness in workplaces, religious institutions, and other community settings.

Inclusive education encompasses comprehensive sex education programs that cover a diverse range of sexual orientations and gender identities. It also involves training educators, healthcare professionals, and other service providers to create safe and inclusive spaces for LGBTQ individuals. By promoting accurate information, dispelling myths, and fostering empathy, education becomes a powerful tool for change.

*Example:* The It Gets Better Project, founded by Dan Savage and Terry Miller in 2010, aims to uplift and support LGBTQ youth by sharing personal stories of hope and resilience. Through online videos and campaigns, it has reached millions of young people worldwide, promoting acceptance, mental health support, and suicide prevention. This initiative highlights the impact of education and awareness in creating a more inclusive and supportive society.

## Collaboration and Intersectionality

Achieving full equality for the LGBTQ community necessitates collaboration and intersectionality. By building alliances with other marginalized communities, including racial, ethnic, and religious minorities, advocates can address the intersecting forms of discrimination many individuals face.

Recognizing that LGBTQ individuals exist in various intersecting identities increases the effectiveness and reach of activism. Supporting causes that promote racial justice, gender equality, and disability rights strengthens the broader fight for equality and amplifies marginalized voices.

*Example:* The intersectional activism of the Black Lives Matter movement has brought attention to the experiences of Black transgender individuals who face disproportionately high levels of violence and discrimination. By centering their advocacy around the most marginalized within the LGBTQ community, activists are working towards a fuller and more comprehensive vision of equality for all.

## Cultivating Supportive Allies

Allies play a vital role in the road to full equality. By amplifying LGBTQ voices, challenging heteronormativity, and advocating for inclusive policies, allies help create a stronger foundation for change.

Cultivating supportive allies involves education and outreach efforts, fostering empathy and understanding, and highlighting the shared values and common humanity that underpin the fight for equality. Allies can use their privilege and influence to uplift marginalized voices and challenge discriminatory practices in their personal and professional lives.

*Example:* The Human Rights Campaign's "Coming Out for Equality" campaign encourages allies, including celebrities, politicians, and public figures, to publicly support LGBTQ rights. By sharing personal stories and using their platforms to advocate for equality, these allies have a significant impact on public opinion and create a safer and more inclusive society.

### The Power of Continued Activism

The road to full equality is a continuous journey that requires sustained activism and dedication. Achieving legal victories and policy changes is not the endpoint but rather a stepping stone towards broader societal change.

Never becoming complacent and continually pushing the boundaries of acceptance and inclusivity ensures that progress is not reversed. As society evolves and new challenges emerge, activists must adapt their strategies and approaches to remain effective in the pursuit of full equality.

*Example:* The ongoing fight for trans rights exemplifies the constant need for continued activism. As more visibility and awareness are brought to the experiences of transgender individuals, advocates push for inclusive policies, access to healthcare, and an end to violence and discrimination. Continued activism is necessary to ensure that transgender individuals are fully included and protected in all aspects of society.

### Conclusion: An Inclusive Future

The road to full equality for the LGBTQ community is a challenging but necessary journey. Through policy advocacy, grassroots activism, education, collaboration, and allyship, we can build a more inclusive future.

By recognizing the intersections of oppression and advocating for the most marginalized within the LGBTQ community, we can ensure that the fight for equality is comprehensive and leaves no one behind. Together, we can break down barriers, challenge prejudices, and create a society that celebrates and embraces the diverse identities of its members.

Let us be inspired by the trailblazers before us, learn from their victories and failures, and forge ahead with determination. The road to full equality may be long, but with perseverance, solidarity, and a commitment to justice, we can build a world where everyone is free to live, love, and thrive without fear of discrimination.

# Awards and Recognition

## Honors for LGBTQ Activism

In recognition of his tireless advocacy for LGBTQ rights and his efforts to bridge LGBTQ and Middle Eastern advocacy, Omar Sharif Jr. has received numerous

# AWARDS AND RECOGNITION

honors and accolades throughout his career. These awards not only highlight his impact as an activist but also serve as a platform to spread awareness and inspire change in the global community.

## The Human Rights Campaign Visibility Award

One of the most prestigious honors Omar Sharif Jr. has received is the Human Rights Campaign (HRC) Visibility Award. The HRC is the largest LGBTQ advocacy group in the United States, and their Visibility Award recognizes individuals who use their platform to bring attention to LGBTQ issues. It is a testament to Omar's courage and dedication to championing LGBTQ rights in both the Middle East and the wider world.

## The GLAAD Media Award

The Gay & Lesbian Alliance Against Defamation (GLAAD) Media Awards celebrate and recognize media for their fair, accurate, and inclusive representation of the LGBTQ community. Omar Sharif Jr. was honored with this award for his work in advocating for LGBTQ rights through various media platforms. From television appearances to magazine features, Omar has used his voice to challenge stereotypes and promote acceptance, making a significant impact on LGBTQ representation in the media.

## The Trevor Hero Award

Omar Sharif Jr. was also recognized as a Trevor Hero by the Trevor Project, a leading organization providing crisis intervention and suicide prevention services to LGBTQ youth. The Trevor Hero Award is given to individuals who actively work to improve the mental health and well-being of LGBTQ young people. Omar's advocacy and commitment to creating safe spaces and support networks for LGBTQ youth align perfectly with the mission of the Trevor Project.

## The Arab Foundation for Freedoms and Equality Award

In acknowledgement of his efforts to advance LGBTQ rights in the Middle East, Omar was honored with the Arab Foundation for Freedoms and Equality (AFE) Award. The AFE plays a significant role in promoting LGBTQ equality and supporting individuals and organizations working to address LGBTQ issues in the Arab region. This award recognizes Omar's substantial impact on LGBTQ advocacy and his dedication to creating positive social change in his home region.

## The Elizabeth Taylor Legacy Award

The Elizabeth Taylor Legacy Award is presented by the Elizabeth Taylor AIDS Foundation to individuals who have shown exemplary commitment to fighting the HIV/AIDS epidemic and promoting awareness and education. Omar Sharif Jr. received this prestigious award for his advocacy work in raising awareness about HIV/AIDS and fighting the stigma associated with the disease within the LGBTQ community. This recognition is a tribute to his efforts to improve the lives of those affected by HIV/AIDS and his contributions to promoting inclusive healthcare and support services.

## Impact on the LGBTQ Community

These honors not only celebrate Omar Sharif Jr.'s accomplishments but also amplify the voices of the LGBTQ community and support ongoing advocacy efforts. They serve as a testament to the progress made in LGBTQ rights, acknowledging the impact of individuals who have dedicated themselves to fighting for equality and inclusion. Through his activism, Omar has inspired countless individuals to embrace their authentic selves, driving positive change in societies around the world.

It is essential to recognize the power of these awards and their ability to shape perceptions and advance LGBTQ rights. They provide a platform for honorees like Omar Sharif Jr. to continue spreading awareness, challenging discrimination, and fostering acceptance. Each accolade symbolizes a step forward in the ongoing struggle for equality and serves as a reminder of the work that still needs to be done.

### The Importance of Recognition

One of the critical aspects of these awards is their ability to elevate the visibility and impact of LGBTQ activists like Omar Sharif Jr. Recognition not only validates their tireless efforts but also provides a platform to reach a broader audience and spark crucial conversations about LGBTQ rights. These accolades encourage other individuals to take a stand and make a difference, creating a ripple effect throughout society.

### Using Awards as a Platform for Change

Omar Sharif Jr. has used the recognition he has received to amplify his advocacy work and shed light on the issues faced by the LGBTQ community. With each award, he leverages his platform to bring attention to the struggles and triumphs of LGBTQ individuals, challenging societal norms and advocating for change.

### Inspiring Others to Get Involved

The honors bestowed upon Omar serve as an inspiration to people from all walks of life, encouraging them to mobilize and join the fight for LGBTQ rights. When individuals see the impact of activism and the recognition it receives, they are motivated to take action and contribute in meaningful ways to create a more inclusive and accepting world.

**Conclusion**

Omar Sharif Jr.'s journey has been marked by the recognition he has received for his LGBTQ advocacy. From prestigious awards to accolades from leading organizations, each honor represents a step forward in the fight for LGBTQ equality. These accolades not only celebrate Omar's accomplishments but also serve as a reminder of the ongoing work needed to create a more inclusive and accepting society. As he continues to make strides in LGBTQ and Middle Eastern advocacy, the recognition he receives paves the way for future generations of activists, empowering them to create their own legacy of change.

## The Role of Awards in Spreading Awareness

Awards play a crucial role in spreading awareness and advancing social movements, and that includes the LGBTQ rights movement. This section explores how awards have contributed to the visibility and progress of this movement, and how they have propelled activists like Omar Sharif Jr. to the forefront of advocacy.

## Recognizing and Honoring LGBTQ Activism

Awards are a powerful way to recognize and honor LGBTQ activists for their contributions. By acknowledging the hard work and dedication of individuals, organizations, and movements, awards bring attention to the important issues being addressed. They celebrate the milestones achieved and inspire others to take action.

One prominent example of an award that recognizes LGBTQ activism is the Harvey Milk Medal of Freedom. Named after the iconic LGBTQ rights activist Harvey Milk, this award is given to individuals who have made significant contributions towards LGBTQ equality. It not only celebrates the achievements of recipients but also serves as a reminder of the ongoing fight for justice and equality.

## Amplifying Voices and Spreading Awareness

Awards provide a platform for LGBTQ activists to amplify their voices and reach a broader audience. When high-profile individuals like Omar Sharif Jr. are honored with awards, it brings attention to their work and allows them to share their experiences and messages with a larger community.

For example, the GLAAD Media Awards recognize and honor the media's fair, accurate, and inclusive representations of LGBTQ individuals and issues. This award not only celebrates the positive portrayals in film, television, and journalism but also encourages media professionals to continue telling diverse stories that accurately represent the LGBTQ community.

Moreover, the visibility and credibility that come with receiving awards help LGBTQ activists gain traction in their advocacy efforts. It opens doors to partnerships, collaborations, and speaking engagements, allowing them to reach even larger audiences and spread awareness about LGBTQ rights.

**Inspiring Others and Fostering Change**

Awards inspire others to follow in the footsteps of LGBTQ activists, emboldening them to take action and make a difference in their own communities. When individuals see someone like Omar Sharif Jr. receiving recognition for their advocacy, it encourages them to embrace their own identities and fight for their rights.

In addition to inspiring individuals, awards also drive institutional change. They put pressure on governments, institutions, and organizations to reflect on their policies and practices regarding LGBTQ rights. The awareness generated by awards often leads to increased support and resources for LGBTQ initiatives, paving the way for meaningful change.

For instance, the Stonewall Book Award is given annually to English-language works of exceptional merit relating to the gay, lesbian, bisexual, and transgender experience. By recognizing outstanding literature that explores LGBTQ themes, this award promotes inclusivity and diversity in literature and educates readers about different perspectives and experiences.

**Promoting Dialogue and Collaboration**

Awards catalyze conversations and promote dialogue across diverse communities. They bring together activists, policymakers, artists, and the general public to discuss and evaluate the progress made in LGBTQ rights. This dialogue allows for the exchange of ideas, the sharing of strategies, and the creation of collaborations that can further advance the movement.

The International LGBTQI Youth and Student Organization (IGLYO) Rainbow Europe Nisimazine Award is a shining example of an award that promotes collaboration and dialogue. This award supports young LGBTQ activists and filmmakers by providing them with a platform to showcase their work and engage with a global audience. By connecting LGBTQ activists from different countries and backgrounds, it fosters international solidarity and sparks conversations on pressing issues related to LGBTQ rights.

## Using Recognition as a Catalyst for Change

When LGBTQ activists like Omar Sharif Jr. receive awards, it serves as a catalyst for further change. It sends a powerful message that their work is valued and impactful, inspiring them to continue their advocacy efforts. This recognition highlights the importance of ongoing activism and encourages others to get involved.

Furthermore, award recipients often leverage their recognition to push for policy changes and legislative reforms. The credibility and visibility that come with receiving awards provide LGBTQ activists with a platform to engage with decision-makers and advocate for comprehensive and inclusive policies.

By using their awards as a voice and a symbol of progress, LGBTQ activists like Omar Sharif Jr. can rally support and overcome challenges on the path to equality.

## Conclusion: The Role of Awards in Spreading Awareness

Awards are essential in the LGBTQ rights movement as they recognize, amplify, and inspire LGBTQ activists and their causes. They serve as a powerful tool for spreading awareness, promoting dialogue, and fostering change around the world.

By acknowledging the achievements and contributions of individuals like Omar Sharif Jr., awards create visibility and inspire others to take action. They provide a platform for activists to share their stories, amplify their voices, and propel their advocacy efforts forward.

Moreover, awards drive institutional change by pressuring governments, organizations, and institutions to reevaluate their policies and practices. They foster collaboration and dialogue, creating opportunities for diverse communities to come together and work towards a more inclusive and equal society.

Awards not only honor the recipients but also uplift the entire LGBTQ community, offering hope for a more inclusive and accepting world. As the LGBTQ rights movement continues to evolve, awards will play a vital role in celebrating achievements, inspiring progress, and ensuring that the voices and struggles of LGBTQ individuals are recognized and valued.

## Omar Sharif Jr.'s Iconic Status

Omar Sharif Jr., the multitalented LGBTQ activist, has not only become an influential figure in the fight for equality but has also achieved iconic status within the community. His relentless dedication to challenging societal norms and advocating for LGBTQ rights has earned him admiration and respect from people all over the world.

Why has Omar Sharif Jr. become an icon? It is because of his courage to be authentically himself and his unwavering commitment to making a difference. By coming out as gay and openly embracing his true identity, Sharif Jr. has shattered stereotypes and become a beacon of hope for countless LGBTQ individuals who struggle with self-acceptance.

His journey to self-discovery was not an easy one. Sharif Jr. went through the internal struggle of hiding his true self, fearing the consequences of being open about his sexuality. However, he found support in unexpected places, including individuals who had faced similar challenges. This support gave him the courage to make the decision to live his life authentically, regardless of the potential backlash.

Through his brave act of coming out, Sharif Jr. has inspired and empowered others to embrace their identities and live openly. He has become a role model for LGBTQ youth who may be struggling with self-acceptance, showing them that being true to themselves is not only possible but also necessary for personal growth and happiness.

In addition to his personal journey, Sharif Jr.'s impact as an LGBTQ icon extends to his activism and advocacy work. By leveraging his fame and visibility, he has been able to bring attention to important issues facing the LGBTQ community, both in the Middle East and globally.

One of the most notable aspects of Sharif Jr.'s iconic status is his ability to bridge cultures. Born into a traditional Middle Eastern family, he faced unique challenges in reconciling his LGBTQ identity with his cultural heritage. Through his advocacy work, Sharif Jr. has strived to break down cultural barriers and change perceptions in the Middle East. His efforts have not only increased acceptance within the LGBTQ community but have also fostered understanding and tolerance among the wider population.

Sharif Jr.'s impact is not limited to his advocacy work alone; he has also actively worked to create safe spaces for LGBTQ individuals. By establishing LGBTQ centers and support networks, he has provided resources for education, support, and empowerment. These safe spaces have become vital in nurturing acceptance and understanding, contributing to the overall well-being of the LGBTQ community.

As an iconic figure, Sharif Jr. has used his platform to challenge prejudice and discrimination through the power of media. By creating LGBTQ-inclusive content and using social media as a tool for activism, he has reached a global audience, challenging misconceptions and promoting acceptance. Through his engaging public speaking, he motivates others to take action and inspires change through his words and actions.

Omar Sharif Jr.'s iconic status is not solely based on his individual achievements; it is a testament to the collective impact of his advocacy. Through collaborations with LGBTQ organizations, governments, and NGOs, he has influenced policy and legislation, pushing for greater equality and rights. His efforts have contributed to significant milestones in LGBTQ rights and have played a pivotal role in conquering homophobia and transphobia.

In recognition of his extraordinary impact, Sharif Jr. has received numerous honors for his LGBTQ activism. These awards not only acknowledge his efforts but also provide a platform for spreading awareness about LGBTQ issues. Sharif Jr. harnesses this recognition to further amplify his message and create lasting change.

Looking to the future, Omar Sharif Jr.'s iconic status will continue to evolve as he takes on new challenges and causes. The fight for LGBTQ rights is a never-ending battle, and Sharif Jr. remains committed to being at the forefront of the movement. His ongoing efforts will shape the future of LGBTQ activism, ensuring progress and a more inclusive world for generations to come.

In conclusion, Omar Sharif Jr.'s iconic status is a result of his personal journey, his unwavering commitment to advocacy, and his ability to bridge cultures. Through his courage and authenticity, he has become an inspiration to LGBTQ individuals worldwide. His impact extends beyond his individual achievements and serves as a beacon of hope for a more inclusive and accepting world.

## Using Recognition as a Platform for Change

In the journey of LGBTQ activism, being recognized for one's contributions is not just a personal achievement, but also a powerful tool to create social change. Recognition can provide a platform for activists like Omar Sharif Jr. to amplify their message, inspire others, and advocate for LGBTQ rights on a global scale. This section explores how recognition serves as a catalyst for change and explores the ways in which Omar Sharif Jr. has utilized his iconic status to make a lasting impact.

## Honors for LGBTQ Activism

Recognition comes in many forms, and for Omar Sharif Jr., it has taken the shape of honors and awards for his tireless activism. Whether it's being honored by LGBTQ organizations, receiving accolades from human rights groups, or even being recognized by governmental bodies, these acknowledgments act as a validation of his work and dedication.

One such example of recognition is the inclusion of Omar Sharif Jr. on prestigious lists of influential LGBTQ figures. Being acknowledged alongside other trailblazers serves to amplify his voice and spread awareness about the LGBTQ rights movement. Awards and honors play a crucial role in shedding light on the importance of LGBTQ advocacy and its impact on society.

## The Role of Awards in Spreading Awareness

Awards and recognition not only validate an individual's efforts but also provide an opportunity to spread awareness about LGBTQ rights on a larger scale. When Omar Sharif Jr. receives an award, it often comes with media attention and public exposure, allowing him to reach a wider audience.

Through interviews, press releases, and acceptance speeches, Omar can use these platforms to educate the public, challenge misconceptions, and advocate for policy change. His ability to convey personal experiences and highlight the struggles of the LGBTQ community helps humanize the movement and encourages empathy and understanding. Award ceremonies become a stage for activism, allowing the audience to witness the power of advocacy firsthand.

## Omar Sharif Jr.'s Iconic Status

Having achieved iconic status, Omar Sharif Jr. possesses a unique platform to raise awareness and inspire change. As the grandson of a legendary actor and a public figure in his own right, he has the attention of both fans and the media. His celebrity status provides him with the visibility and influence needed to tackle LGBTQ issues on a global scale.

Through interviews, red carpet appearances, and social media presence, Omar is able to reach millions of people who may not otherwise engage with LGBTQ activism. By sharing his story and advocating for inclusion and equality, he effectively uses recognition as a stepping stone to drive social change. His commitment to activism transcends borders and cultures and captures the attention of diverse audiences worldwide.

## Using Recognition as a Platform

Recognition alone is not enough to bring about meaningful change. It is how individuals like Omar Sharif Jr. leverage that recognition that truly makes a difference. By utilizing his platform, Omar expands his reach beyond the LGBTQ community and engages with allies, policymakers, and influencers.

To use recognition as a platform for change, Omar employs various strategies. He partners with organizations that share his vision, advocates for policy reform, and campaigns for LGBTQ rights. By leveraging his connections and influence, he can bring about systemic change that benefits not only LGBTQ individuals but society as a whole.

## Impact of Recognition on the LGBTQ Movement

Recognition helps create a ripple effect within the LGBTQ movement. When influential figures like Omar Sharif Jr. are acknowledged for their activism, it encourages others to join the cause, empowers LGBTQ individuals to embrace their identities, and instills hope that change is possible.

Moreover, recognition amplifies the voices of marginalized communities within the LGBTQ umbrella. By being celebrated and honored, activists like Omar Sharif Jr. bring attention to intersectionality, ensuring that the movement is inclusive and representative of all identities and experiences.

## Using Recognition as a Call to Action

Beyond personal achievements, recognition can serve as a call to action for both individuals and society. It reminds us that progress has been made but emphasizes the work that still needs to be done. By celebrating LGBTQ activists like Omar Sharif Jr., we highlight the importance of continuing the fight for equality and justice.

Recognition also compels individuals to educate themselves and take an active role in creating change. It encourages conversations, prompts donations to LGBTQ causes, and motivates others to use their own platforms for advocacy. The impact goes beyond the individual being recognized, inspiring a collective effort towards a more inclusive and accepting world.

## Conclusion: A Hero for Our Times

Omar Sharif Jr.'s journey, fueled by recognition and activism, has paved the way for a new generation of LGBTQ advocates. By using his platform to educate, inspire, and challenge societal norms, he has left an indelible mark on the LGBTQ and Middle Eastern advocacy landscape.

Recognition serves as a cornerstone for change, allowing individuals like Omar Sharif Jr. to effect lasting progress in the pursuit of LGBTQ rights. Through his work, he has demonstrated the transformative power of recognition as a catalyst for social change, bridging cultures, and breaking down barriers.

As we celebrate his contributions and the impact he continues to make, we are reminded of the power each individual possesses to create a more inclusive world. Omar Sharif Jr.'s legacy will continue to inspire future activists, both within the LGBTQ community and beyond, providing hope and inspiration for generations to come.

## Lessons Learned

### Reflections on a Lifetime of Activism

Throughout his lifetime, Omar Sharif Jr. has been a relentless advocate for LGBTQ rights and Middle Eastern advocacy. In this section, we will delve into his reflections on his journey and the personal growth he experienced through his activism. We will explore the insights gained from his tireless work, the challenges faced, and the legacy he hopes to leave behind.

### The Power of Personal Growth

Omar Sharif Jr. acknowledges that his activism has not only brought about change in his community, but has also transformed him as an individual. He reflects on the countless conversations, debates, and encounters he has had, which have broadened his perspectives and deepened his understanding of the world.

Engaging with diverse individuals and communities has challenged his own preconceptions and biases, pushing him towards personal growth. It is through this process that he has come to appreciate the beauty of humanity's shared experiences and the importance of empathy in advocacy.

### Lessons Learned Along the Way

Omar Sharif Jr. offers valuable insights gained from his years of activism. He emphasizes the significance of perseverance and resilience in the face of adversity. Despite the personal and professional challenges he has encountered, he remains steadfast in his commitment to fostering change.

He highlights the importance of finding allies and building coalitions with like-minded individuals and organizations. By coming together, activists can amplify their voices and create a powerful force for change. Additionally, he emphasizes the role of education as a tool for empowerment and breaking down barriers.

### Inspiring the Next Generation

Omar Sharif Jr. is passionate about inspiring and empowering the next generation of activists. He believes in the power of mentorship and nurturing young voices. In his reflections, he encourages young LGBTQ individuals and advocates to embrace their identities and use their unique stories as catalysts for change.

Through his own journey, he has learned the importance of self-care and maintaining balance in one's personal and professional life. He encourages young activists to prioritize their well-being and seek support when needed. He also urges them to remain adaptable and open-minded in the face of changing societal landscapes.

### The Intersectionality of Activism

One of the key lessons Omar Sharif Jr. reflects upon in his lifetime of activism is the importance of intersectionality. He recognizes that the fight for LGBTQ rights intersects with various other social justice issues such as gender equality, racial justice, and economic disparity.

He emphasizes the need for collaborative activism that takes into account the unique challenges different communities face. By working together, activists can create a more inclusive and equitable society for all.

### Leaving a Lasting Impact

In contemplating his legacy, Omar Sharif Jr. hopes to leave a lasting impact on LGBTQ activism and Middle Eastern advocacy. He envisions a world where the LGBTQ community in the Middle East is embraced and celebrated for their contributions to society.

He hopes his work will inspire future generations to carry on the fight for equality and justice. He encourages his fellow activists to continue challenging societal norms, pushing for policy changes, and fostering understanding and acceptance.

### Embracing Hope for a Better Future

As he concludes his reflections, Omar Sharif Jr. expresses his unwavering optimism for a more inclusive world. He believes that by sharing our stories and persistently advocating for change, we can create a future where LGBTQ individuals in the Middle East and beyond can live openly and authentically.

He reminds us that the journey towards equality is ongoing, and urges us all to stand together in solidarity. It is through collective action and a sense of shared humanity that we can build a brighter and more inclusive world for future generations.

In Omar Sharif Jr.'s reflections on a lifetime of activism, we find inspiration, wisdom, and hope. His journey serves as a reminder that change begins with individual voices, but it is through collective efforts that we can truly transform society.

### Personal Growth through Advocacy

Personal growth is an essential aspect of any journey, especially when it comes to activism. For Omar Sharif Jr., his advocacy work has not only impacted others but has also played a significant role in his own personal growth. Through his experiences, challenges, and triumphs, Omar has discovered profound insights and developed as an individual. In this section, we will delve into the transformative power of advocacy in shaping Omar's character and worldview.

One of the foundational aspects of personal growth through advocacy is self-reflection. As Omar embarked on his journey of LGBTQ activism, he had to confront his own beliefs, biases, and prejudices. This introspection allowed him to challenge societal norms and rethink his understanding of identity and inclusivity. It required him to question deeply ingrained attitudes and develop a more empathetic and compassionate mindset. In doing so, he not only expanded his worldview but also enhanced his ability to connect with diverse communities.

Advocacy also teaches individuals the importance of resilience and perseverance. Throughout his activism, Omar faced numerous challenges and setbacks. Whether it was backlash from conservative communities or threats to his personal safety, he had to navigate through difficult situations with unwavering determination. These experiences not only strengthened his resolve but also contributed to his personal growth. By confronting adversity head-on, he gained valuable insights into his own strength and resilience.

Another significant aspect of personal growth through advocacy is the development of effective communication skills. As Omar became a public figure, he realized the power of his voice in inspiring change. He honed his public speaking abilities, gained confidence, and learned how to effectively convey his message to various audiences. Through his appearances in media and engagements with different communities, he refined his skills in articulating social issues, sharing personal stories, and fostering understanding.

Moreover, advocacy often leads to personal growth through building relationships and forming alliances. As Omar connected with LGBTQ communities around the world, he experienced the transformative power of solidarity and collaboration. Through partnerships with other activists and organizations, he learned the value of collective action and the strength in unity. These relationships not only provided support and encouragement but also challenged his perspective and widened his understanding of the LGBTQ movement.

Advocacy, at its core, is about making a positive impact in society. Through his activism, Omar witnessed firsthand the transformative power of his efforts in changing lives and communities. This sense of purpose and fulfillment fueled his personal growth, as it reinforced his dedication to his cause and motivated him to continue fighting for equality. It allowed him to recognize the immense potential of individuals to effect change and inspired him to leave a lasting legacy.

In conclusion, personal growth is an integral aspect of advocacy, and Omar Sharif Jr.'s journey is a testament to its transformative power. Through self-reflection, resilience, effective communication, and building relationships, he has experienced significant personal growth while making a positive impact on LGBTQ advocacy. His story serves as a reminder that the pursuit of justice not only impacts society but also has the potential to profoundly shape individuals on their journey of self-discovery and growth.

## Insights for Future Activists

In this section, we will explore the invaluable insights and advice that Omar Sharif Jr. has for future activists. Through his own journey and experiences, he has gained a wealth of knowledge and understanding of the LGBTQ rights movement and the challenges that come with it. Let's delve into the lessons he has learned and the wisdom he has to offer.

### Embrace Your Authenticity

One of the most powerful messages that Omar Sharif Jr. shares is the importance of embracing your authenticity. He encourages future activists to be true to themselves and to never compromise their identity. It is through living authentically that true change and progress can occur.

*Example*: Omar recalls his own struggles with hiding his true self and the toll it took on his mental and emotional wellbeing. Once he made the decision to live openly and authentically, he felt a profound sense of liberation and empowerment. This personal journey serves as a reminder to future activists that embracing their authenticity is not only liberating for themselves but also inspiring for others.

## Find Support and Build Communities

Building strong support networks and communities is essential for activists. Omar emphasizes the importance of finding like-minded individuals who share similar values and goals. These communities provide a safe space for individuals to connect, grow, and support each other in their advocacy work.

*Example*: Omar highlights the pivotal role that LGBTQ organizations played in his own journey. These organizations provided him with a sense of belonging, support, and guidance. Through these networks, he was able to connect with other activists, share experiences, and collaborate on projects that furthered the cause of LGBTQ rights.

## Adopt an Intersectional Approach

Omar stresses the need for activists to adopt an intersectional approach in their advocacy. This means recognizing and addressing the interconnected nature of various forms of oppression, such as racism, sexism, and ableism. By acknowledging and centering the experiences of marginalized communities, activists can create a more inclusive and equitable movement.

*Example*: Omar draws from his own experiences as a LGBTQ individual from a Middle Eastern background to highlight the significance of intersectionality. He emphasizes the need to understand and address the unique challenges faced by LGBTQ individuals in different cultural contexts, recognizing that their struggles are shaped by both their sexual orientation and their cultural background.

## Educate and Raise Awareness

Education and raising awareness are critical tools for driving change. Omar emphasizes the importance of educating oneself and others on LGBTQ rights, history, and the impact of discrimination. By sharing knowledge and promoting understanding, activists can challenge misconceptions and foster empathy and acceptance.

*Example*: Omar recounts his own experience of using education and awareness to challenge cultural norms and stereotypes. Through interviews, public speaking engagements, and media appearances, he has been able to educate audiences and break down barriers. By sharing personal stories and insights, he has helped people to see LGBTQ individuals in a new light and spark important conversations.

## Engage in Collaboration and Allyship

Collaboration and allyship are essential components of effective activism. Omar encourages future activists to seek out opportunities for collaboration with individuals and organizations that are aligned with their cause. By working together, activists can amplify their impact and create a united front for change.

*Example*: Omar highlights his collaborations with LGBTQ organizations, governments, and NGOs as key moments of success in his advocacy work. By joining forces with other advocates, he has been able to lobby for policy changes, raise awareness on a larger scale, and push for greater equality.

## Persevere and Stay Resilient

Activism is often a long and challenging journey, filled with victories and setbacks. Omar emphasizes the importance of perseverance and resilience in the face of adversity. He encourages future activists to stay hopeful, maintain their determination, and find strength in their cause.

*Example*: Omar recalls the personal and professional challenges he has faced as an LGBTQ activist. From threats and backlash to the exhaustion of fighting for change, he persevered by keeping his focus on his mission. His resilience serves as an inspiration for future activists who may encounter similar challenges.

## Think Globally, Act Locally

Finally, Omar encourages activists to think globally but act locally. While global advocacy is crucial, creating change at the local level can have a profound impact on communities. By engaging with local organizations, schools, and communities, activists can effect tangible change and lay the foundation for broader transformation.

*Example*: Omar shares how he has worked closely with Middle Eastern LGBTQ organizations to create safe spaces and foster acceptance. By focusing on local initiatives, he has instigated change in the communities that need it the most. This approach demonstrates the power of grassroots activism in building a more inclusive society.

In conclusion, future activists can draw valuable insights from Omar's journey. From embracing authenticity to educating others, collaborating with allies, and persevering in the face of adversity, his experiences offer guidance and inspiration for those passionate about LGBTQ rights and broader social justice causes. By internalizing these lessons, activists can make a lasting impact and create a more inclusive world.

## The Legacy of Omar Sharif Jr.'s Journey

Omar Sharif Jr.'s journey as an LGBTQ activist has left an indelible mark on the world. His bravery, passion, and unwavering commitment to equality have paved the way for a more inclusive and accepting society. As we reflect on his remarkable legacy, we can trace the impact he has made in several key areas: personal transformation, community empowerment, policy change, and global recognition.

## Personal Transformation: Inspiring Change from Within

Omar's personal transformation serves as a powerful testament to the human capacity for growth and self-discovery. Through his journey of self-acceptance and coming out as a gay man, he has empowered countless individuals to embrace their true selves, regardless of societal norms or expectations. By openly sharing his own struggles and triumphs, Omar has provided solace and hope to those grappling with their own identities.

Omar's courage to live authentically has challenged societal norms and shattered stereotypes, encouraging others to break free from the constraints of heteronormativity and embrace their diverse identities. His journey reminds us that the path towards self-acceptance and love is never easy, but always worthwhile.

## Community Empowerment: Amplifying Voices and Fostering Acceptance

Throughout his advocacy work, Omar has championed the rights and voices of LGBTQ individuals, particularly those in the Middle Eastern community. By leveraging his platform, he has created safe spaces for dialogue and discussion, fostering a sense of belonging and empowerment for individuals who have long been marginalized.

Omar's commitment to bridging LGBTQ and Middle Eastern advocacy has served as a catalyst for change, challenging cultural norms and promoting understanding. Through his collaborations with local organizations and community leaders, he has helped dismantle systemic barriers and foster acceptance in societies where LGBTQ rights are still viewed with skepticism.

## Policy Change: Influencing Governments and Institutions

Omar's advocacy extends beyond individual transformation and community empowerment. His relentless pursuit of policy change has been instrumental in advancing LGBTQ rights and legal protections. By engaging with governments, non-governmental organizations, and policymakers, he has provided crucial insight into the unique challenges faced by LGBTQ individuals in the Middle East and beyond.

Omar's lobbying efforts and collaborative initiatives have played a significant role in shaping legislation and policies that protect LGBTQ individuals from discrimination, ensuring their right to live authentically and without fear. His work has also sought to create inclusive and empowering spaces within institutions, challenging discriminatory practices and fostering a culture of acceptance.

## Global Recognition: Elevating the LGBTQ Movement

Omar's global impact as an LGBTQ activist is undeniable. Through his presence at international conferences and collaborations with queer activists worldwide, he has amplified the voices of those fighting for equality and justice. Each platform he engages with becomes an opportunity to challenge preconceived notions, dispel stereotypes, and promote acceptance.

By utilizing the power of media, particularly social media, Omar has effectively disseminated his message to a global audience. His inclusive content and engagement with diverse communities have sparked conversations and encouraged individuals from all walks of life to examine their own biases, generating support for the LGBTQ movement on an unprecedented scale.

## Preserving History: A Lasting Legacy

As we reflect on Omar's legacy, it is crucial to acknowledge the importance of preserving LGBTQ history. Omar's journey has become a part of that history, representing the struggles and triumphs of countless individuals. By sharing his story and experiences, he ensures that future generations will have access to a narrative that speaks to their own struggles and aspirations.

Omar's commitment to preserving LGBTQ history goes beyond his own journey. Through collaborations with archival institutions and academic organizations, he has paved the way for the documentation and preservation of

LGBTQ experiences, ensuring that the stories of those who have fought for equality will never be forgotten.

In conclusion, Omar Sharif Jr.'s journey as an LGBTQ activist leaves behind a legacy of personal transformation, community empowerment, policy change, global recognition, and the preservation of LGBTQ history. His unwavering dedication to inclusivity and equality has inspired individuals around the world to challenge societal norms, embrace their identities, and work towards a more inclusive future. As we continue on the path towards equality, may Omar's legacy serve as a guiding light and a reminder of the power of advocacy and authentic self-expression.

# Chapter 4: Beyond Borders: The Global Impact

## Chapter 4: Beyond Borders: The Global Impact

### Chapter 4: Beyond Borders: The Global Impact

In this chapter, we explore the remarkable global impact of LGBTQ activist Omar Sharif Jr. His tireless efforts in advocating for LGBTQ rights have transcended borders, creating positive change not only in the Middle East but also on a global scale. Through his work, Omar has broken down barriers, challenged stereotypes, and built bridges between LGBTQ communities around the world.

### Speaking at Global LGBTQ Conferences

Omar Sharif Jr.'s influence reaches far beyond his immediate community. He has been invited to speak at numerous global LGBTQ conferences, where he shares his experiences and insights with a diverse array of activists, allies, and policymakers. These conferences provide a platform for Omar to inspire and empower others to take action in their own communities.

During these speaking engagements, Omar emphasizes the importance of intersectionality in activism. He highlights the need for collaboration and solidarity among different marginalized groups, recognizing that the fight for LGBTQ rights intersects with other social justice issues such as gender equality, racial justice, and immigrant rights. By addressing the interconnected nature of these struggles, Omar encourages a more inclusive and comprehensive approach to activism.

## Amplifying Voices of Queer Activists Worldwide

Omar Sharif Jr. understands the power of using his platform to amplify the voices of queer activists worldwide. He actively engages with these individuals, listening to their stories and experiences, and sharing them with a broader audience. By sharing these stories, Omar helps to humanize the LGBTQ experience and create empathy and understanding among people from different cultures and backgrounds.

Through interviews, social media campaigns, and collaborations with LGBTQ organizations, Omar ensures that the stories and perspectives of LGBTQ individuals from diverse backgrounds are heard and valued. This inclusive approach not only fosters greater acceptance and understanding but also helps to dismantle stereotypes and misconceptions about the LGBTQ community.

## Global Partnerships and Collaborations

Omar Sharif Jr. recognizes the importance of building partnerships and collaborations to effect change on a global scale. He actively seeks out like-minded organizations and individuals who share his commitment to LGBTQ rights and works together with them to create impactful initiatives.

These partnerships may involve joint advocacy campaigns, community outreach programs, or collaborative research projects. By joining forces with other LGBTQ activists, human rights organizations, and NGOs, Omar amplifies the impact of his advocacy efforts and fosters a sense of unity within the global LGBTQ community.

## Connecting LGBTQ Communities on a Global Scale

One of Omar Sharif Jr.'s primary goals is to connect LGBTQ communities from around the world. He uses his position as a global LGBTQ icon to foster connections, build bridges, and create networks of support and solidarity.

Through online platforms, social media campaigns, and in-person gatherings, Omar facilitates conversations and exchanges of ideas among LGBTQ individuals and organizations. These connections strengthen the global LGBTQ movement, enabling activists to learn from one another, share best practices, and collectively work towards a more inclusive and accepting world.

## The Power of Social Media in Activism

Omar recognizes the immense power of social media in driving activism and raising awareness. He has leveraged platforms like Instagram, Twitter, and YouTube to share his message, reach a broader audience, and inspire change.

Through engaging and thought-provoking content, Omar sparks conversations, educates his followers, and challenges societal norms and prejudices. Social media has allowed him to transcend geographical boundaries and connect with individuals who may not have access to LGBTQ resources or support in their own communities.

## Creating LGBTQ-Inclusive Content

As a media personality, Omar Sharif Jr. understands the influential role that media plays in shaping public opinion. He actively works towards creating LGBTQ-inclusive content that represents the diverse experiences of the community.

Whether it's through his own productions or collaborations with media organizations, Omar strives to promote positive and accurate portrayals of LGBTQ individuals. By showcasing a range of narratives and experiences, he aims to challenge stereotypes, combat homophobia and transphobia, and foster greater acceptance and understanding.

## Using Media to Challenge Prejudice and Discrimination

Media has the power to challenge deep-rooted prejudices and discrimination. Omar Sharif Jr. utilizes various media platforms to challenge harmful narratives and promote acceptance.

Through interviews, documentaries, op-eds, and opinion pieces, Omar confronts discriminatory practices, policies, and attitudes. By sharing personal stories and shining a light on the experiences of LGBTQ individuals, he aims to shift public opinion and create a more inclusive and empathetic society.

## The Reach and Influence of Omar Sharif Jr.'s Message

Omar Sharif Jr.'s global impact is not limited to the LGBTQ community. His message of equality, acceptance, and respect resonates with people from all walks of life.

Through his charismatic and engaging communication style, Omar captures the attention and imagination of audiences worldwide. Whether it's speaking at conferences, writing articles, or appearing in media interviews, he effectively communicates the urgency and importance of LGBTQ rights, inspiring others to join the fight for equality.

### Establishing LGBTQ Centers and Support Networks

Understanding the role of local communities in activism, Omar Sharif Jr. recognizes the importance of establishing LGBTQ centers and support networks around the globe. These safe spaces provide essential resources, support, and community for LGBTQ individuals.

Omar actively collaborates with local organizations and community leaders to establish and sustain these spaces. Through funding initiatives, capacity-building, and sharing best practices, he helps create a network of LGBTQ centers that empower and uplift individuals and communities.

### Fostering Acceptance and Understanding

Omar's work in creating safe spaces and supporting LGBTQ organizations is driven by a desire to foster greater acceptance and understanding. He believes that education and exposure are key to dispelling stereotypes and prejudices.

Through workshops, seminars, and community dialogues, Omar facilitates conversations about LGBTQ rights, gender identity, and sexual orientation. By inviting people to ask questions, share their concerns, and engage in open dialogue, he helps break down barriers and foster empathy and understanding among individuals from diverse backgrounds.

### The Importance of Local Communities in Activism

While global impact is essential, Omar Sharif Jr. emphasizes the significance of local communities and grassroots movements in effecting meaningful change. He recognizes that activism is most effective when it comes from the ground up.

Omar actively engages with local LGBTQ activists and organizations, supporting their initiatives and advocating for their needs. By nurturing these local movements, he ensures that the fight for LGBTQ rights is rooted in the experiences and realities of the communities who need it most.

## Conclusion: A Hero for Our Times

Omar Sharif Jr.'s global impact as an LGBTQ activist is undeniable. By speaking at global conferences, amplifying voices, fostering collaborations, and connecting communities, he has played a significant role in the advancement of LGBTQ rights worldwide.

Through his use of social media, creation of LGBTQ-inclusive content, and challenge of prejudice and discrimination, Omar has effectively used media as a tool for change. His efforts to establish LGBTQ centers and foster acceptance and understanding have made a difference in the lives of countless individuals.

As Omar continues his advocacy journey, his legacy serves as an inspiration to future generations of activists. His indomitable spirit, dedication to equality, and commitment to creating a more inclusive world ensure that his impact will be felt for years to come.

Let us now delve into the challenges and triumphs that Omar Sharif Jr. has faced along his journey in the next chapter.

# International Activism

## Speaking at Global LGBTQ Conferences

Speaking at global LGBTQ conferences is a significant aspect of Omar Sharif Jr.'s advocacy work. These conferences serve as important platforms for sharing knowledge, experiences, and strategies in the fight for LGBTQ rights. In this section, we will explore the role of these conferences, the impact they have, and how Omar Sharif Jr. actively contributes to these gatherings.

## The Importance of Global LGBTQ Conferences

Global LGBTQ conferences bring together activists, scholars, policymakers, and community members from around the world. These conferences provide a space for individuals to exchange ideas, learn from one another, and strengthen the global LGBTQ movement. By fostering connections and networks, these conferences facilitate a collective effort in advancing LGBTQ rights on a global scale.

These gatherings focus on various aspects of LGBTQ advocacy, including legal reforms, health and well-being, intersectionality, and representation. They provide a platform to discuss challenges, share success stories, and develop strategies to address the unique issues faced by the LGBTQ community.

## Omar Sharif Jr.'s Active Involvement

Omar Sharif Jr. is a prominent speaker and advocate at global LGBTQ conferences. His participation serves as a source of inspiration for attendees and amplifies the voices of LGBTQ individuals from the Middle East.

As a LGBTQ rights advocate, Omar Sharif Jr. shares his personal experiences, challenges, and successes at these conferences. By openly discussing his journey and the obstacles he has faced, he empowers others to embrace their identities and fight for equality. His speeches are a powerful blend of personal anecdotes, statistics, and calls to action, leaving a lasting impact on the audience.

Omar also actively engages in panel discussions, workshops, and breakout sessions during these conferences. Through his participation, he contributes to critical conversations about LGBTQ rights, cultural sensitivities, and strengthening alliances across borders. His insights, gained through years of experience in advocacy work, offer valuable perspectives for both newcomers and seasoned activists attending these events.

## Leveraging Conferences for Global Impact

Omar Sharif Jr.'s presence at global LGBTQ conferences extends beyond individual speeches and panel discussions. He utilizes these gatherings as opportunities to create meaningful connections and form alliances with fellow LGBTQ advocates, organizations, and policymakers.

By networking with other activists, Omar establishes collaborations that extend long after the conference ends. These partnerships enable the sharing of resources, expertise, and support, ultimately strengthening the impact and reach of LGBTQ advocacy efforts globally. Through these connections, he helps to bridge gaps between different regions and cultures, fostering a sense of solidarity within the diverse LGBTQ community.

## Challenges and Opportunities

Participating in global LGBTQ conferences also presents challenges and opportunities for Omar Sharif Jr. and other activists. The conferences often highlight the progress made in some parts of the world while shedding light on the struggles faced by LGBTQ individuals in others. These disparities offer a chance to learn from successful advocacy strategies and adapt them to different cultural contexts.

However, navigating cultural sensitivity is crucial when discussing LGBTQ issues at international conferences. Omar Sharif Jr. approachesthis challenge by providing insights into the unique dynamics of LGBTQ activism in the Middle East. By sharing his experiences and perspectives, he raises awareness of the specific challenges faced by LGBTQ individuals in the region and promotes a more nuanced understanding of the Middle Eastern context.

## Advocacy Beyond the Conferences

Global LGBTQ conferences act as catalysts for change and inspiration. However, Omar Sharif Jr. understands that advocacy work extends far beyond these gatherings. He recognizes the importance of taking the lessons learned and the connections made at these conferences back to the field, where real change happens.

Omar actively carries the spirit of the conferences into his everyday activism. He leverages his platform, both online and offline, to educate and raise awareness about LGBTQ rights. By maintaining an active presence in social media, he continues to engage his audience and further the conversation on a global scale. Additionally, he collaborates with local organizations in the Middle East, utilizing the knowledge and connections gained from conferences to drive change at a grassroots level.

## Inspiration for Future Activists

Omar Sharif Jr.'s active involvement in global LGBTQ conferences sets an example for future activists. His commitment, resilience, and dedication to creating a more inclusive world inspire emerging advocates to find their own voice and contribute to the LGBTQ movement.

As Omar Sharif Jr. continues to speak at global LGBTQ conferences, his impact on the international stage grows. He remains a powerful force in advocating for LGBTQ rights, bridging cultures, and amplifying the voices of LGBTQ individuals worldwide.

Through his participation in these conferences, Omar Sharif Jr. demonstrates the significance of coming together as a global community to achieve meaningful change. His continued efforts serve as a reminder that progress is possible when passionate individuals gather, share their stories, and work tirelessly towards a future where LGBTQ individuals are truly equal in every corner of the world.

## Amplifying Voices of Queer Activists Worldwide

In the world of LGBTQ activism, the power of amplifying voices cannot be underestimated. It is through the collective strength and resilience of queer activists worldwide that significant progress and change are achieved. In this section, we will explore the various ways in which Omar Sharif Jr. has been instrumental in amplifying the voices of queer activists globally, and the impact this has had on the LGBTQ movement.

## Understanding the Importance of Amplification

Amplifying voices refers to the act of giving marginalized individuals a platform to share their experiences, stories, and perspectives with a wider audience. For queer activists, this is crucial as they often face discrimination, marginalization, and lack of representation in mainstream media and society. By amplifying their voices, we can shed light on the challenges they face, raise awareness about LGBTQ issues, and foster empathy and understanding among the general public.

## Building Bridges and Creating Alliances

Omar Sharif Jr. understands the power of building bridges and creating alliances to amplify queer voices worldwide. Through his extensive network and collaborations with LGBTQ organizations and activists, he has been able to connect individuals and communities across different regions and cultures. By fostering these connections, he has facilitated the sharing of knowledge, resources, and strategies among activists, allowing for the creation of a global movement that transcends borders.

## Providing Platforms for Engagement

One of the key ways in which Omar Sharif Jr. amplifies the voices of queer activists is by providing platforms for engagement. By leveraging his influence and visibility as a public figure, he has been able to secure opportunities for queer activists to be heard on various media platforms, conferences, and events. The inclusion of queer voices in mainstream media not only provides individuals with a chance to share their stories but also helps in challenging stereotypes and promoting acceptance.

## Empowering Local Activists

Omar Sharif Jr. recognizes the importance of empowering local activists and grassroots organizations in marginalized communities. He actively seeks out opportunities to collaborate with and uplift individuals who may not have the same access and resources as their counterparts in more privileged regions. By investing in the leadership and capacity-building of local activists, he ensures that their voices are amplified not only within their communities but also on a global scale.

## Utilizing the Power of Social Media

In today's digital age, social media has become a powerful tool for activism and amplifying voices. Omar Sharif Jr. has embraced this platform as a means to connect with and amplify the voices of queer activists worldwide. Through strategic use of social media platforms, he has been able to reach a global audience, engage in meaningful conversations, and bring attention to pressing LGBTQ issues. This online presence has allowed him to share powerful stories, garner support, and mobilize individuals to take action.

### Advocacy Through Artistic Expression

Artistic expression has long been a powerful tool for social change and amplifying marginalized voices. Omar Sharif Jr. recognizes the significance of art in the LGBTQ movement and actively supports artists and creatives who use their work to advocate for change. By showcasing their art, whether through film, literature, visual arts, or performance, he amplifies their voices and provides a platform for their messages to be heard loud and clear.

### Engaging Allies and Supporters

Amplifying the voices of queer activists does not solely rely on the efforts of the LGBTQ community. Allies and supporters play a crucial role in ensuring that marginalized voices are heard. Omar Sharif Jr. actively engages allies and supporters, calling upon them to use their platforms and influence to uplift and amplify queer voices. By fostering these relationships, he creates a robust network of individuals committed to the cause of LGBTQ rights and advocacy.

### Unconventional Endeavors

To truly amplify the voices of queer activists worldwide, it is necessary to think outside the box and engage in unconventional endeavors. Omar Sharif Jr. has been a strong advocate for unconventional approaches to activism, such as using humor, art, storytelling, and even popular culture references to spark conversations and challenge societal norms. By adopting these unconventional approaches, he breaks through barriers and reaches audiences that may not have otherwise been receptive to LGBTQ issues.

### Exercises and Reflection

1. Research and identify queer activists from different parts of the world whose voices need to be amplified. Share their stories and messages on your social media platforms to raise awareness about their work.

2. Reflect on your own privileges and consider ways in which you can use your platform, whether big or small, to amplify the voices of marginalized LGBTQ individuals in your community.

3. Engage in discussions with friends, family, and colleagues about LGBTQ issues, and share stories and perspectives of queer activists to help challenge stereotypes and promote understanding.

4. Create or contribute to an LGBTQ-inclusive artistic project, such as a short film, poetry collection, or visual art exhibition, that aims to amplify queer voices and raise awareness about LGBTQ issues.

Remember, amplifying queer voices is an ongoing process that requires consistent effort and allyship. By actively engaging in these exercises and incorporating them into your daily life, you can contribute to the global movement for LGBTQ rights and create a more inclusive world.

## Global Partnerships and Collaborations

Global partnerships and collaborations have been instrumental in Omar Sharif Jr.'s advocacy work, allowing him to amplify his message and effect meaningful change on a global scale. Through forging alliances with like-minded organizations and influential individuals, he has been able to connect with LGBTQ communities worldwide and work towards a more inclusive future. This section explores the impact of these partnerships and collaborations and highlights their significance in creating a united front for LGBTQ rights.

### Forming Alliances

Building global partnerships requires a delicate balance of shared values, common goals, and mutual trust. Omar Sharif Jr. has been successful in forming alliances with both LGBTQ-focused organizations and broader human rights groups, recognizing the interconnected nature of social justice issues.

One such partnership is with the International Lesbian, Gay, Bisexual, Trans and Intersex Association (ILGA), a prominent global organization working towards LGBTQ equality. ILGA's extensive network and resources have provided Omar Sharif Jr. with a platform to spread his message and collaborate with activists from diverse backgrounds. Through this partnership, he has been able to contribute to ILGA's mission of advancing LGBTQ rights worldwide.

Additionally, Sharif Jr. has engaged in collaborations with leading human rights organizations like Amnesty International and Human Rights Watch. By aligning with these respected entities, he has leveraged their expertise and expanded his reach to broader audiences. These alliances not only grant him credibility but also enable him to advocate for LGBTQ rights within a wider human rights framework.

## Joint Campaigns and Initiatives

Global partnerships often involve joint campaigns and initiatives that leverage the collective influence of organizations and individuals. Omar Sharif Jr. has actively participated in several such endeavors to promote LGBTQ acceptance and equality.

One notable example is his involvement in the United Nations' Free & Equal campaign. This global initiative seeks to raise awareness and promote LGBTQ rights through media campaigns, events, and educational programs. Sharif Jr.'s collaboration with the United Nations has significantly amplified his activism, allowing him to reach a vast audience and inspire change on an international level.

In addition to his work with established organizations, Sharif Jr. has also formed collaborations with fellow LGBTQ activists and influencers. These partnerships capitalize on the power of social media and popular culture to spread awareness and advocate for LGBTQ rights. By working together, they create a united front, enhancing the impact of their collective efforts.

## Cultural Sensitivity and Local Collaborations

When engaging in global partnerships, cultural sensitivity is of utmost importance. Recognizing the distinct challenges faced by LGBTQ communities in different regions of the world, Omar Sharif Jr. actively seeks collaborations with local organizations and individuals to ensure that his advocacy work is contextually relevant and respectful.

By partnering with LGBTQ organizations in the Middle East, for instance, Sharif Jr. has contributed to breaking down cultural barriers and challenging societal norms. These collaborations not only provide valuable insights and perspectives but also empower local activists to drive change within their communities.

Moreover, partnering with influential figures from the Middle East, such as acclaimed artists, musicians, and writers, allows Sharif Jr. to bridge the gap between LGBTQ advocacy and Middle Eastern culture. These collaborations foster dialogue and promote acceptance, highlighting the shared humanity of all individuals irrespective of their sexual orientation or gender identity.

## Unconventional Actions for Global Change

Sometimes, unconventional actions can lead to unexpected breakthroughs in global partnerships and collaborations. Omar Sharif Jr. has been a trailblazer in his approach, constantly seeking innovative ways to promote LGBTQ rights worldwide.

For example, he has taken advantage of his platform as a public figure to engage with diplomats, politicians, and policymakers through unconventional means. By attending international diplomatic events, film festivals, and high-profile gatherings, Sharif Jr. has found unique opportunities to spark conversations about LGBTQ rights and influence decision-makers at the highest levels.

Additionally, he has utilized his background in the media and entertainment industry to create LGBTQ-inclusive content that challenges stereotypes and breaks down barriers. Through collaborations with filmmakers and production companies, he has brought LGBTQ narratives into mainstream media, fostering understanding and empathy among viewers globally.

## Conclusion

Global partnerships and collaborations have played a pivotal role in Omar Sharif Jr.'s journey as an LGBTQ advocate. By forming alliances with organizations, individuals, and communities around the world, he has been able to amplify his message and create lasting change on a global scale.

Through joint campaigns, cultural sensitivity, and unconventional actions, Sharif Jr. continues to foster connections and collaborations that strengthen the LGBTQ movement. By working together with diverse partners, he inspires hope for a more inclusive world where LGBTQ individuals can live openly and authentically, regardless of their geographical location.

The next chapter will explore the rise of Omar Sharif Jr. as an LGBTQ icon, delving into his personal journey and the challenges he faced on the path to becoming a prominent advocate and role model.

## Connecting LGBTQ Communities on a Global Scale

In the ever-expanding digital age, the world has become more connected than ever before. Distance and borders are no longer insurmountable barriers to communication and collaboration. This has opened up incredible opportunities for LGBTQ communities across the globe to connect, share experiences, and unite in their fight for equality and acceptance.

## The Power of Online Platforms

The internet has revolutionized the way we connect with one another, and it has played an integral role in the global LGBTQ movement. Online platforms such as social media, blogs, and forums have provided spaces where individuals can come together, share stories, and build supportive communities.

For instance, LGBTQ individuals from conservative countries with oppressive laws now have the opportunity to connect with those from more progressive regions. This allows for the exchange of ideas, strategies, and support, offering a lifeline to those who may be isolated and threatened in their own countries.

These online platforms have also given a voice to LGBTQ activists who are unable to speak out in their own communities for fear of persecution. By using pseudonyms or remaining anonymous, they can advocate for LGBTQ rights and share their stories without putting themselves at immediate risk.

## Virtual Conferences and Summits

In addition to online platforms, virtual conferences and summits have become significant avenues for connecting LGBTQ communities on a global scale. These events bring together LGBTQ activists, scholars, and leaders from all corners of the world to engage in discussions, share experiences, and collaborate on solutions.

Virtual conferences offer a unique opportunity to break down geographic barriers and financial limitations. LGBTQ individuals who may not have the means to travel to physical conferences can now participate from the comfort of their homes. This inclusion ensures a more diverse range of perspectives and experiences.

Furthermore, virtual conferences often provide simultaneous translation services, making it easier for individuals who are not fluent in English to actively participate and contribute. This inclusive approach allows for a truly global conversation surrounding LGBTQ rights and advocacy.

## Transnational Activism

Transnational activism plays a crucial role in connecting LGBTQ communities globally. It involves collaboration and solidarity between activists and organizations across different countries and regions. By working together, they can address common issues, share resources, and amplify their collective voices.

One notable example of transnational activism is the Global Equality Caucus, a network of parliamentarians from around the world who advocate for LGBTQ rights. This caucus connects legislators from different countries, enabling them to share best practices, coordinate efforts, and advance LGBTQ-inclusive policies on an international level.

Similarly, LGBTQ organizations from various countries often form partnerships and alliances to support each other's initiatives. This collaborative approach allows for the exchange of knowledge and expertise, ultimately strengthening the fight for LGBTQ rights worldwide.

## Supporting Local LGBTQ Organizations

Connecting LGBTQ communities on a global scale involves supporting and uplifting local LGBTQ organizations. These grassroots organizations understand the unique challenges faced by LGBTQ individuals in their respective countries and can effectively address these issues.

By providing financial aid, resources, and technical support, global LGBTQ networks can help empower local organizations to effect change at the grassroots level. This support may involve facilitating networking opportunities, offering capacity-building programs, or assisting in advocacy efforts.

Furthermore, global LGBTQ networks can help amplify the voices of local organizations by providing them with platforms and visibility. This can be achieved through collaborative campaigns, media partnerships, or showcasing their success stories on international platforms.

## Caveats and Challenges

While the ability to connect LGBTQ communities on a global scale is a powerful tool for advocacy, it does come with its own set of challenges. It is essential to be mindful of cultural and contextual differences when building connections and collaborations.

Cultural sensitivity is crucial in ensuring that the messages and approaches used by LGBTQ activists resonate with individuals from diverse backgrounds. This requires a deep understanding of local customs, beliefs, and historical contexts to avoid unintentionally causing offense or misunderstanding.

Additionally, it is essential to recognize and address the power dynamics that exist within global LGBTQ networks. Ensuring equal representation and giving agency to marginalized voices is crucial to avoid perpetuating existing inequalities within the movement.

## Conclusion

Connecting LGBTQ communities on a global scale is a vital aspect of the fight for equality and acceptance. Online platforms, virtual conferences, transnational activism, and support for local LGBTQ organizations all contribute to building a global movement that is united in its pursuit of justice.

This interconnectedness allows for the sharing of knowledge, resources, and experiences, ultimately strengthening the advocacy efforts of LGBTQ communities worldwide. By breaking down barriers and fostering collaboration, we can create a more inclusive world where LGBTQ individuals are celebrated and respected.

# Breaking Barriers through Media

## The Power of Social Media in Activism

In today's digital age, social media has emerged as a powerful tool for activism, providing individuals and communities with a platform to raise awareness, mobilize support, and advocate for change. Omar Sharif Jr. recognizes the immense potential of social media and has effectively harnessed its power in his LGBTQ advocacy work. In this section, we explore the ways in which social media has revolutionized activism and examine the strategies employed by Omar Sharif Jr. to amplify his message.

## The Rise of Social Media Activism

With the advent of platforms like Facebook, Twitter, Instagram, and TikTok, the world has witnessed a paradigm shift in how social movements are organized and amplified. Activists can now bypass traditional gatekeepers of information and directly communicate with their target audience, breaking down barriers of distance and time. Social media has facilitated real-time conversations, enabling activists like Omar Sharif Jr. to engage with a global audience instantaneously.

## The Reach and Impact of Social Media

One of the greatest strengths of social media is its potential to reach a wide audience. By leveraging various platforms, Omar Sharif Jr. has been able to expand the visibility of LGBTQ issues beyond traditional boundaries. Through compelling storytelling, engaging visuals, and strategic use of hashtags, he has captured the attention of millions. Social media allows him to connect with individuals who may not have previously been exposed to LGBTQ rights, thereby broadening the scope of his advocacy.

Moreover, social media platforms provide a space for like-minded individuals to connect, creating virtual communities where people can share experiences, offer support, and mobilize for collective action. This sense of community fosters solidarity and empowers individuals to take a stand for LGBTQ equality, both online and offline.

## Strategies for Effective Social Media Activism

While social media provides a powerful platform for activism, success hinges on utilizing effective strategies. Omar Sharif Jr. has employed several key approaches to maximize the impact of his social media advocacy:

1. **Authenticity and Vulnerability:** By sharing personal stories and vulnerabilities, Omar Sharif Jr. humanizes the LGBTQ experience, fostering empathy and understanding among his audience. Authenticity resonates with people and helps build genuine connections, encouraging others to join the cause.

2. **Engaging Content:** In a fast-paced online environment, attention-grabbing content is essential. Omar Sharif Jr. employs captivating visuals, videos, and infographics to convey his message effectively and leave a lasting impression. He creatively uses storytelling techniques to evoke emotions, spark conversations, and promote dialogue.

3. **Strategic Hashtagging:** Hashtags are a powerful tool for increasing the discoverability of content and connecting with a broader audience. By carefully selecting and utilizing relevant hashtags, Omar Sharif Jr. ensures that his advocacy reaches beyond his immediate followers to a wider network of individuals who are interested in LGBTQ rights.

4. **Collaboration and Amplification:** Building alliances and partnering with influential individuals or organizations amplifies the reach and impact of social media activism. Omar Sharif Jr. actively collaborates with other LGBTQ activists, celebrities, and organizations to combine efforts, cross-promote content, and engage with new audiences.

5. **Dialogue and Engagement:** Social media is not a one-way street. Omar Sharif Jr. recognizes the importance of engaging in conversations with his followers and actively responding to comments, messages, and concerns. By

fostering dialogue, he creates a safe and inclusive space where individuals feel heard and valued.

6. **Call-to-Action:** To truly effect change, social media activism must go beyond awareness-raising. Omar Sharif Jr. uses his social media presence to encourage his followers to take concrete actions, such as signing petitions, attending events, or donating to LGBTQ organizations. By providing clear calls-to-action, he empowers others to join the movement and make a tangible impact.

## Caveats and Challenges

While social media offers immense opportunities for activism, it is not without its challenges. The open nature of online platforms invites both support and opposition, and Omar Sharif Jr. has faced his fair share of backlash and hate. Trolling, harassment, and threats can pose significant mental and emotional challenges for activists. Safeguarding personal well-being and implementing strategies to manage online negativity are crucial aspects of social media activism.

Moreover, the algorithms and algorithms used by different platforms play a significant role in information dissemination. Content visibility can be influenced by various factors, including user behavior, platform policies, and paid advertising. Understanding and navigating these dynamics is key to ensuring that advocacy efforts on social media reach the intended audience.

## The Unconventional Approach: Using Memes for Change

In the realm of social media activism, one unconventional yet incredibly effective approach that Omar Sharif Jr. has embraced is the use of memes. Memes, often humorous or satirical, have become a popular form of communication on social media and can convey powerful messages in a relatable and engaging way. By capitalizing on this viral content format, Omar Sharif Jr. taps into the collective consciousness of online users, using humor and wit to challenge stereotypes, tackle misconceptions, and promote LGBTQ acceptance.

For instance, he has created memes that juxtapose societal expectations with the realities faced by LGBTQ individuals, highlighting the absurdity of homophobia and discrimination. These memes provide a fresh and light-hearted perspective, enabling individuals to reflect on their own beliefs and potentially reconsider their prejudices.

## Conclusion

Social media has emerged as a game-changer in the realm of activism, enabling voices like Omar Sharif Jr.'s to be heard louder and farther than ever before. By leveraging the power of social media, he has effectively raised awareness, mobilized support, and catalyzed change on LGBTQ rights. The strategies discussed in this section, such as authenticity, engaging content, strategic hashtagging, collaboration, and call-to-action, have significantly contributed to the success of his social media activism. However, it is essential to remain vigilant of the challenges and dynamics of online spaces, ensuring a safe and inclusive environment for all. As social media continues to evolve, it is through savvy and innovative approaches like using memes that activists can continue to inspire, educate, and advocate for a more inclusive and equal world.

## Creating LGBTQ-Inclusive Content

Creating LGBTQ-inclusive content is an essential aspect of LGBTQ activism. By promoting positive and accurate representation of LGBTQ individuals in various forms of media, we can challenge stereotypes, reduce stigma, and foster greater acceptance and understanding. In this section, we will explore the importance of creating LGBTQ-inclusive content, discuss strategies for implementation, and provide examples of successful initiatives.

### Why LGBTQ-Inclusive Content Matters

LGBTQ individuals have long been marginalized and misrepresented in mainstream media. Negative portrayals often perpetuate harmful stereotypes and contribute to societal prejudice. By creating LGBTQ-inclusive content, we can counteract these biases and promote a more inclusive and equitable society.

LGBTQ-inclusive content matters for several reasons. Firstly, it provides representation for LGBTQ individuals who have historically been underrepresented or inaccurately depicted. Seeing themselves portrayed positively in media can have a profound impact on the self-esteem and well-being of LGBTQ individuals, helping them feel accepted and valued.

Secondly, inclusive content helps to educate and build empathy among broader audiences. By showcasing diverse LGBTQ experiences, challenges, and triumphs, we can challenge preconceived notions and foster greater understanding. This not only benefits the LGBTQ community but also promotes a more inclusive society overall.

Lastly, inclusive content has the power to drive social change and advocate for LGBTQ rights. By showcasing the realities faced by LGBTQ individuals, media can raise awareness, engage audiences, and mobilize support for equal rights and protections. It can also serve as a platform for important conversations about LGBTQ issues, spurring further activism and progress.

## Strategies for Creating LGBTQ-Inclusive Content

Creating LGBTQ-inclusive content requires careful consideration and sensitivity. Here are some strategies to guide content creators in their efforts:

1. Representation: Ensure that LGBTQ characters and stories are authentically portrayed. Consult with members of the LGBTQ community to avoid stereotypes and misrepresentations. Include diverse intersections of LGBTQ identities, including race, gender, and disability.

2. Accuracy: Research LGBTQ experiences, terminology, and history to accurately represent the community. Avoid using outdated or offensive language and consult appropriate resources to maintain accuracy.

3. Queer Creatives: Encourage the participation of LGBTQ individuals in the creation and production process. This includes hiring LGBTQ writers, directors, and actors to contribute their unique perspectives and insights.

4. Collaboration: Seek input and feedback from LGBTQ organizations and activists to ensure the content aligns with community values and needs. Collaborating with experts can help create content that is impactful and resonates with the intended audience.

5. Intersectionality: Recognize and address the intersections of LGBTQ identities with other marginalized groups. Addressing issues of racial, economic, and gender inequality can foster a more comprehensive understanding of LGBTQ experiences.

6. Audience Engagement: Encourage audience engagement through interactive content and campaigns. This can include social media initiatives, public discussions, and educational resources that encourage dialogue and understanding.

## Examples of Successful LGBTQ-Inclusive Content

1. "Pose" (TV Series): This groundbreaking series created by Ryan Murphy explores the New York ballroom culture of the 1980s and '90s, showcasing the lives and struggles of predominantly LGBTQ+ characters, including transgender women of color. The show has been praised for its authentic representation,

accurate portrayal of LGBTQ history, and its positive impact on LGBTQ communities.

2. "Love, Simon" (Film): This coming-of-age romantic comedy-drama film follows Simon Spier, a gay high school student navigating his sexuality and coming out. The film garnered critical acclaim for its heartfelt storytelling, relatable characters, and its ability to resonate with LGBTQ youth. It has been lauded as a landmark film in LGBTQ+ cinema.

3. "#VisibleMe" (Social Media Campaign): This social media campaign encouraged LGBTQ individuals to share their stories and experiences using the hashtag #VisibleMe. The campaign aimed to start a dialogue, increase visibility, and reduce stigma surrounding LGBTQ identities. It was successful in creating a supportive online community and inspiring others to share their own stories.

4. LGBTQ+ Book Clubs: Online and offline LGBTQ+ book clubs provide a platform for LGBTQ individuals and allies to engage with LGBTQ-inclusive literature. These book clubs foster discussion, broaden perspectives, and help to normalize LGBTQ experiences in literary spaces.

## Unconventional Wisdom: Fostering Creativity and Authenticity

Creating LGBTQ-inclusive content often requires fostering creativity and authenticity. One unconventional approach is to facilitate collaborations between LGBTQ artists and content creators from diverse backgrounds. By encouraging the intersection of different art forms and perspectives, we can generate unique and innovative LGBTQ-inclusive content. This approach can challenge traditional norms and expand the boundaries of LGBTQ representation.

For example, a collaboration between a LGBTQ musician and a visual artist could result in a powerful music video that explores LGBTQ themes from a fresh and imaginative perspective. By encouraging unconventional collaborations, we can break free from the limitations of traditional storytelling and create art that truly captures the essence of the LGBTQ experience.

## Conclusion: Promoting Acceptance through Inclusive Content

Creating LGBTQ-inclusive content is an essential tool for fostering acceptance, education, and social change. By representing LGBTQ individuals authentically and promoting positive narratives, we can challenge stereotypes, reduce stigma, and build a more inclusive society.

Through strategies such as accurate representation, collaboration, and audience engagement, content creators can make a meaningful impact on LGBTQ visibility and acceptance. By showcasing diverse LGBTQ experiences and fostering creativity, we can amplify marginalized voices and advocate for LGBTQ rights on a global scale.

As we continue to embrace LGBTQ-inclusive content, it is crucial to learn from successful examples and embrace unconventional approaches that push the boundaries of traditional storytelling. By doing so, we can create a future where LGBTQ individuals are celebrated, understood, and embraced by all.

## Using Media to Challenge Prejudice and Discrimination

One of the most powerful tools in the fight against prejudice and discrimination is the use of media. The ability to broadcast messages, tell stories, and share experiences has the potential to transform societal attitudes and challenge deeply ingrained biases. In this section, we will explore how Omar Sharif Jr. has utilized the media to challenge prejudice and discrimination faced by the LGBTQ community, both in the Middle East and globally.

### Harnessing the Power of Social Media

In today's digital age, social media platforms such as Twitter, Instagram, and Facebook serve as dynamic spaces for advocacy and activism. With their wide reach and ability to connect individuals across borders, these platforms offer an unparalleled opportunity to challenge prejudice and discrimination.

Omar Sharif Jr. understands the immense power of social media and has harnessed it to amplify LGBTQ voices, inspire change, and counteract harmful narratives. By sharing personal stories, promoting inclusive content, and engaging with followers, Omar has built a strong online presence that reaches millions.

For example, he often shares his own experiences as an openly gay man, shedding light on the challenges faced by LGBTQ individuals in discriminatory societies. Through heartfelt, authentic posts, he builds empathy among his followers, encouraging them to challenge their own prejudices. Omar also collaborates with other LGBTQ activists and influencers to create digital campaigns that make a powerful statement against discrimination.

### Creating LGBTQ-Inclusive Content

Representation in mainstream media plays a crucial role in challenging prejudice and discrimination. By showcasing diverse LGBTQ characters and stories, media outlets have the ability to shape public opinion, break down stereotypes, and foster empathy.

As an LGBTQ icon, Omar Sharif Jr. understands the importance of inclusive representation. He has actively collaborated with media organizations, filmmakers, and writers to promote narratives that challenge prejudices and highlight the lived experiences of LGBTQ individuals. Through his involvement in film and television projects, Omar has paved the way for increased LGBTQ visibility and acceptance.

Furthermore, Omar has used his platform to call out instances of homophobia and transphobia in media. By holding media outlets accountable for harmful portrayals of LGBTQ individuals, he challenges discriminatory norms and encourages more inclusive content creation.

## Countering Prejudice and Misconceptions

Media often perpetuates stereotypes and misconceptions about marginalized communities. Omar Sharif Jr. recognizes the power of media in shaping perceptions and actively works to counter these negative narratives.

Through interviews, articles, and op-eds, Omar shares his own personal journey and challenges common misconceptions about the LGBTQ community, particularly in the Middle East. He uses his platform to dismantle stereotypes and highlight the richness and diversity of LGBTQ experiences.

Moreover, Omar engages in public debates, panel discussions, and media campaigns to challenge discriminatory practices and promote inclusivity. By offering well-reasoned arguments, backed by evidence and personal experience, he effectively counters prejudice and discrimination perpetuated by the media.

## The Reach and Influence of Omar Sharif Jr.'s Message

Omar Sharif Jr.'s advocacy through media has had a far-reaching impact, both locally and globally. His use of social media platforms allows him to connect with individuals who may not have access to LGBTQ-inclusive resources or who live in regions where LGBTQ rights are limited.

By engaging with followers from diverse backgrounds, Omar encourages dialogue about LGBTQ issues, challenging prejudices that may exist even within progressive societies. His willingness to address difficult topics openly and honestly fosters understanding and empathy, ultimately leading to change.

Omar's media presence also extends to traditional outlets, such as mainstream news channels, magazines, and newspapers, ensuring that his message reaches a wide audience. Through these platforms, he has been able to challenge stereotypes, spark conversations, and inspire individuals to question their own biases.

## Empowering Action for Change

Media has the extraordinary ability to empower individuals to take action and create change. Omar Sharif Jr.'s advocacy through media not only challenges prejudice and discrimination but also inspires others to join the fight for LGBTQ rights.

By sharing stories of resilience, showcasing success stories, and highlighting the progress made in LGBTQ activism, Omar ignites hope and motivates individuals to become activists in their own right. He emphasizes that anyone, regardless of their background, can make a difference by using the power of media to challenge prejudice and discrimination.

In conclusion, Omar Sharif Jr.'s utilization of media platforms to challenge prejudice and discrimination has been instrumental in advancing LGBTQ rights. Through social media, LGBTQ-inclusive content creation, countering misconceptions, and reaching a wide audience, he has effectively challenged societal norms and fostered acceptance. By harnessing the power of media, Omar Sharif Jr. continues to inspire change and leave a lasting impact on the fight against prejudice and discrimination.

## The Reach and Influence of Omar Sharif Jr.'s Message

Omar Sharif Jr.'s message of love, acceptance, and equal rights has resonated with people all over the world. Through his powerful advocacy work, he has been able to reach a wide audience and create a lasting impact on society. Sharif's influence extends far beyond his immediate circle, as his message has reached millions through various platforms and mediums.

## Harnessing the Power of Social Media

One of the key ways in which Omar Sharif Jr. has been able to spread his message is through the use of social media. He understands the importance of utilizing these platforms to reach a global audience and connect with individuals who may be experiencing similar struggles or seeking support.

Through the strategic use of platforms such as Instagram, Twitter, and Facebook, Sharif has been able to engage with his followers by sharing personal stories, thought-provoking messages, and informative content. By consistently posting and interacting with his followers, he has created a virtual community where individuals can find solace, inspiration, and information.

### Creating LGBTQ-Inclusive Content

One of the most impactful ways in which Omar Sharif Jr. has influenced society is through the creation of LGBTQ-inclusive content. Whether through his own personal storytelling or collaborations with various media outlets, he has helped break down barriers and challenge prejudices.

By sharing his own experiences and vulnerabilities, Sharif has humanized the LGBTQ experience, allowing others to relate and empathize. His interviews, articles, and speeches have shed light on the struggles faced by LGBTQ individuals and offered a platform for meaningful discussions.

### Using Media to Challenge Prejudice and Discrimination

Omar Sharif Jr. recognizes the power of media in shaping public opinion and challenging societal norms. Through his work as an actor, TV presenter, and public speaker, he has used these platforms as vehicles for driving change.

In TV appearances, Sharif has eloquently addressed issues related to LGBTQ rights, highlighting the need for acceptance and understanding. He has gracefully challenged stereotypes and misconceptions surrounding the LGBTQ community, providing an alternative perspective rooted in empathy and education.

### The Reach and Impact of Collaborations

A crucial aspect of Omar Sharif Jr.'s message is his ability to collaborate with other advocates and organizations. By joining forces with like-minded individuals, he has been able to amplify his voice and extend his reach.

Collaborations with LGBTQ organizations, human rights groups, and influential figures in the entertainment industry have allowed Sharif to engage with diverse audiences and make a greater impact. Together, these collaborations have fostered understanding, raised awareness, and provided resources and support to LGBTQ individuals in need.

Through these partnerships, Sharif has been able to tap into existing networks, allowing his message to reach corners of society that may have previously been unreached or difficult to access.

### Inspiring Change and Empowering Others

Perhaps the most significant aspect of Omar Sharif Jr.'s reach and influence is his ability to inspire change and empower others. Through his activism, he has sparked

CREATING SAFE SPACES 177

conversations, challenged societal norms, and provided hope for a more inclusive future.

By living authentically and unapologetically embracing his identity, Sharif has become a role model for LGBTQ individuals around the world. His courage has given others the strength to embrace their true selves and stand up for their rights.

Furthermore, through his charitable initiatives and philanthropic efforts, Sharif has provided resources and support to LGBTQ individuals in need, ensuring that they have the tools to overcome challenges and thrive.

### Conclusion: A Lasting Impact

Omar Sharif Jr.'s reach and influence extend far beyond the boundaries of his immediate circle. Through his strategic use of social media, creation of LGBTQ-inclusive content, utilization of media platforms, collaborations with advocates and organizations, and ability to inspire change and empower others, he has made a lasting impact on LGBTQ advocacy.

Sharif's message of love, acceptance, and equal rights has touched the lives of millions, and his legacy will continue to inspire future generations of activists. By challenging societal norms, breaking down barriers, and tirelessly advocating for LGBTQ rights, Omar Sharif Jr. has left an indelible mark on the fight for equality and a more inclusive world.

# Creating Safe Spaces

## Establishing LGBTQ Centers and Support Networks

Establishing LGBTQ centers and support networks is a crucial step in creating inclusive and safe spaces for the LGBTQ community. These centers serve as vital resources for education, support, and advocacy. They provide a sense of belonging, promote acceptance, and address the unique challenges faced by LGBTQ individuals. In this section, we will explore the importance of LGBTQ centers, the benefits they offer, and strategies for their establishment.

### The Need for LGBTQ Centers

LGBTQ individuals often face discrimination, marginalization, and societal stigmatization. Consequently, they require specialized support systems to address their unique needs. LGBTQ centers play a crucial role in providing a safe and welcoming environment where individuals can find the assistance, resources, and community they need.

These centers provide a range of services that directly benefit LGBTQ individuals and their allies. They offer counseling and mental health support tailored to the specific challenges faced by the LGBTQ community, including coming out, family acceptance, and dealing with discrimination. LGBTQ centers also serve as hubs for information, providing resources on healthcare, legal rights, and community events.

## The Benefits of LGBTQ Centers

Establishing LGBTQ centers yields numerous benefits for both individuals and the community as a whole. These centers create a sense of community and belonging, fostering social support networks that help combat isolation and loneliness. By providing a safe space, LGBTQ centers encourage individuals to embrace their authentic selves, leading to improved mental health and overall well-being.

Furthermore, LGBTQ centers serve as platforms for educational programs and workshops, promoting a better understanding of LGBTQ issues among both the LGBTQ community and the general public. They offer opportunities for training in cultural competency and sensitivity, helping to reduce discrimination and prejudice. Additionally, LGBTQ centers often host support groups that allow individuals to connect with peers who share similar experiences, ensuring a sense of solidarity and camaraderie.

## Strategies for Establishing LGBTQ Centers

Establishing LGBTQ centers requires careful planning, collaboration, and community involvement. Here are some strategies to consider:

1. **Needs Assessment:** Conduct a comprehensive assessment of the needs and resources available within the local LGBTQ community. This will help identify gaps and determine the services and support required.

2. **Community Partnerships:** Forge partnerships with local organizations, institutions, and government entities to garner support and resources. Collaborative efforts can lead to shared funding, increased visibility, and a broader impact.

3. **Securing Funding:** Develop a sustainable funding plan for the establishment and ongoing operation of the LGBTQ center. Seek grants, fundraising opportunities, and community donations to ensure long-term viability.

4. **Staffing and Volunteers:** Recruit qualified and compassionate staff members who are knowledgeable about LGBTQ issues. Additionally, build a team of dedicated volunteers who can contribute their time and expertise to support the center's activities.

5. **Physical Space:** Identify a suitable location for the LGBTQ center that is accessible, safe, and welcoming. Ensure that the space meets the unique needs of the community, including privacy considerations.

6. **Programming and Services:** Develop a diverse range of programming and services to address the needs of various subgroups within the LGBTQ community. This may include support groups, counseling services, educational workshops, and community-building events.

7. **Outreach and Marketing:** Raise awareness about the LGBTQ center through effective outreach and marketing strategies. Engage with local media, community events, and social media platforms to promote the center's services and resources.

## Example: The Rainbow Hub

To illustrate the impact of LGBTQ centers, let's consider the example of the "Rainbow Hub," an LGBTQ center established in a Midwestern city in the United States. The Rainbow Hub offers a wide range of services, including counseling, support groups, legal assistance, and educational workshops.

One of the center's unique programs is the "Rainbow Mentors" initiative, which pairs experienced LGBTQ individuals with those who are newly out or struggling with acceptance. Mentors provide guidance, support, and a listening ear, helping mentees navigate their journey with compassion and empathy.

To ensure the center's sustainability, the Rainbow Hub implements a diverse funding strategy. It receives grants from LGBTQ-focused foundations, collaborates with local businesses for sponsorship, and organizes community fundraising events. The center also actively engages with local politicians and organizations to advocate for LGBTQ rights and foster community partnerships.

By providing a safe and supportive environment, the Rainbow Hub has significantly enhanced the well-being and quality of life for LGBTQ individuals in the community. It serves as a beacon of hope, empowering individuals to embrace their identities and fostering a culture of acceptance and inclusivity.

## Conclusion

Establishing LGBTQ centers and support networks is a vital step towards creating a more inclusive and accepting society. These centers provide a range of services, support, and resources tailored to the unique needs of the LGBTQ community. By fostering a sense of belonging, offering educational programs, and combating discrimination, LGBTQ centers play a crucial role in promoting the well-being and empowerment of LGBTQ individuals. Through strategic planning, community partnerships, and sustainable funding, these centers can continue to make a significant impact in the fight for LGBTQ equality and rights.

## Offering Resources for Education and Support

In order to create real change and foster a more inclusive society, it is crucial to provide education and support for LGBTQ individuals and their allies. Omar Sharif Jr. understands the power of knowledge and resources in empowering marginalized communities. In this section, we will explore the various ways in which he offers educational resources and support to those in need.

### Creating LGBTQ-Inclusive Curricula

One of the key ways in which Omar Sharif Jr. promotes education is by advocating for LGBTQ-inclusive curricula in schools. He recognizes the importance of teaching young people about diversity, acceptance, and the LGBTQ experience. Through partnerships with educational institutions, he works towards developing comprehensive curricula that address LGBTQ issues in age-appropriate and sensitive ways.

For example, Omar collaborates with teachers and educators to design lesson plans that incorporate LGBTQ topics into various subjects, such as history, literature, and social studies. By integrating LGBTQ history and stories into the curriculum, young people learn about the struggles and contributions of the LGBTQ community, fostering empathy and understanding.

### Support Networks and Helplines

In addition to educational resources, Omar Sharif Jr. recognizes the need for support networks and helplines to assist LGBTQ individuals who may be facing challenges or seeking guidance. He collaborates with organizations to establish helplines that provide a safe and confidential space for individuals to seek support, ask questions, and receive information.

These helplines are staffed by trained professionals who have an understanding of the unique challenges faced by LGBTQ individuals. They provide emotional support, resources, and referrals to services such as mental health professionals, legal aid, and LGBTQ support groups. By offering this lifeline, Omar ensures that LGBTQ individuals have access to the help they need, regardless of their location or circumstances.

## Online Educational Platforms

Omar Sharif Jr. recognizes the power of technology in reaching a wide audience. To extend the reach of his educational initiatives, he establishes online platforms that provide accessible and inclusive educational resources. These platforms include informative articles, videos, and interactive tools that aim to educate and empower individuals in their journey towards LGBTQ acceptance.

For example, one of Omar's online initiatives is a comprehensive LGBTQ glossary that defines and explains key terms and concepts. This resource serves as a valuable tool for individuals who are exploring their LGBTQ identities, as well as for allies who seek to better understand the LGBTQ community. By offering these resources online, Omar ensures that educational content is easily accessible to those who may not have access to LGBTQ-inclusive education in their local communities.

## Workshops and Training Programs

Another important aspect of Omar Sharif Jr.'s educational initiatives is the organization of workshops and training programs. These programs are designed to educate individuals from various sectors, including educational institutions, corporations, and community organizations, on LGBTQ inclusion and support.

These workshops cover a range of topics, such as understanding LGBTQ identities, addressing LGBTQ issues in the workplace, and creating inclusive spaces for LGBTQ individuals. By providing practical tools and strategies, Omar empowers participants to become advocates for change within their own spheres of influence.

## Collaboration with LGBTQ Organizations

Omar Sharif Jr. understands the value of collaboration in creating lasting change. He actively seeks partnerships with LGBTQ organizations to amplify his educational initiatives. By working together, they can pool their resources, expertise, and networks to reach a wider audience and maximize their impact.

Through these collaborations, Omar supports and promotes existing LGBTQ organizations that provide education and support services. He helps raise awareness about their programs and initiatives, assisting them in their goal of creating a more inclusive and accepting society.

### Unconventional Approach: Connecting Education with the Arts

In his quest to offer resources for education and support, Omar Sharif Jr. also embraces unconventional approaches that combine education with the arts. He recognizes that art has the power to inspire, challenge, and transform hearts and minds.

For example, he collaborates with artists to create LGBTQ-themed films, plays, and visual art exhibitions. These artistic endeavors not only entertain but also educate and provoke meaningful conversations. Through storytelling and artistic expression, he engages audiences in a way that fosters empathy and understanding.

### Conclusion: Empowering Through Education and Support

In this section, we explored the various ways in which Omar Sharif Jr. offers resources for education and support to LGBTQ individuals and their allies. From creating LGBTQ-inclusive curricula and online educational platforms to establishing support networks and organizing workshops, Omar recognizes that education is a crucial tool for empowering marginalized communities.

By providing knowledge, resources, and support, he helps individuals navigate their journey towards acceptance and create a more inclusive society. Through his collaborative and unconventional approaches, Omar strives to make a lasting impact and inspire others to embrace LGBTQ equality and understanding.

### Fostering Acceptance and Understanding

In this section, we delve into the important work of fostering acceptance and understanding within the LGBTQ community and beyond. Omar Sharif Jr. has played a pivotal role in this area, working tirelessly to bridge gaps and promote a culture of tolerance and empathy. Through his advocacy efforts and initiatives, he has sought to create safe spaces and foster an environment where everyone can be accepted and understood, regardless of their sexual orientation or gender identity.

## The Importance of Dialogue

One of the key ways to foster acceptance and understanding is through open and honest dialogue. Omar Sharif Jr. recognizes the power of conversation in breaking down barriers and dispelling misconceptions. By engaging in meaningful conversations, he encourages individuals to question their biases and preconceived notions, opening the door to greater understanding and empathy.

To facilitate dialogue, Omar Sharif Jr. has organized numerous community events, panel discussions, and workshops. These platforms provide a safe space for individuals to share their stories, ask questions, and learn from one another. By bringing together diverse voices and perspectives, he helps create an inclusive environment that encourages dialogue and cultivates a sense of community.

## Educational Initiatives

Education is another crucial aspect of fostering acceptance and understanding. In order to combat discrimination and prejudice, it is essential to provide accurate and comprehensive information about LGBTQ issues. Omar Sharif Jr. has been a strong advocate for LGBTQ-inclusive education, working tirelessly to ensure that schools and educational institutions promote inclusivity and provide resources for LGBTQ students.

Through his work, he has collaborated with educators, curriculum developers, and policymakers to develop LGBTQ-inclusive curricula and training programs. These initiatives aim to raise awareness, challenge harmful stereotypes, and promote understanding among students and educators alike. By incorporating LGBTQ topics into the curriculum, Omar Sharif Jr. believes that we can create a more inclusive and accepting society.

## Empathy and Allyship

Fostering acceptance and understanding also requires cultivating empathy and allyship. Omar Sharif Jr. emphasizes the importance of individuals, regardless of their sexual orientation or gender identity, standing up for one another and being allies in the fight for equality.

To promote empathy, he encourages individuals to listen to the stories and experiences of LGBTQ individuals, recognizing the common humanity and struggles that connect us all. By fostering empathy, he believes that we can build bridges of understanding and break down the walls of prejudice and discrimination.

Furthermore, Omar Sharif Jr. actively promotes allyship by providing resources, guidance, and support for individuals who aspire to be allies to the LGBTQ community. He emphasizes the need for allies to educate themselves, challenge their own biases, and actively advocate for LGBTQ rights. By fostering a strong network of allies, he believes we can create a more inclusive and accepting society.

## Challenging Stereotypes Through Media

Media plays a powerful role in shaping societal perceptions and attitudes. Omar Sharif Jr. recognizes this and has worked within the entertainment industry to challenge harmful stereotypes and promote LGBTQ visibility. Through his involvement in film and television, he has used his platform to portray diverse LGBTQ characters and storylines, showcasing the richness and complexity of LGBTQ experiences.

In addition to his work in traditional media, Omar Sharif Jr. has harnessed the power of social media to amplify marginalized voices and drive conversations around LGBTQ issues. Through his active online presence, he shares personal stories, highlights important LGBTQ milestones, and engages with individuals from all walks of life. By utilizing social media as a tool for education and advocacy, he aims to challenge stereotypes and misconceptions, fostering a greater understanding and acceptance of the LGBTQ community.

## Promoting Cultural Sensitivity

A crucial aspect of fostering acceptance and understanding is promoting cultural sensitivity. Omar Sharif Jr. understands the importance of approaching LGBTQ advocacy in a way that respects and acknowledges different cultural contexts and traditions, especially in the Middle Eastern region.

He engages with local organizations and collaborates with community leaders to develop strategies that are sensitive to cultural norms and values. By combining LGBTQ advocacy with a deep understanding and appreciation of Middle Eastern cultures, he aims to create a more inclusive and accepting environment for LGBTQ individuals in the region.

Ultimately, fostering acceptance and understanding requires an ongoing commitment to compassion, education, and dialogue. Omar Sharif Jr.'s tireless efforts in this area have made a significant impact, bridging gaps between communities and creating a more inclusive world. By fostering acceptance and understanding, we can build a society where everyone is free to live and love authentically.

## The Importance of Local Communities in Activism

Local communities play a vital role in shaping activism and driving meaningful change. Their involvement is essential to create an inclusive and supportive environment for LGBTQ individuals. In this section, we will explore the significance of local communities in activism and how they contribute to the overall progress of LGBTQ rights.

### Creating Safe Spaces

One of the most critical aspects of community activism is the creation of safe spaces. LGBTQ individuals often face discrimination, exclusion, and violence in their daily lives. Local communities have the power to establish safe spaces where individuals can express themselves authentically without fear of judgment or harm.

These safe spaces can take various forms, such as community centers, support groups, and social events. They provide a sense of belonging, acceptance, and understanding for LGBTQ individuals who might otherwise feel isolated. Safe spaces allow people to connect, share experiences, and gain support from others who have gone through similar struggles.

### Educating the Community

Local communities have a unique opportunity to educate their members about LGBTQ issues and foster understanding. By organizing workshops, seminars, and awareness campaigns, they can challenge stereotypes, debunk myths, and provide accurate information about sexual orientation and gender identity.

Education is a powerful tool to combat ignorance and prejudice. It can contribute to the overall acceptance and inclusion of LGBTQ individuals within the community. Through education, local communities can help individuals recognize their biases, question societal norms, and develop empathy and compassion.

### Building Alliances and Partnerships

Successful activism requires collaboration and partnerships with various stakeholders. Local communities play a crucial role in building these alliances by reaching out to other organizations, institutions, and community leaders. By forging connections, activists can amplify their message and create a broader impact.

These alliances can take different forms, such as partnering with educational institutions to implement LGBTQ-inclusive curricula or collaborating with local businesses to promote LGBTQ-friendly policies. By working together, local communities can leverage their collective power to effect change on a larger scale.

## Advocating for Policy Change

Local communities are at the forefront of advocating for policy change that protects and promotes LGBTQ rights. Through grassroots initiatives, they can influence local governments, advocate for LGBTQ-inclusive policies, and lobby for the enforcement of existing laws.

By engaging with local representatives and policymakers, activists can highlight the needs of the LGBTQ community and emphasize the importance of equal rights and protections. Local communities can organize rallies, demonstrations, and public hearings to raise awareness about specific issues and generate public support for policy changes.

## Supporting LGBTQ Youth

LGBTQ youth often face unique challenges, including higher rates of homelessness, mental health issues, and bullying. Local communities can provide vital support systems for these vulnerable individuals, ensuring their well-being and empowering them to navigate the hurdles they face.

Supportive local communities can establish mentorship programs, counseling services, and provide resources for LGBTQ youth. By offering a safe and nurturing environment, they can help young individuals develop resilience, self-acceptance, and the skills necessary to lead successful lives.

## Harnessing Social Media and Technology

In today's digital age, social media and technology have become indispensable tools for activism. Local communities can utilize these platforms to amplify their message, raise awareness, and mobilize support.

By creating online communities, local activists can connect with a broader audience and reach individuals who may not have access to physical community spaces. They can share stories, engage in discourse, and organize virtual events to promote LGBTQ rights.

Furthermore, technological advancements enable local communities to provide resources, information, and support online. It reduces barriers of access to knowledge and creates opportunities for individuals to seek help and connect with others.

## Conclusion

Local communities are the heart of activism. Their efforts, support, and dedication are indispensable in the fight for LGBTQ rights. By creating safe spaces, educating the community, building alliances, advocating for policy change, supporting LGBTQ youth, and leveraging technology, local communities contribute significantly to the progress of activism. They play a vital role in fostering acceptance, promoting equality, and creating a more inclusive world for all individuals.

# Public Speaking and Engaging the Masses

## The Art of Powerful Public Speaking

Public speaking is an art form that can captivate and inspire audiences. In this section, we will explore the principles and techniques behind powerful public speaking and how Omar Sharif Jr. has used his skills to advocate for change and make a lasting impact on the LGBTQ community.

## The Importance of Authenticity

One of the key aspects of powerful public speaking is authenticity. Audiences can sense when a speaker is genuine and passionate about their message, and this creates a deeper connection and resonates with listeners. Omar Sharif Jr. understands the power of authenticity and uses it to communicate his experiences as an LGBTQ activist.

Being true to oneself allows the speaker to create a sense of trust and credibility with the audience. By sharing personal stories and experiences, Omar Sharif Jr. invites the audience into his world, helping them to understand the struggles and triumphs of being LGBTQ in the Middle East. This vulnerability not only showcases his authenticity but also creates empathy and understanding among listeners.

## Crafting a Compelling Narrative

A powerful public speaker knows how to craft a compelling narrative that engages and captivates the audience. Omar Sharif Jr., through his storytelling abilities, has been able to communicate the challenges faced by the LGBTQ community and the importance of advocacy in a way that resonates with people from all walks of life.

Effective storytelling involves structuring the speech in a way that builds tension and emotion. Omar Sharif Jr. often begins with personal anecdotes and experiences, drawing the audience in with relatable and heartfelt stories. He then transitions to broader societal issues, painting a vivid picture of the struggles faced by the LGBTQ community in the Middle East.

By weaving personal stories with broader societal issues, Omar Sharif Jr. creates a compelling narrative that educates, inspires, and motivates his audience to take action and support the LGBTQ cause.

## Empathy and Connection

Empathy is a crucial component of powerful public speaking. Effective speakers have the ability to connect with their audience on an emotional level, creating a shared understanding and sense of belonging. Omar Sharif Jr. excels in establishing this connection by relating his experiences to universal emotions and values.

He taps into the common desire for love, acceptance, and equality, reminding the audience that these are fundamental human rights that everyone deserves. Through empathy, he encourages listeners to see beyond their differences and embrace diversity.

Furthermore, Omar Sharif Jr. actively engages with his audience during his speeches. He creates a dialogue by asking thought-provoking questions, encouraging reflection and introspection. This interactive approach not only keeps the audience engaged but also fosters a deeper connection between the speaker and the listeners.

## Utilizing Non-Verbal Communication

Non-verbal communication plays a significant role in public speaking. From facial expressions to body language, these cues can enhance or detract from the speaker's message. Omar Sharif Jr. has honed his non-verbal communication skills to complement his spoken words, making his speeches more impactful and engaging.

For instance, he uses eye contact to establish a sense of connection and trust with individual audience members. By scanning the room and making eye contact with different individuals, he ensures that everyone feels involved and heard.

Additionally, Omar Sharif Jr. employs gestures and body movements to emphasize key points and add visual interest to his speeches. These non-verbal cues help to convey his passion and conviction, making his message all the more powerful and persuasive.

## Inspiring Action and Change

The ultimate goal of powerful public speaking is to inspire action and drive change. Omar Sharif Jr. has made a significant impact through his speeches by motivating his audience to become advocates for LGBTQ rights and work towards a more inclusive society.

During his speeches, he provides tangible steps and resources for individuals to get involved in activism, such as supporting local LGBTQ organizations or engaging with policymakers. By empowering his audience with actionable takeaways, Omar Sharif Jr. ensures that his speeches are not just inspirational but also catalysts for real change.

Moreover, he encourages his audience to utilize their own voices and platforms to amplify the LGBTQ movement. By highlighting the power of collective action, he demonstrates that everyone has a role to play in advancing LGBTQ rights, regardless of their background or position.

## Embracing Vulnerability

In addition to all the techniques mentioned above, a truly powerful public speaker is willing to be vulnerable and share their own struggles and insecurities. Omar Sharif Jr., by openly discussing his personal journey as an LGBTQ individual in a traditional Middle Eastern family, invites the audience to join him in embracing vulnerability and confronting social stigmas.

Vulnerability can be transformative, as it allows the speaker to connect with their audience on a deeper level. By sharing both the triumphs and challenges of his life as an LGBTQ advocate, Omar Sharif Jr. creates a safe space for open dialogue and understanding.

Through vulnerability, he fosters a sense of courage and resilience within his audience, inspiring them to confront their own fears and prejudices. This transformative power of vulnerability is a testament to the strength and impact of Omar Sharif Jr.'s public speaking.

## Conclusion: Making a Lasting Impact

Powerful public speaking is an essential tool for activists like Omar Sharif Jr. who wish to make a lasting impact on society. By embracing authenticity, crafting compelling narratives, establishing connections through empathy and non-verbal communication, inspiring action and change, and embracing vulnerability, Omar Sharif Jr. has been able to captivate audiences and advocate for LGBTQ rights on a global scale.

His ability to engage with different audiences, from local communities to international stages, has helped bridge gaps and foster understanding between LGBTQ and Middle Eastern advocacy. Through his speeches, Omar Sharif Jr. continues to inspire future generations of activists and pave the way towards a more inclusive and accepting world.

## Engaging with Different Audiences

Engaging with different audiences is a crucial aspect of activism. In order to create change and spread awareness, it is important for activists like Omar Sharif Jr. to connect with people from various backgrounds and demographics. Whether it's speaking at a conference, giving a TED talk, or participating in a panel discussion, effective communication is key to reaching and inspiring different audiences.

### Understanding Your Audience

Before engaging with any audience, it is essential to have a deep understanding of their needs, concerns, and beliefs. This requires research and empathy. By gaining insights into the specific challenges faced by different communities, activists can tailor their message and approach accordingly. For instance, when speaking to LGBTQ youth, Omar Sharif Jr. would focus on issues such as bullying and acceptance, whereas when addressing policymakers, he would emphasize the importance of implementing LGBTQ-inclusive policies and legislation.

### Adapting Communication Styles

To engage effectively, activists must adapt their communication styles to resonate with different audiences. This involves using language and terminology that is accessible and relatable. For instance, when speaking to LGBTQ communities, using inclusive language and addressing specific challenges faced by queer individuals can create a sense of connection. On the other hand, when engaging with conservative or religious groups, it is important to frame the conversation in a way that aligns with their values and emphasizes the common ground.

## Telling Personal Stories

One of the most powerful ways to engage with audiences is by sharing personal stories. By openly discussing his own journey of self-discovery and the challenges he has faced, Omar Sharif Jr. can create a sense of empathy and connection with his listeners. Personal stories humanize the issues at hand and help the audience see the real-life impact of discrimination and prejudice. This can be particularly effective in changing hearts and minds, as people often respond more positively to personal experiences than to abstract concepts or statistics.

## Using Visual Aids and Technology

In today's digital age, visual aids and technology play a crucial role in engaging with different audiences. Activists like Omar Sharif Jr. can utilize multimedia presentations, videos, and infographics to enhance their message and captivate their audience. These tools can help simplify complex topics, provide visual representations of data, and make the content more engaging and memorable.

Furthermore, social media platforms offer a powerful way to connect with diverse audiences. By leveraging platforms like Instagram, Twitter, and YouTube, activists can reach millions of people and educate them about LGBTQ rights and Middle Eastern advocacy. Sharing personal stories, organizing online campaigns, and fostering discussions can amplify the message and extend the reach of the advocacy work.

## Creating Interactive Experiences

Another effective way to engage with different audiences is through interactive experiences. Omar Sharif Jr. can organize workshops, seminars, or town hall meetings where attendees can actively participate and contribute to the conversation. This allows for a two-way dialogue, enabling activists to address concerns, answer questions, and provide support. Interactive experiences create a sense of community and empower individuals to take action, fostering a deeper connection to the cause.

### Collaborating with Other Activists

Engaging with different audiences becomes even more impactful when activists from diverse backgrounds come together. Collaborating with other activists allows for a wider range of perspectives and increases the reach of the advocacy work. By forming alliances and partnerships, Omar Sharif Jr. can tap into different networks and amplify the message to reach new audiences. This collaborative approach also helps foster a sense of solidarity among activists, creating a more united front for change.

### Unconventional Approach: Artistic Expression

Activism doesn't always have to follow a traditional script. In fact, sometimes the most effective way to engage with different audiences is through artistic expression. Omar Sharif Jr. can explore mediums such as music, poetry, or visual arts to convey messages of inclusivity, acceptance, and equality. Art has a universal language that can touch hearts and minds in a unique way, transcending barriers and challenging preconceived notions. This unconventional approach allows for a deeper emotional connection with the audience and has the potential to create lasting impact.

In conclusion, engaging with different audiences is a critical aspect of activism. By understanding the needs and concerns of various communities, adapting communication styles, sharing personal stories, utilizing visual aids and technology, creating interactive experiences, collaborating with other activists, and exploring unconventional approaches, activists like Omar Sharif Jr. can effectively spread awareness, create change, and build a more inclusive world for all.

## Motivating Others to Take Action

Motivating others to take action is a crucial aspect of any successful activism movement. In the context of LGBTQ advocacy, it becomes even more essential as we strive for equality, acceptance, and inclusion for all. Omar Sharif Jr. serves as a powerful catalyst for change, inspiring individuals from all walks of life to join the fight for LGBTQ rights. Let's explore some of the key strategies and principles that can effectively motivate others to take action.

### The Power of Personal Stories

One of the most potent tools in motivating others is the power of personal stories. Omar Sharif Jr. shares his own experiences, struggles, and triumphs to create a connection with his audience. By openly discussing his journey of self-discovery and the challenges he has faced as a LGBTQ Middle Eastern activist, he humanizes the LGBTQ rights movement and makes it relatable to individuals who may not have previously understood or empathized with the cause.

When individuals hear personal stories that resonate with their own experiences or challenges, it can ignite a sense of solidarity and inspire them to take action. Sharif Jr. encourages others to share their stories, creating a ripple effect that amplifies the voices of the LGBTQ community and strengthens the movement as a whole.

**Empathy and Understanding**

Motivating others to take action requires cultivating empathy and understanding. Sharif Jr. emphasizes the importance of education and awareness in challenging the stereotypes and misconceptions that surround LGBTQ individuals, particularly in the Middle East. By providing accurate information, fostering open dialogue, and creating safe spaces for discussions, Sharif Jr. helps others understand the struggles faced by LGBTQ individuals and the urgency for change.

Through empathy, individuals can develop a deeper understanding of the impact of discrimination and prejudice. Showing compassion for the experiences of others can move people to take action, whether it's engaging in conversations with their families, friends, or colleagues, or actively participating in advocacy efforts.

**Creating Opportunities for Involvement**

Motivation is often sparked by providing individuals with opportunities to get involved. Omar Sharif Jr. organizes events, workshops, and campaigns that encourage individuals to join the movement as allies, advocates, and volunteers. By actively engaging with community members, he cultivates a sense of ownership and connection to the cause.

In the workshops he hosts, participants learn about the history of LGBTQ activism, the current challenges faced by the community, and the various tactics for effecting change. Through this hands-on approach, individuals are empowered to make a difference through their own actions, whether it's through organizing local events, fundraising, or leveraging their skills and expertise to support the cause.

**Promoting Collaboration and Intersectionality**

Motivating others to take action also requires recognizing the importance of collaboration and intersectionality. Omar Sharif Jr. actively collaborates with LGBTQ organizations, human rights groups, and activists from various social justice movements. By embracing intersectionality, he understands that the

LGBTQ struggle does not exist in isolation but is connected to broader issues of gender, race, class, and religion.

Sharif Jr. encourages others to seek partnerships and coalitions with diverse communities and organizations that share common goals. By acknowledging the interconnectedness of different struggles, individuals are motivated to work collectively towards a more just and inclusive society.

**Recognizing Small Victories**

Finally, motivating others requires celebrating small victories along the way. Omar Sharif Jr. emphasizes the importance of acknowledging progress and recognizing the efforts of individuals and organizations dedicated to LGBTQ rights. By highlighting achievements, even modest ones, he instills a sense of hope and optimism in others.

Recognizing small victories not only boosts morale but also inspires individuals to continue their involvement and contributions to the cause. Sharif Jr. believes that celebrating milestones along the journey is vital to sustaining long-term motivation and commitment.

**Conclusion**

Motivating others to take action in the fight for LGBTQ rights is a complex and multifaceted process. Omar Sharif Jr. has mastered the art of motivation through personal storytelling, empathy, creating opportunities for involvement, promoting collaboration, and recognizing small victories. Through his tireless efforts, he has sparked a ripple effect of change, inspiring individuals worldwide to join the movement and work towards a more inclusive and accepting world. The strategies and principles he employs serve as a blueprint for motivating others to take action in any advocacy cause, ultimately paving the way for a brighter and more equitable future for all.

**Inspiring Change through Words and Actions**

In this section, we explore how Omar Sharif Jr. has inspired change through the power of his words and actions. His ability to engage and motivate others has been a driving force behind his successful advocacy work. Let's delve into the principles that guide him and the strategies he employs to inspire change.

## The Power of Storytelling

One of the most powerful tools in inspiring change is storytelling. By sharing personal experiences, struggles, and triumphs, Omar has been able to connect with people on a deep and emotional level. He uses his own journey of self-discovery and acceptance to break down barriers and challenge stereotypes.

Through his speeches, interviews, and written pieces, Omar conveys the importance of embracing one's true identity, even in the face of adversity. He paints a vivid picture of the challenges he has faced and the strength he has gained through his advocacy work. By sharing his story, he inspires others to find their own voice and share their experiences, ultimately fostering a sense of belonging and solidarity within the LGBTQ community.

## Leading by Example

Actions speak louder than words, and Omar understands the significance of leading by example. He consistently demonstrates courage, resilience, and authenticity in his advocacy efforts, setting a powerful precedent for others to follow.

Whether it is participating in public demonstrations, attending LGBTQ events, or collaborating with organizations fighting for equality, Omar consistently shows up and actively engages in the cause. His commitment to showing up for both himself and others inspires individuals to step out of their comfort zones and take action in their own communities.

## Creating Empowering Communities

Omar recognizes that change cannot happen in isolation; it requires a collective effort. He has been instrumental in creating empowering communities where individuals can come together, share ideas, and support one another.

Through his involvement in LGBTQ centers and support networks, Omar fosters an environment of acceptance and understanding. These spaces provide individuals with the resources and support needed to navigate their own journeys of self-discovery. By creating safe spaces where people feel seen and heard, he empowers others to embrace their identities and join the fight for equality.

## Building Bridges and Collaboration

Omar believes in the power of collaboration and building bridges between diverse communities. He actively seeks out opportunities to work with individuals and organizations that may not initially seem aligned with his cause. This approach allows him to reach a wider audience and challenge preconceived notions.

By engaging in constructive dialogue and finding common ground, Omar encourages empathy, understanding, and collaboration. He understands that change is more likely to occur when people with different perspectives and experiences come together to find common solutions.

## Utilizing Social Media and Technology

In the digital age, social media and technology have become powerful tools for advocacy. Omar leverages these platforms to amplify his message and reach a global audience. His strategic use of social media allows him to connect with individuals from all walks of life, engage in meaningful conversations, and inspire change on a broader scale.

From live Q&A sessions to posting impactful stories and articles, Omar utilizes social media to create awareness, challenge stereotypes, and educate others. Through these digital platforms, he encourages individuals to get involved, take action, and be part of the movement for LGBTQ rights.

## Example: Empowering LGBTQ Youth through Education

To illustrate the impact of inspiring change through words and actions, let's consider the example of empowering LGBTQ youth through education. One of the key aspects of Omar's advocacy work is his dedication to creating inclusive educational environments.

Problem: LGBTQ youth often face discrimination, bullying, and lack of support in educational settings, leading to lower academic achievement and psychological distress.

Solution: Omar works tirelessly to advocate for LGBTQ-inclusive education by collaborating with schools, educators, and policymakers. He emphasizes the importance of creating safe and nurturing spaces where LGBTQ youth feel validated and supported.

Explanation: By providing resources, training, and workshops for educators, Omar enables them to create LGBTQ-inclusive curricula and implement policies that protect LGBTQ students from discrimination. He also encourages schools to establish LGBTQ support groups and to educate all students about diversity, acceptance, and respect.

Example: Omar partners with a local high school to implement LGBTQ-inclusive education. He gives a compelling presentation to the school board, demonstrating the positive impact inclusive education can have on LGBTQ students' mental health and academic performance.

Resources: Omar collaborates with LGBTQ youth organizations, mental health professionals, and educational experts to develop resources such as lesson plans, toolkits, and training programs for educators. These resources provide practical guidance and support for creating inclusive classrooms.

Caveat: Implementing LGBTQ-inclusive education may face resistance from certain individuals or groups who hold discriminatory beliefs. It is important to engage in respectful dialogue and address concerns, emphasizing the importance of creating an inclusive and safe learning environment for all students.

Ultimately, by empowering LGBTQ youth through education, Omar believes in nurturing the next generation of advocates who will continue to inspire change, creating a more inclusive society for everyone.

In conclusion, Omar Sharif Jr. has inspired change through his impactful words and actions. By sharing his story, leading by example, creating empowering communities, building bridges, and utilizing technology, he has ignited a movement for LGBTQ rights and Middle Eastern advocacy. His dedication to inspiring change serves as a beacon of hope for a more inclusive and equal world.

# The Continued Journey

## Never-Ending Advocacy

Advocacy is not just a journey with a final destination; it is a lifelong commitment to fighting for what is right. For Omar Sharif Jr., this means that his work for LGBTQ rights and Middle Eastern advocacy is never-ending. In this section, we will explore the various aspects of his ongoing advocacy and how he continues to make a difference in the world.

## Staying Informed and Evolving

To be an effective advocate, one must stay informed and constantly adapt to the changing landscape of LGBTQ rights and Middle Eastern activism. Omar Sharif Jr. understands the importance of ongoing education and growth in his advocacy work. He stays connected to LGBTQ communities, attends conferences, and engages with experts to deepen his understanding of the challenges faced by the community and the evolving strategies to address them.

Omar recognizes that the fight for equality is not static; it requires continuous evolution and adaptation. He keeps a close eye on the global LGBTQ rights movement, seeking inspiration and learning from other activists and organizations across the world. By staying informed and evolving his approach, he ensures that his advocacy remains relevant and impactful.

## Expanding the Scope

While Omar Sharif Jr. began his advocacy work focusing on LGBTQ rights and Middle Eastern advocacy, he understands the importance of intersectionality. He acknowledges that various forms of discrimination and inequality intersect and amplify one another. Therefore, he expands the scope of his advocacy beyond LGBTQ rights to tackle issues such as racial discrimination, gender inequality, and refugee rights.

By addressing these intersecting issues, Omar creates a more comprehensive and inclusive advocacy that recognizes the interconnectedness of various struggles for justice and equality. He uses his platform to shed light on the experiences of marginalized communities, amplifying their voices and advocating for change.

## Harnessing the Power of Technology

In the modern world, technology has become an undeniable force of change and a powerful tool for advocacy. Omar Sharif Jr. recognizes the potential of technology to reach wider audiences and generate meaningful impact. He leverages social media platforms, online campaigns, and digital storytelling to raise awareness, educate, and mobilize support for LGBTQ rights and Middle Eastern advocacy.

One of the unconventional yet effective strategies Omar adopts is using virtual reality (VR) and augmented reality (AR) to create immersive experiences that promote empathy and understanding. Through these innovative technologies, he transports people into the lives of LGBTQ individuals and those affected by discrimination in the Middle East, fostering a deeper connection and empathy.

## Collaboration and Coalition Building

Omar Sharif Jr. understands that no significant change can be achieved alone. He recognizes the power of collaboration and coalition building to tackle complex societal issues. He actively seeks out partnerships with other organizations, activists, and influencers to amplify the collective efforts towards social change.

By collaborating with others who share his passion for LGBTQ rights and Middle Eastern advocacy, Omar creates a united front that is stronger and more impactful than individual efforts. He fosters dialogue, facilitates connections, and encourages the exchange of ideas and strategies. Through these collaborations, he builds bridges between diverse communities and ensures that the fight for equality is inclusive and intersectional.

### Engaging with the Youth

The youth are at the forefront of social change, and Omar Sharif Jr. recognizes their power and potential. He is dedicated to engaging with young people, empowering them to become advocates for LGBTQ rights and Middle Eastern activism. He visits schools and universities to deliver inspiring talks, conducts workshops, and mentors young activists.

Omar firmly believes that investing in the youth is an investment in the future of advocacy. He encourages young people to embrace their identities, embrace activism, and make their voices heard. By empowering the youth, he ensures that the fight for equality continues beyond his own endeavors.

### Continuing the Conversation

Advocacy is a never-ending conversation. Omar Sharif Jr. understands that his work is not just about achieving specific goals or milestones but about fostering a long-lasting dialogue. He actively maintains a presence in public discourse, engaging with media, participating in panel discussions, and writing op-eds to continue the conversation on LGBTQ rights and Middle Eastern advocacy.

By keeping the conversation alive, Omar ensures that the struggles and achievements of the LGBTQ community and marginalized groups in the Middle East remain visible and relevant. He sparks debate, challenges prejudices, and encourages critical thinking, thereby paving the way for a more inclusive and accepting society.

As Omar Sharif Jr.'s advocacy journey continues, the fight for LGBTQ rights and Middle Eastern advocacy remains as important as ever. Through ongoing education, expanding the scope of his work, harnessing technology, collaborating with others, engaging with the youth, and continuing the conversation, he is making a lasting impact on the world. His example serves as an inspiration for future generations of activists, showing them that the fight for equality is a never-ending endeavor that requires unwavering dedication and a commitment to progress.

### Taking on New Challenges and Causes

As Omar Sharif Jr. continues his extraordinary journey of LGBTQ and Middle Eastern advocacy, he constantly seeks out new challenges and causes to champion. With his unyielding spirit and passion for social justice, he is determined to make a lasting impact on the world. In this section, we will explore some of the new challenges and causes Omar has taken on, showcasing his unwavering commitment to creating a more inclusive and equal society.

## Addressing Mental Health in the LGBTQ Community

One of the pressing challenges that Omar Sharif Jr. has taken on is addressing the mental health issues faced by LGBTQ individuals. Recognizing the high rates of depression, anxiety, and suicide among this community, Omar has been a fierce advocate for mental health support and resources.

Through partnerships with mental health organizations, he has helped raise awareness about the unique challenges LGBTQ individuals face and the importance of accessible and inclusive mental health services. He has actively campaigned for increased funding for LGBTQ-specific mental health programs and continuously works to reduce the stigma surrounding mental health within the community.

Omar's efforts have resulted in the establishment of LGBTQ-focused mental health centers, support networks, and helplines, providing essential resources to those in need. By shining a light on this critical issue, he has empowered countless individuals to seek help and find solace in a community that understands and supports them.

## Advancing Transgender Rights

Recognizing the heightened discrimination and marginalization faced by transgender individuals, Omar Sharif Jr. has taken on the cause of advancing transgender rights both locally and globally. He understands that the struggle for transgender equality is multifaceted and requires a comprehensive approach to address social, legal, and healthcare issues.

Omar has worked tirelessly to educate the public about transgender identities, dispel myths and misconceptions, and foster empathy and understanding. Through collaborations with transgender activists, organizations, and healthcare professionals, he has been instrumental in advocating for gender-affirming healthcare, legal protections, and inclusive policies.

In addition to his advocacy, Omar has actively supported the creation of safe spaces for transgender individuals, such as shelters and community centers, where they can find support, resources, and affirmation. He believes that by uplifting the voices and experiences of transgender individuals, society can move closer to true equality and acceptance for all.

## Fighting for Intersectional Justice

Understanding the interconnectedness of various forms of oppression, Omar Sharif Jr. has embraced the importance of intersectionality in his advocacy work. He recognizes that marginalized communities often face multiple forms of discrimination based on their race, gender, sexuality, or socio-economic status.

Omar has actively collaborated with organizations and activists working on a wide range of social justice issues, including racial equality, women's rights, and income inequality. By centering intersectionality in his activism, he amplifies the voices and experiences of those who are often overlooked or silenced.

Through his collaborations, Omar has promoted the understanding that true equality can only be achieved by addressing all forms of oppression simultaneously. By advocating for intersectional justice, he aims to build a more inclusive and equitable world, where every individual's rights and dignity are respected.

## Promoting LGBTQ-Inclusive Faith Communities

Recognizing the profound impact of religion on the lives of individuals in the Middle East and beyond, Omar Sharif Jr. has taken on the cause of promoting LGBTQ-inclusive faith communities. He believes that no individual should have to choose between their faith and their identity.

Omar has engaged in conversations with religious leaders, scholars, and communities to foster dialogue and understanding about LGBTQ individuals' place within diverse religious traditions. By challenging homophobic interpretations of religious texts and promoting inclusive interpretations, he has paved the way for acceptance within religious spaces.

Through partnerships with grassroots organizations and faith leaders, Omar has helped create safe and inclusive spaces within religious communities, where LGBTQ individuals can practice their faith without fear or judgment. His efforts have inspired other religious leaders to speak out in support of LGBTQ rights, fostering greater acceptance and understanding within faith communities.

## Embracing Environmental Activism

Recognizing that environmental issues deeply impact marginalized communities, Omar Sharif Jr. has recently embarked on a new challenge: embracing environmental activism. He understands that the fight for social justice cannot be achieved without addressing the urgent need to protect the planet.

Omar has collaborated with environmental organizations, participated in climate change conferences, and used his platform to raise awareness about the intersection of environmental and social issues. By emphasizing the disproportionate impact of climate change on vulnerable communities, including LGBTQ individuals, people of color, and those living in poverty, he has amplified their voices and advocated for environmental justice.

With his newfound passion for environmentalism, Omar aims to inspire others to join the fight for a sustainable future, where justice, equality, and environmental stewardship go hand in hand. Through education and action, he strives to create a world in which all individuals, regardless of their background, can thrive in harmony with nature.

## Conclusion: A Hero for Our Times

Omar Sharif Jr. continues to push the boundaries of LGBTQ and Middle Eastern advocacy, fearlessly tackling new challenges and causes. Through his relentless commitment to social justice, he has become a beacon of hope for millions around the world.

From addressing mental health in the LGBTQ community to advancing transgender rights, fighting for intersectional justice, promoting LGBTQ-inclusive faith communities, and embracing environmental activism, Omar exemplifies the power of individual activism to bring about positive change.

As a global icon, Omar Sharif Jr.'s impact extends far beyond his personal journey. By inspiring others and challenging the status quo, he leaves an indelible legacy that will shape the future of LGBTQ and Middle Eastern advocacy for generations to come.

In the final chapter, we will reflect on his contributions, celebrate his remarkable journey, and explore the lasting legacy of LGBTQ and Middle Eastern advocacy.

## The Evolution of LGBTQ Activism

The evolution of LGBTQ activism is a testament to the power of collective action and the relentless pursuit of equality. Over the years, LGBTQ activists have fought tirelessly to dismantle discriminatory laws, challenge societal norms, and create a more inclusive world for all. This section explores the key milestones and strategies that have shaped the evolution of LGBTQ activism.

## Historical Context

To understand the evolution of LGBTQ activism, it is important to first appreciate the historical context in which it emerged. LGBTQ individuals have faced widespread discrimination, persecution, and marginalization throughout history.

Homosexuality was criminalized in many countries, and same-sex relationships were considered taboo or even pathological.

The Stonewall Riots in 1969 marked a turning point in LGBTQ activism. In response to a police raid on the Stonewall Inn, a gay bar in New York City, LGBTQ individuals and allies fought back, sparking days of protests and demonstrations. This event galvanized the LGBTQ community, leading to the formation of advocacy organizations and the birth of the modern LGBTQ rights movement.

## Strategies and Tactics

In the early stages of LGBTQ activism, the focus was primarily on visibility and destigmatization. Coming out, sharing personal stories, and humanizing LGBTQ experiences became powerful tools for challenging societal prejudices. LGBTQ individuals and their allies worked to create safe spaces where they could gather, organize, and advocate for their rights.

As LGBTQ activism gained momentum, it became clear that legal and policy changes were crucial for achieving equality. Activists focused on lobbying for anti-discrimination laws, marriage equality, and protections against hate crimes. Legal victories, such as the decriminalization of homosexuality and the legalization of same-sex marriage in various countries, marked significant milestones in the evolution of LGBTQ activism.

With the advent of the internet and social media, digital platforms became powerful tools for organizing and mobilizing activists. Online campaigns, petitions, and viral hashtags have allowed LGBTQ activists to reach broader audiences, raise awareness, and challenge discriminatory practices.

Intersectionality has also played a crucial role in the evolution of LGBTQ activism. Recognizing the interconnectedness of various forms of oppression and discrimination, activists have worked to build alliances with other marginalized communities, such as racial and ethnic minorities, people with disabilities, and gender non-conforming individuals. This intersectional approach has strengthened the movement and allowed for a more inclusive understanding of equality.

## Key Milestones

The evolution of LGBTQ activism can be traced through key milestones that have shaped the movement. Some notable milestones include:

1. Decriminalization: In the late 20th century, several countries, including the United Kingdom, Canada, and Australia, decriminalized homosexuality, removing legal penalties for consensual same-sex relationships.

2. AIDS Crisis: The devastating impact of the HIV/AIDS epidemic in the 1980s brought attention to the health disparities faced by LGBTQ individuals. Activists fought for access to healthcare, research funding, and an end to discrimination against people living with HIV/AIDS.

3. Marriage Equality: The fight for marriage equality took center stage in the early 2000s. Landmark cases, such as the United States Supreme Court's ruling in Obergefell v. Hodges in 2015, legalized same-sex marriage nationwide.

4. Transgender Rights: The visibility and advocacy of transgender activists have pushed for greater recognition and protection of transgender rights. The inclusion of gender identity and expression in anti-discrimination laws and policies has been a significant milestone in LGBTQ activism.

5. Global Efforts: LGBTQ activism has extended beyond national borders, with activists partnering globally to support LGBTQ communities worldwide. International organizations like the United Nations have recognized the importance of LGBTQ rights and have worked towards global accountability and equality.

## Challenges and Future Outlook

Despite the significant progress made in LGBTQ activism, challenges remain. Many countries still have laws that criminalize homosexuality or fail to protect LGBTQ individuals from discrimination and violence. LGBTQ youth continue to face bullying and exclusion in schools, and transgender individuals often experience societal rejection and limited access to healthcare.

Moving forward, LGBTQ activism will continue to evolve to address these challenges. Advocates will work to broaden the understanding of gender and sexuality, challenge binary norms, and fight for comprehensive LGBTQ-inclusive education. They will also prioritize the needs of intersectional communities, recognizing the unique challenges faced by LGBTQ individuals at the intersection of other marginalized identities.

In conclusion, the evolution of LGBTQ activism is a testament to the power of collective action and the resilience of the LGBTQ community. From its early beginnings centered around visibility and destigmatization to its current focus on policy change, the movement has made significant strides in the fight for equality. However, challenges persist, and the ongoing efforts of activists are necessary to create a more inclusive future for all.

## Omar Sharif Jr's Ongoing Impact

Throughout his journey as an LGBTQ activist and advocate for Middle Eastern rights, Omar Sharif Jr. has made a significant and lasting impact on both local and global communities. His relentless dedication to creating positive change has paved the way for a more inclusive world. In this section, we will explore the ongoing influence of his activism and the legacy he continues to build.

## Driving Progress through Collaboration

Omar Sharif Jr.'s impact extends beyond his individual efforts. He has actively sought out collaborations with other activists, organizations, and governments to drive progress and create sustainable change. By working together, they have been able to amplify their voices and achieve more significant results.

One of the key aspects of his ongoing impact is his ability to bridge the gap between LGBTQ and Middle Eastern advocacy. He recognizes the interconnectedness of these movements and understands the importance of addressing intersectional issues. Through his collaborations, he has facilitated dialogue and fostered understanding between different communities, creating a space for shared goals and collective action.

## Amplifying Voices on a Global Scale

Omar Sharif Jr.'s media presence has played a vital role in amplifying the voices of LGBTQ individuals and activists worldwide. Through traditional media outlets, social media platforms, and his own personal platforms, he has consistently used his voice to challenge prejudice and discrimination.

In the digital age, he recognizes the power of social media in mobilizing communities and shaping public opinion. As a result, he has been strategic in leveraging platforms like Twitter, Instagram, and YouTube to reach a global audience and inspire change. By sharing his personal experiences, insights, and messages of empowerment, he has motivated others to take action and break down barriers in their own communities.

## Creating Safe Spaces for LGBTQ Individuals

Creating safe spaces for LGBTQ individuals is paramount to fostering acceptance and understanding. Omar Sharif Jr. understands the importance of providing resources, support, and education to LGBTQ individuals who may face discrimination, rejection, or isolation.

He has been instrumental in establishing LGBTQ centers and support networks in various regions. These spaces not only provide valuable resources but also serve as beacons of hope for LGBTQ individuals who may be struggling with their identities or facing adversity.

Moreover, Sharif Jr. recognizes that change begins at the grassroots level. By engaging with local communities, he has helped create an environment where LGBTQ individuals can thrive and find acceptance. Through his ongoing efforts, he continues to promote inclusivity, understanding, and empathy within these communities.

## Inspiring the Next Generation

A crucial part of Omar Sharif Jr.'s ongoing impact is his role in inspiring the next generation of activists. Through his journey, he has shown LGBTQ youth that their voices matter and that no dream is too big to achieve.

By openly sharing his story and experiences, Sharif Jr. has become a symbol of hope and resilience. He encourages LGBTQ youth to embrace their authentic selves, regardless of the challenges they may face. His advocacy serves as a reminder that change is possible and that their actions can shape a more inclusive future.

Furthermore, he emphasizes the importance of education and empowerment in creating lasting change. By engaging with educational institutions and advocating for LGBTQ-inclusive curricula, he ensures that the next generation is equipped with the knowledge and understanding to challenge discrimination and foster acceptance.

## Continuing the Fight for Equality

Omar Sharif Jr.'s ongoing impact is not limited to the present. He is committed to continuing the fight for LGBTQ and Middle Eastern equality, understanding that the struggle for true equality is an ongoing process.

He recognizes the evolving nature of LGBTQ activism and the importance of adaptability. As new challenges arise and societal norms shift, he remains at the forefront of the movement, seeking innovative approaches to address the needs of LGBTQ individuals.

Through his consistent dedication to LGBTQ rights, he inspires others to join the cause and leverage their unique skills and talents. By fostering a sense of unity and collaboration, he ensures that the fight for equality remains a collective effort.

## Conclusion: A Hero for Our Times

Omar Sharif Jr.'s ongoing impact is a testament to his unwavering commitment to creating a more inclusive world. By bridging LGBTQ and Middle Eastern advocacy, amplifying voices on a global scale, creating safe spaces, inspiring the next generation, and continuing the fight for equality, he has become a hero for our times.

His legacy extends far beyond his activism. His story serves as a reminder that one person can make a difference, and their impact can be felt for generations to come.

As we reflect on the remarkable journey of Omar Sharif Jr., we are inspired to take action and continue the fight for LGBTQ and Middle Eastern rights. His ongoing impact serves as a powerful reminder that change is possible, and our collective efforts can create a better, more inclusive future.

# Chapter 5: Legacy and Future Endeavors

## Chapter 5: Legacy and Future Endeavors

### Chapter 5: Legacy and Future Endeavors

In this final chapter, we explore the lasting impact of Omar Sharif Jr.'s activism and his vision for the future of LGBTQ and Middle Eastern advocacy. As a tireless advocate for equality, Omar has left an indelible mark on the movement and continues to inspire future generations of activists. His journey is a testament to the power of perseverance, compassion, and a belief in the possibility of change.

#### The Impact of Omar Sharif Jr.'s Activism

Omar Sharif Jr.'s activism has had a profound impact on both LGBTQ rights and Middle Eastern advocacy. By sharing his personal story and speaking out about the challenges faced by LGBTQ individuals in the Middle East, Omar has raised awareness and sparked crucial conversations. His courage has inspired countless others to live authentically and fight for their rights.

Omar's advocacy has helped to break down barriers and challenge cultural norms. Through his work, he has advocated for LGBTQ inclusion and acceptance in the Middle East, working to create safe spaces for queer individuals and fostering a sense of belonging. His efforts have helped to dismantle prejudice and discrimination, paving the way for a more equitable society.

#### Inspiring Future Generations of Activists

One of Omar's most significant contributions is the inspiration he provides to future generations of activists. By fearlessly sharing his truth and advocating for change, he has become a role model for individuals around the world. His work has shown that one person can make a difference and that every voice matters.

Omar's ability to connect with diverse audiences has made him a powerful advocate. He has engaged with both LGBTQ communities and Middle Eastern organizations, fostering dialogue and understanding. Through his words and actions, he challenges individuals to confront their biases and embrace the importance of equality and acceptance.

## The Indomitable Spirit of Advocacy

Advocacy is an ongoing journey, and Omar's journey is far from over. His indomitable spirit ensures that he will continue to fight for LGBTQ and Middle Eastern rights, even in the face of adversity. The challenges and triumphs he has experienced have only served to fuel his passion and commitment.

Omar's advocacy extends beyond his individual efforts. He recognizes the importance of collaboration and partnership in creating lasting change. By working with other activists, organizations, and governments, he seeks to amplify the impact of his work and build a united front in the fight for equality.

## Preserving History for the LGBTQ Community

As Omar Sharif Jr.'s activism continues to shape the world, preserving history becomes a crucial endeavor. The LGBTQ community has a rich and diverse past, filled with trailblazers and unsung heroes. Omar believes in the importance of documenting and sharing these stories, ensuring that future generations understand the struggles and triumphs of the movement.

By preserving LGBTQ history, Omar aims to foster a sense of pride and resilience within the community. He encourages LGBTQ individuals to embrace their heritage and find strength in the stories of those who came before them. Through this preservation, he hopes to inspire a deep appreciation for the progress made and a commitment to fighting for continued equality.

## Conclusion: A Hero for Our Times

In concluding our biography of Omar Sharif Jr., we celebrate his contributions as a hero for our times. His legacy lies not only in his achievements as an LGBTQ activist and advocate for Middle Eastern rights but also in his unwavering dedication to creating a more inclusive world.

Omar's journey has been marked by challenges, triumphs, and an unwavering commitment to social justice. Through his activism, he has shattered stereotypes, challenged cultural norms, and paved the way for change. His fearlessness, authenticity, and compassion have inspired individuals across the globe and ignited a movement that will continue to shape the future.

As we reflect on Omar Sharif Jr.'s remarkable journey, we are reminded of the power of one individual to make a difference. His legacy serves as a beacon of hope for a more inclusive world, where LGBTQ individuals in the Middle East and beyond can live authentically and without fear. Let us carry forward his vision, creating a brighter future for all.

# Leaving a Lasting Legacy

## The Impact of Omar Sharif Jr.'s Activism

Omar Sharif Jr.'s activism has had a profound impact on the LGBTQ community and Middle Eastern advocacy. Through his tireless efforts and unwavering dedication, he has helped pave the way for a more inclusive and accepting world. In this section, we will explore some of the key areas in which Omar's activism has made a significant difference.

### LGBTQ Visibility

One of the most significant contributions of Omar Sharif Jr.'s activism is his role in increasing LGBTQ visibility. By publicly coming out as gay, he has shattered stereotypes and challenged societal norms in the Middle Eastern region. His courage to live authentically and proudly has inspired countless individuals struggling with their own identities and has shown them that it is possible to be true to oneself, even in challenging environments.

Through interviews, media appearances, and social media engagement, Omar has used his platform to share his personal story, raise awareness, and advocate for LGBTQ rights. By putting a face and a voice to the LGBTQ community in the Middle East, he has humanized the experiences of those who have long been marginalized and ignored.

### Promoting Acceptance and Understanding

Omar Sharif Jr.'s activism has been instrumental in promoting acceptance and understanding of LGBTQ individuals in the Middle East. Through his advocacy, he has worked tirelessly to challenge deeply ingrained prejudices and misconceptions surrounding homosexuality and gender identity.

By engaging in dialogue with various religious and cultural leaders, Omar has sought to bridge the gap between LGBTQ rights and the values of Middle Eastern societies. His approach, grounded in empathy and respect, has enabled him to build bridges and foster greater understanding between LGBTQ individuals and their communities.

Furthermore, Omar has actively participated in public speaking engagements, workshops, and panel discussions on LGBTQ acceptance and inclusion. His ability to articulate the importance of equality and respect has resonated with both LGBTQ individuals and allies, furthering the cause of acceptance and understanding in the region.

## Legal and Policy Change

Omar Sharif Jr.'s advocacy has also been instrumental in driving legal and policy change for LGBTQ rights in the Middle East. By leveraging his influence, he has worked closely with governments, NGOs, and international organizations to push for policy reforms that protect the rights and well-being of LGBTQ individuals.

Through strategic partnerships and collaborations, Omar has played an active role in advocating for the decriminalization of homosexuality, the protection against discrimination, and the recognition of same-sex relationships. His efforts have been particularly impactful in countries where the LGBTQ community faces severe legal challenges and societal backlash.

Omar's relentless pursuit of legal and policy change signifies his commitment to securing equal rights for LGBTQ individuals in the Middle East. By challenging discriminatory laws and championing inclusive policies, he has paved the way for a more equitable society that embraces diversity and values human rights.

## Empowering LGBTQ Youth

Omar Sharif Jr.'s activism has had a profound impact on LGBTQ youth in the Middle East, providing them with hope, inspiration, and a sense of belonging. By openly sharing his own struggles and triumphs, he has become a role model for countless young individuals grappling with their sexual orientation or gender identity.

Through various initiatives, including mentorship programs and educational campaigns, Omar has actively worked towards empowering LGBTQ youth. By providing them with guidance, resources, and a safe space to explore their identities, he has helped foster a generation of resilient and confident LGBTQ advocates.

Furthermore, Omar's work with LGBTQ-inclusive education has had far-reaching effects on how LGBTQ issues are addressed in schools and educational institutions. By advocating for comprehensive sex education, inclusive curriculum, and training for educators, he has paved the way for a more inclusive and accepting learning environment that recognizes and affirms the rights and identities of all students.

## Conclusion

Omar Sharif Jr.'s activism has had a transformative effect on LGBTQ advocacy and Middle Eastern societies. Through his visibility, dialogues promoting acceptance, legal and policy change, and empowering LGBTQ youth, he has left an indelible mark on the world.

His courageous journey and unwavering commitment to equality and justice continue to inspire individuals globally. Omar Sharif Jr.'s impact extends far beyond his own personal achievements, as he has confidently and authentically painted a picture of hope and acceptance for future generations.

As we reflect on the impact of Omar's activism, we are reminded of the power of an individual's voice, determination, and unwavering belief in a more inclusive world. His ongoing legacy serves as a reminder that the fight for LGBTQ rights is far from over, and that each and every one of us can make a difference by championing equality and justice for all.

## Inspiring Future Generations of Activists

In this section, we explore how Omar Sharif Jr. has become a beacon of inspiration for future generations of activists. Through his tireless advocacy work and unwavering commitment to LGBTQ rights and Middle Eastern advocacy, he has laid a solid foundation for the next wave of changemakers. Let's delve deeper into the ways in which he continues to inspire and empower others.

### Leading by Example

One of the most powerful tools for inspiring others is leading by example. Omar Sharif Jr.'s personal journey of self-acceptance and coming out serves as a shining example of courage, resilience, and authenticity. By sharing his story openly and honestly, he has shown countless individuals that it is possible to overcome societal expectations and embrace one's true identity.

Through his willingness to navigate the complexities of his cultural background and LGBTQ identity, Omar Sharif Jr. has become a role model for individuals who may be struggling with similar circumstances. His ability to bridge the gap between LGBTQ and Middle Eastern advocacy has not only shattered stereotypes but also serves as a testament to the power of personal authenticity in creating social change.

## Educating and Empowering

Inspiring future activists also involves providing them with the knowledge and tools they need to create meaningful change. Omar Sharif Jr. understands the importance of education as a catalyst for social transformation. Through his advocacy work, he emphasizes the need for LGBTQ-inclusive education, both in the Middle East and globally.

By advocating for LGBTQ-inclusive curricula, he aims to foster greater understanding, acceptance, and empathy among students and educators. Omar Sharif Jr. utilizes his platform to raise awareness about the importance of LGBTQ history and visibility, ensuring that future generations are equipped with the necessary knowledge to challenge discrimination and advocate for equality.

Furthermore, he actively participates in educational initiatives and workshops, empowering young activists to find their voices and take action. He encourages them to utilize social media and technology to amplify their messages, connect with like-minded individuals, and create networks that foster collective action.

## Encouraging Intersectionality

True progress in the fight for equality can only be achieved by recognizing and addressing the intersectionality of various identities and social justice issues. Omar Sharif Jr. emphasizes the importance of intersectional activism in inspiring future generations of activists.

He champions the rights of LGBTQ individuals within the broader context of human rights, recognizing that multiple forms of discrimination and oppression intersect. By actively collaborating with organizations and advocates fighting for racial, gender, and economic justice, Omar Sharif Jr. encourages young activists to adopt an intersectional approach in their advocacy work.

Through his own collaborations and partnerships, he demonstrates the power of uniting diverse communities in the pursuit of justice and equality. By highlighting the interconnectedness of various struggles, he empowers future activists to challenge systemic oppression and work towards a more inclusive world.

### Nurturing Compassion and Empathy

Inspiring future generations of activists goes beyond providing them with knowledge and tools; it also involves nurturing compassion and empathy. Omar Sharif Jr. embodies these qualities in his advocacy work, serving as a living example of the transformative power of empathy.

By openly discussing his personal experiences and engaging in meaningful dialogue, he fosters understanding and empathy among individuals who may hold different beliefs or perspectives. By emphasizing the shared humanity of all individuals, regardless of sexual orientation, gender identity, or cultural background, he encourages future activists to approach advocacy with compassion and open-mindedness.

Through his speeches, interviews, and personal interactions, Omar Sharif Jr. leaves a lasting impact on those he encounters, cultivating a sense of empathy and understanding that is essential for inclusive activism.

### Conclusion: A Hero for Our Times

Omar Sharif Jr.'s unwavering commitment to LGBTQ rights and Middle Eastern advocacy has not only made him an iconic figure but also a hero for our times. Through his tireless efforts, he has not only created positive change but has also inspired future generations of activists to continue the fight for equality.

By leading by example, educating and empowering others, encouraging intersectionality, and nurturing compassion and empathy, Omar Sharif Jr. has left an indelible mark on the LGBTQ rights movement and Middle Eastern advocacy. His legacy will continue to inspire and shape the work of future activists, ensuring that the fight for equality transcends borders and leads to a more inclusive world for all.

### The Indomitable Spirit of Advocacy

The indomitable spirit of advocacy is a driving force that fuels change and propels movements forward. It is the unwavering determination to fight for what is right, regardless of the challenges and obstacles that may arise. In the context of LGBTQ and Middle Eastern advocacy, the indomitable spirit is the driving force behind Omar Sharif Jr.'s journey and the continued fight for equality and acceptance.

Advocacy is not simply about making noise or raising awareness; it is a lifelong commitment to creating meaningful and lasting change. The indomitable spirit of advocacy is a mindset that requires resilience, perseverance, and courage. It is the unwavering belief that every individual deserves to live authentically and freely, without fear of discrimination or persecution.

In his advocacy work, Omar Sharif Jr. has faced numerous challenges. He has endured personal and professional obstacles, threats, and attacks. However, it is his indomitable spirit that has allowed him to overcome these challenges and emerge stronger than ever.

The indomitable spirit of advocacy is rooted in a deep sense of purpose and the unwavering belief in the importance of the cause. It is the driving force that propels individuals to push beyond their comfort zones and challenge the status quo. It fuels the determination to make a difference, no matter how small or seemingly insignificant the actions may appear.

Omar Sharif Jr.'s indomitable spirit is evident in his tireless efforts to bridge the gap between LGBTQ and Middle Eastern advocacy. He recognizes the importance of intersectionality and understands that true progress cannot be achieved by focusing on just one aspect of identity. It is this holistic approach that sets him apart and makes his advocacy work so impactful.

The indomitable spirit of advocacy is not limited by geographical boundaries or cultural differences. It transcends borders, connecting like-minded individuals and communities around the world. Omar Sharif Jr. has leveraged his international platform to amplify the voices of queer activists worldwide, ensuring that their struggles and triumphs are heard and recognized.

While the path of advocacy may be challenging, the indomitable spirit is what keeps activists going. It fuels hope, resilience, and the unwavering belief in a better future. This spirit is contagious and spreads to those who witness the passion and dedication of advocates like Omar Sharif Jr.

To cultivate the indomitable spirit of advocacy, one must be willing to push beyond their comfort zone, challenge the status quo, and persist in the face of adversity. It requires a deep understanding that change takes time and requires collective action. Advocates must be willing to collaborate with others, share resources, and support each other along the way.

In the journey of advocacy, setbacks are inevitable. However, it is the indomitable spirit that enables activists to rise above them and continue their fight for justice and equality. It is this spirit that inspires future generations of activists and ensures that the struggle for LGBTQ and Middle Eastern rights will never be forgotten.

In conclusion, the indomitable spirit of advocacy is a powerful force that propels individuals like Omar Sharif Jr. forward in their quest for equality and acceptance. It is a mindset that embraces resilience, perseverance, and courage, and fuels the determination to make a lasting impact. By embodying this spirit, we can create a more inclusive and accepting world for all.

## Preserving History for the LGBTQ Community

Preserving the history of the LGBTQ community is crucial in order to ensure that the struggles, triumphs, and contributions of queer individuals are not forgotten. By documenting and sharing our history, we can inspire future generations, educate the public, and validate the lived experiences of LGBTQ people.

### The Importance of LGBTQ History

LGBTQ history is rich with stories of resilience, activism, and cultural significance. It serves as a reminder of the struggles that queer individuals have faced throughout history, the progress that has been made, and the work that still needs to be done. By understanding our collective history, we can gain a sense of identity, pride, and community.

Preserving LGBTQ history is especially crucial because queer narratives have often been erased or marginalized. Many historical figures who were part of or supported the LGBTQ community have been omitted from mainstream historical accounts. By bringing these stories to light, we can challenge heteronormative narratives and provide representation for marginalized communities.

### Methods of Preservation

Preserving LGBTQ history requires a multifaceted approach that combines archival work, oral history, digital platforms, and community engagement. Here are some methods and tactics that can be employed:

**Archives and Museums:** Establishing dedicated LGBTQ archives and museums is vital in preserving historical documents, artifacts, photographs, and personal testimonies. These institutions serve as repositories for LGBTQ history and provide a physical space for education and reflection. They also contribute to the process of reclaiming and asserting LGBTQ narratives.

**Oral Histories and Interviews:** Documenting the lived experiences of LGBTQ individuals through oral histories and interviews helps to capture personal stories that may not be found in traditional archives. This method allows for a diversity of voices and perspectives to be included in the historical record. These recordings can be transcribed, digitized, and made accessible online, ensuring that they are widely available for research and educational purposes.

**Digital Preservation:** In the digital age, it is essential to utilize online platforms to preserve and share LGBTQ history. Creating digital archives, websites, and databases allows for easy access to historical materials and facilitates community engagement. Interactive features, such as curated exhibitions and online exhibits, can enhance the learning experience and attract a wider audience.

**Community Involvement:** Engaging the LGBTQ community in the preservation of their own history is crucial. Encouraging individuals to donate their personal archives, photographs, and memorabilia ensures that valuable materials are not lost. Collaborating with LGBTQ organizations, community centers, and activists can also help to amplify and validate LGBTQ narratives.

## Challenges and Solutions

Preserving LGBTQ history comes with its own set of challenges. Many LGBTQ individuals faced discrimination and persecution, leading to the destruction of personal records, photographs, and other historical documentation. Additionally, the hidden nature of LGBTQ history often means that resources and information are scattered and difficult to locate.

To overcome these challenges, collaboration and resource-sharing among archival institutions and organizations are essential. By pooling resources and expertise, institutions can provide a more comprehensive view of LGBTQ history. Sharing digitized collections and creating inter-institutional partnerships can also increase accessibility for researchers, educators, and the general public.

## Unconventional Approach: LGBTQ Histories in Popular Culture

One unconventional approach to preserving LGBTQ history is integrating queer narratives into popular culture. Films, television shows, and literature that depict LGBTQ characters and stories play a vital role in raising awareness and fostering understanding. By highlighting historical events and figures in mainstream entertainment, we can reach a wider audience and ensure that LGBTQ history becomes an integral part of the collective memory.

For example, producing historically accurate films or documentaries about influential LGBTQ figures can educate and inspire viewers. Including LGBTQ history in school curricula and textbooks is another way to ensure that the knowledge is passed down to future generations.

## Conclusion

Preserving LGBTQ history is a crucial task that must be undertaken to validate the experiences of LGBTQ individuals, inspire future generations, and challenge social stigma. Through archival work, oral histories, digital preservation, and community involvement, we can ensure that LGBTQ narratives are included in the broader historical record. By embracing an unconventional approach and integrating queer stories into popular culture, we can reach a wider audience and create a more inclusive society. Let us remember and honor the rich history of the LGBTQ community and let it guide us towards a more equitable future.

# Expanding the Middle Eastern LGBTQ Movement

## Strengthening LGBTQ Organizations in the Middle East

The Middle East is a region that poses unique challenges for LGBTQ individuals. Deeply rooted cultural and religious beliefs often create an environment that is hostile towards the LGBTQ community, making it difficult for them to find acceptance and support. However, there is hope on the horizon, as there is a growing movement to strengthen LGBTQ organizations in the Middle East. These organizations play a crucial role in advocating for the rights and well-being of LGBTQ individuals, creating safe spaces, and fostering social change. In this section, we will explore the importance of strengthening LGBTQ organizations in the Middle East, the challenges they face, and strategies for their growth and success.

## Understanding the Challenges

Before delving into strategies to strengthen organizations, it is crucial to understand the unique challenges faced by LGBTQ individuals and organizations in the Middle East. The region's societal, cultural, and legal landscape often imposes significant barriers to LGBTQ rights and organizations.

One of the biggest challenges is the prevailing social stigma and discrimination against LGBTQ individuals. Many Middle Eastern societies view homosexuality as morally wrong, and LGBTQ individuals often face ostracization, harassment, and even violence. Consequently, LGBTQ organizations must navigate through these societal attitudes while trying to be catalysts for change.

Another challenge lies in the legal framework of many Middle Eastern countries. In several nations, laws criminalize consensual same-sex relationships, making it difficult for LGBTQ organizations to operate openly. Organizational leaders and members must navigate the legal landscape carefully to ensure their advocacy work does not put them at risk of legal repercussions.

Moreover, religious conservatism in the Middle East can further complicate the work of LGBTQ organizations. Islamic interpretations, which hold significant influence in the region, often condemn homosexual relationships. Balancing religious values and LGBTQ advocacy is a complex task that requires careful navigation and nuanced approaches.

## Promoting Visibility and Education

One of the key strategies to strengthen LGBTQ organizations in the Middle East is to promote visibility and education. Visibility plays a crucial role in challenging societal stigmas and promoting acceptance. By showcasing the diversity and humanity of LGBTQ individuals, organizations can chip away at deeply held prejudices.

LGBTQ organizations can engage in various visibility-building activities. These include hosting Pride events, organizing panel discussions, and participating in media interviews. By taking up space and making their presence known, organizations can create a platform for dialogue and understanding.

Education is also essential in creating lasting change. LGBTQ organizations can develop educational programs aimed at dispelling myths and misconceptions about LGBTQ individuals. These programs can be tailored for different audiences, including schools, religious institutions, and community centers. By providing accurate information and promoting empathy, organizations can contribute to a more informed and inclusive society.

## Building Strategic Partnerships

Building strategic partnerships with other human rights organizations, both within and outside the Middle East, is another crucial strategy for strengthening LGBTQ organizations. Solidarity and collaboration with organizations working on related issues, such as gender equality, women's rights, and freedom of expression, can amplify the impact of LGBTQ advocacy.

Collaboration can take various forms, such as joint campaigns, shared resources, and capacity-building initiatives. By partnering with established organizations, LGBTQ groups can leverage existing networks and expertise, expanding their reach and influence.

It is also important to foster partnerships with international organizations that prioritize LGBTQ rights. These partnerships can provide financial support, technical assistance, and access to global platforms for advocacy. Working together, LGBTQ organizations can create a strong, united front in the fight for equality.

## Supporting Organizational Development

To ensure the long-term sustainability and effectiveness of LGBTQ organizations in the Middle East, support for organizational development is crucial. This includes capacity building, mentorship programs, and resource mobilization.

Capacity building workshops can enhance the skills and knowledge of organizational leaders and members. Topics such as strategic planning, fundraising, networking, and advocacy techniques can empower LGBTQ organizations to operate more efficiently and effectively.

Mentorship programs that pair experienced activists with emerging LGBTQ leaders can provide invaluable guidance and support. Mentorship allows for the transfer of knowledge, skills, and connections, ensuring the continuation of the LGBTQ advocacy movement.

Resource mobilization is essential for organizational growth and impact. LGBTQ organizations can explore diverse fundraising strategies such as grant writing, crowdfunding, and corporate partnerships. By diversifying their funding sources, organizations can become more resilient and sustainable, allowing them to expand their programs and services.

## Promoting Legal Reforms

Legal reforms are critical for securing the rights and protections of LGBTQ individuals in the Middle East. LGBTQ organizations play a vital role in advocating for these reforms and challenging discriminatory laws and practices.

Working towards legal reforms requires a multi-pronged approach. LGBTQ organizations can engage in strategic litigation, filing lawsuits to challenge discriminatory laws and seek legal remedies for victims of human rights abuses. This can help pave the way for progressive legal interpretations and precedents.

Advocacy efforts targeting policymakers, lawmakers, and government officials can also contribute to legal change. Organizing workshops, awareness campaigns, and lobbying initiatives can help raise awareness about the importance of LGBTQ rights and build support for reforms.

Additionally, LGBTQ organizations can collaborate with international human rights organizations to exert pressure on governments and legal bodies to enact reforms. Advocacy at the international level can bring attention to human rights violations in the Middle East and mobilize global support for change.

## An Unconventional Tactic

In addition to conventional strategies, an unconventional yet effective tactic for strengthening LGBTQ organizations in the Middle East is the use of art and creative expression. Art has a unique power to transcend cultural barriers and challenge societal norms.

LGBTQ organizations can collaborate with local artists to create thought-provoking art installations, music, theater, and film. These creative expressions can serve as powerful tools for starting conversations, challenging stereotypes, and humanizing LGBTQ experiences.

Art can also act as an outlet for LGBTQ individuals to express themselves and find healing in the face of discrimination. By supporting artistic endeavors, LGBTQ organizations can foster a sense of community, resilience, and empowerment.

## Conclusion

Strengthening LGBTQ organizations in the Middle East is an ongoing and challenging task. By addressing the unique challenges and applying a strategic approach, these organizations can play a vital role in promoting LGBTQ rights and fostering social change.

Through promoting visibility and education, building partnerships, supporting organizational development, advocating for legal reforms, and embracing unconventional tactics, LGBTQ organizations can lay the groundwork for a more inclusive Middle East. It is through their unwavering commitment and resilience that lasting change can be achieved, creating a future where every individual can live authentically and without fear of discrimination.

## Developing Strategies for Sustainable Change

In the fight for LGBTQ rights, one of the key challenges is developing strategies for sustainable change. While progress has been made, there is still a long way to go in achieving full equality and acceptance for the LGBTQ community, particularly in the Middle East. In this section, we will explore some effective strategies that can help advance the cause of LGBTQ rights in a sustainable manner.

## Understanding the Local Context

To develop effective strategies, it is crucial to have a deep understanding of the local context, culture, and challenges. The Middle East is a diverse region with unique cultural, religious, and political dynamics. Each country within the region has its own specificities and nuances when it comes to LGBTQ issues. It is essential to engage with local LGBTQ organizations, activists, and communities to gain insights and perspectives on the ground realities.

## Building Alliances and Partnerships

Collaboration and coalition-building are critical in advocating for sustainable change. To strengthen the LGBTQ movement in the Middle East, it is essential to build alliances with various stakeholders, including human rights organizations, women's rights groups, religious leaders, and policymakers. By working together, it becomes possible to create a united front and amplify the voices of the LGBTQ community. These partnerships help in influencing public opinion, challenging discriminatory laws, and fostering societal acceptance.

## Empowering Local LGBTQ Organizations

Supporting and empowering local LGBTQ organizations is essential for sustainable change. These organizations play a crucial role in advocating for LGBTQ rights, providing support to community members, and raising awareness about the challenges faced by the LGBTQ community. By providing resources, funding, and capacity-building opportunities to these organizations, we ensure their sustainability and effectiveness in bringing about change at the grassroots level.

## Lobbying and Policy Advocacy

Engaging in lobbying and policy advocacy is vital for achieving sustainable change. By working with governments, lawmakers, and international bodies, it becomes possible to influence legislation and promote policies that protect the rights of LGBTQ individuals. This includes advocating for the repeal of discriminatory laws, the introduction of LGBTQ-inclusive policies, and the implementation of comprehensive anti-discrimination measures. Lobbying efforts should not only focus on national governments but also extend to regional and international platforms.

## Educating the Public and Promoting Awareness

Education and awareness are crucial components of sustainable change. It is essential to engage in public education campaigns to challenge stereotypes, misinformation, and prejudice against the LGBTQ community. This can be done through various channels, including public events, workshops, media campaigns, and digital platforms. By promoting inclusive and accurate narratives, we can generate empathy, understanding, and acceptance among the wider public.

## Supporting LGBTQ-Inclusive Education

Education plays a vital role in creating a more accepting and inclusive society. Supporting LGBTQ-inclusive education is crucial for long-term sustainable change. This includes advocating for LGBTQ-inclusive curriculum, providing training for educators, and promoting safe and inclusive school environments for LGBTQ students. By embedding LGBTQ issues within educational systems, we promote understanding, acceptance, and equality from an early age.

## Creating Safe Spaces and Support Networks

Creating safe spaces and support networks is essential for the well-being of the LGBTQ community. These spaces provide a sense of belonging, support, and empowerment, especially in societies where LGBTQ individuals face discrimination and marginalization. Efforts should be made to establish LGBTQ community centers, helplines, and online platforms that offer resources, services, and a supportive environment. These safe spaces help in building resilience, fostering community engagement, and providing a platform for collective action.

## Harnessing Technology for Advocacy

In the digital age, technology and social media have become powerful tools for advocacy. Harnessing the potential of technology can enable the LGBTQ community to reach a wider audience, organize campaigns, and share stories. It allows for the amplification of voices, facilitates global connections, and helps break barriers across borders. It is crucial to stay updated with the latest digital platforms and adapt communication strategies to effectively utilize technology for sustainable change.

## Promoting Economic Inclusion and Equality

Economic inclusion and equality are key aspects of sustainable change for the LGBTQ community. Discrimination and lack of opportunities in the workplace not only impact individuals' livelihoods but also hinder progress in achieving equality. Efforts should be made to promote inclusive employment policies, establish LGBTQ-friendly workplaces, and support entrepreneurship among LGBTQ individuals. Economic empowerment helps build resilience, enhances social acceptance, and contributes to the overall advancement of LGBTQ rights.

## Nurturing Future LGBTQ Leaders

Sustainable change requires nurturing future LGBTQ leaders. Investing in leadership development programs, mentorship initiatives, and capacity-building opportunities is crucial for the long-term success of the LGBTQ movement. By equipping young activists with the necessary skills, knowledge, and networks, we ensure the continuity of the struggle for LGBTQ rights. These leaders become agents of change, shaping the future of LGBTQ advocacy and driving sustainable progress.

In conclusion, developing strategies for sustainable change is essential in advancing LGBTQ rights in the Middle East. By understanding the local context, building alliances, empowering local organizations, advocating for policy change, promoting awareness, creating safe spaces, harnessing technology, promoting economic inclusion, and nurturing future leaders, we can lay the foundation for lasting progress. The journey towards full equality and acceptance may be challenging, but with strategic and sustainable approaches, we can bring about meaningful change for LGBTQ individuals in the Middle East and beyond.

## Nurturing Partnerships in the Region

Nurturing partnerships in the Middle East is crucial for advancing LGBTQ rights and creating a more inclusive society. By collaborating with organizations and individuals in the region, Omar Sharif Jr. has been able to make significant strides in advocating for change. This section explores the importance of these partnerships, the challenges involved, and the strategies employed to foster collaboration.

## Understanding the Importance of Partnerships

Partnerships play a vital role in amplifying the impact of LGBTQ advocacy efforts. By joining forces with like-minded organizations and individuals, Omar Sharif Jr. has been able to broaden his reach and create lasting change. These partnerships serve several crucial purposes:

- **Increased visibility**: Collaborating with local organizations helps bring LGBTQ rights to the forefront of public discourse in the Middle East. It allows for a more extensive reach and greater influence among key stakeholders.

- **Capacity building**: Partnerships enable the sharing of knowledge, skills, and resources. By working together, LGBTQ organizations can enhance their effectiveness and develop innovative strategies for advancing equality.

- **Establishing trust**: Building partnerships with local organizations and individuals helps establish trust within the community. It ensures that LGBTQ advocacy efforts are seen as authentic, culturally sensitive, and driven by the needs of the community itself.

- **Creating a united front**: Collaborative efforts foster a sense of solidarity among LGBTQ activists in the region. By working together, they can better address common challenges, share best practices, and coordinate efforts towards a common goal.

## Challenges in Nurturing Partnerships

While partnerships are essential for LGBTQ advocacy in the Middle East, they do come with their fair share of challenges. Some of the common obstacles faced in nurturing partnerships include:

- **Cultural barriers:** The Middle East is a diverse region with varying cultural norms and values. It can be challenging to navigate these cultural barriers while building partnerships. Respect for cultural sensitivities and the need for open dialogue are essential in overcoming these obstacles.

- **Legal constraints:** Many countries in the Middle East have laws that criminalize homosexuality, which can hinder partnership efforts. Negotiating these legal constraints requires careful consideration of the potential risks and working within the boundaries set by local laws.

- **Social stigma:** Homophobia and transphobia are prevalent in the Middle East, which can create resistance to partnerships and collaborations. Overcoming social stigma requires patience, education, and a commitment to fostering understanding and acceptance.

- **Lack of resources:** LGBTQ organizations in the region often face resource constraints, making it challenging to establish and maintain partnerships. Creative solutions, such as leveraging digital platforms and seeking international support, can help address this barrier.

## Strategies for Fostering Collaboration

Despite the challenges, Omar Sharif Jr. has employed various strategies to foster collaboration and nurture partnerships in the region. These strategies include:

- **Building bridges through dialogue:** Engaging in open and respectful dialogue with local organizations and individuals is essential for building trust and establishing partnerships. By actively listening to the concerns and perspectives of stakeholders, common ground can be identified and collaborations can be forged.

- **Providing support and resources:** Omar Sharif Jr. has extended support and resources to LGBTQ organizations in the Middle East, recognizing the importance of empowering local activists. This support can range from financial assistance to sharing expertise and providing capacity-building opportunities.

- **Cultivating cultural sensitivity:** Understanding cultural nuances is crucial when nurturing partnerships in the Middle East. Omar Sharif Jr. has emphasized the importance of cultural sensitivity, ensuring that advocacy efforts are respectful of local traditions and customs.

- **Leveraging international alliances:** Partnering with international LGBTQ organizations and allies can help bridge the gap between global and local advocacy efforts. Collaborating with organizations that have experience working in similar contexts can provide valuable insights and resources.

## An Unconventional Approach: Art as a Catalyst for Change

An unconventional yet powerful approach to nurturing partnerships in the region is through the use of art as a catalyst for change. Omar Sharif Jr. has recognized the transformative power of art and has actively supported initiatives that promote LGBTQ rights through artistic expression.

By collaborating with local artists, filmmakers, and performers, Omar Sharif Jr. has been able to create platforms for LGBTQ voices to be heard. Art can serve as a medium for raising awareness, challenging stereotypes, and pushing the boundaries of social norms. It can spark conversations, evoke emotions, and inspire people to question deeply ingrained prejudices.

Through art exhibitions, film festivals, theater productions, and music performances, partnerships are formed between LGBTQ activists, artists, and the broader community. These partnerships not only foster acceptance and understanding but also provide a space for dialogue and collaboration. They create opportunities for the LGBTQ community to share their experiences, express their narratives, and challenge societal perceptions of gender and sexuality.

## Conclusion

Nurturing partnerships in the Middle East is essential for advancing LGBTQ rights and creating a more inclusive society. Despite the challenges posed by cultural norms, legal constraints, and social stigma, collaborating with local organizations and individuals allows for increased visibility, capacity building, trust-building, and the creation of a united front.

Strategies employed by Omar Sharif Jr. to foster collaboration include dialogue, support and resources, cultural sensitivity, and leveraging international alliances. Additionally, an unconventional approach using art as a catalyst for change has proven to be effective in nurturing partnerships and amplifying LGBTQ voices in the region.

By continuously nurturing and strengthening partnerships, Omar Sharif Jr. and other LGBTQ activists in the Middle East are paving the way for sustainable change and a more inclusive future.

## Working Towards Full Equality in the Middle East

The journey towards achieving full equality for LGBTQ individuals in the Middle East is undoubtedly a challenging one. The region is known for its complex cultural, religious, and political landscape, which often presents hurdles for LGBTQ rights and acceptance. However, despite these obstacles, activists like Omar Sharif Jr. are paving the way for change and working tirelessly to create a more inclusive Middle East.

## Understanding the Challenges

To effectively work towards full equality in the Middle East, it is essential to comprehend the specific challenges that exist within the region. One of the most significant obstacles is the prevailing conservative attitudes towards LGBTQ individuals. Many Middle Eastern societies adhere to traditional gender roles and perceive homosexuality as morally wrong or against religious teachings.

Legal frameworks also pose a significant challenge. Several Middle Eastern countries have laws that criminalize same-sex activity, which not only perpetuates discrimination but also infringes upon the basic human rights of LGBTQ individuals. These laws often lead to harassment, arrest, and even violence against the LGBTQ community.

Furthermore, societal stigmatization and lack of education create environments wherein LGBTQ individuals face discrimination and marginalization. Access to comprehensive sexual education is limited in many Middle Eastern countries, leading to misinformation and perpetuating harmful stereotypes.

## Promoting Dialogue and Awareness

One crucial step towards achieving full equality in the Middle East is promoting open dialogue and raising awareness about LGBTQ rights and issues. Activists like Omar Sharif Jr. play a crucial role in initiating conversations and challenging societal norms. By using their platform and visibility, they can amplify the voices of the LGBTQ community and advocate for their rights.

Educational initiatives and awareness campaigns are also essential in breaking down stereotypes and dispelling misconceptions. These programs can be implemented in schools, religious institutions, and community centers to foster a greater understanding of LGBTQ issues and promote acceptance.

## Advocating for Legal Reform

To achieve full equality, it is imperative to advocate for legal reform in the Middle East. Activists can work with local and international organizations to push for the decriminalization of same-sex activity and the enactment of comprehensive anti-discrimination laws that protect LGBTQ individuals.

Lobbying efforts should target lawmakers, religious leaders, and civil society organizations, highlighting the importance of equal rights for all individuals, regardless of their sexual orientation or gender identity. Engaging in dialogue with policymakers and presenting evidence-based arguments can help challenge existing discriminatory laws and shape more LGBTQ-inclusive legislation.

## Supporting LGBTQ Organizations

Supporting and strengthening LGBTQ organizations in the Middle East is crucial for achieving full equality. These organizations provide essential resources, support networks, and safe spaces for LGBTQ individuals in a region where acceptance can be challenging to find.

By collaborating and partnering with local LGBTQ organizations, activists can help amplify their work and provide the necessary tools and resources to advance their goals. This support can range from financial assistance to capacity building and training programs, empowering these organizations to be effective advocates for change.

## Engaging with Religious Leaders

Religion plays a significant role in the lives of many people across the Middle East. To work towards full equality, it is essential to engage with religious leaders and promote a more inclusive interpretation of religious teachings.

By fostering dialogue and building bridges between LGBTQ activists and religious leaders, common ground can be found. This can contribute to the development of LGBTQ-inclusive religious teachings and challenge the negative stereotypes associated with homosexuality within religious contexts.

## Creating International Alliances

Achieving full equality in the Middle East requires collaborative efforts on an international scale. Activists and organizations can form alliances with global LGBTQ rights movements and engage in cross-cultural exchanges of knowledge and experiences.

These alliances can facilitate the sharing of best practices, strategies, and resources, helping activists in the Middle East to overcome challenges more effectively. By joining forces with international advocates, the LGBTQ movement in the Middle East gains visibility, support, and solidarity.

## Embracing Intersectionality

In the fight for full equality in the Middle East, it is essential to recognize and address the intersectionality of identities. LGBTQ individuals in the region often face multiple forms of discrimination and marginalization based on factors such as gender, religion, and socioeconomic status.

Activists must work towards a comprehensive and inclusive approach that takes into account the diverse experiences and challenges faced by LGBTQ individuals. Intersectional advocacy acknowledges the complexities of identity and ensures that the fight for equality does not leave anyone behind.

## Unconventional Solution: Art as a Catalyst for Change

Art and creative expression have the power to transcend cultural barriers and open conversations about LGBTQ issues. In the Middle East, artists and performers can use their craft to challenge societal norms and foster empathy and understanding.

By utilizing mediums such as film, music, theater, and visual arts, artists can humanize LGBTQ experiences and challenge preconceived notions. Artistic collaborations and exhibitions can create safe spaces for discussion, allowing individuals to engage with LGBTQ narratives and perspectives.

## Conclusion

Working towards full equality in the Middle East requires a multifaceted approach that addresses legal, societal, and cultural challenges. Through dialogue, education, advocacy, and international collaboration, activists like Omar Sharif Jr. are making significant strides in creating a more inclusive and accepting Middle East. By embracing intersectionality and unconventional solutions, we can build a future where LGBTQ individuals are valued and celebrated throughout the region.

# The Future of Activism

## The Global Fight for LGBTQ Rights

The global fight for LGBTQ rights is an ongoing battle that aims to promote equality and inclusivity for individuals of diverse sexual orientations and gender identities around the world. It is a cause that has gained significant traction in recent years, thanks to the tireless efforts of activists, organizations, and allies who are committed to creating a more accepting and tolerant society.

## The Importance of International Recognition

One of the key aspects of the global fight for LGBTQ rights is the push for international recognition and acknowledgment of the challenges faced by LGBTQ individuals. This recognition is vital because it helps bring attention to the struggles endured by LGBTQ communities in different parts of the world and fosters a sense of solidarity among activists.

The United Nations has played a crucial role in this fight by advocating for LGBTQ rights through various bodies, including the Human Rights Council and the General Assembly. Resolutions and reports addressing LGBTQ issues have been instrumental in raising awareness and building momentum for LGBTQ equality on a global scale.

## Legal Reforms and Decriminalization

A significant part of the global fight for LGBTQ rights involves advocating for legal reforms and decriminalization of same-sex relationships. In many countries, consensual same-sex activity is still considered a criminal offense, with severe penalties ranging from imprisonment to the death penalty.

Activists and human rights organizations work tirelessly to challenge and overturn these discriminatory laws. They engage in strategic litigation, lobby for policy reforms, and collaborate with local LGBTQ organizations to raise awareness and promote change. The ultimate goal is to achieve decriminalization of homosexuality worldwide and ensure that LGBTQ individuals can live their lives free from prosecution and discrimination.

## Fighting Discrimination and Violence

Discrimination and violence against LGBTQ individuals remain pervasive issues in many parts of the world. LGBTQ people often face social stigma, harassment, and even physical violence due to their sexual orientation or gender identity. The global fight for LGBTQ rights aims to address these injustices and create safe environments where LGBTQ individuals can fully express themselves without fear of reprisal.

Efforts to combat discrimination and violence include advocating for comprehensive anti-discrimination laws, promoting inclusive education and awareness programs, and supporting LGBTQ-friendly policies and practices in various institutions. By fostering understanding, acceptance, and respect, activists and organizations strive to build a world where LGBTQ individuals can thrive and be treated with dignity.

## International Collaboration and Solidarity

The global fight for LGBTQ rights thrives on international collaboration and solidarity. Activists, organizations, and movements from different parts of the world join forces to share knowledge, resources, and strategies, with the aim of creating a more inclusive and equitable future for all.

Global LGBTQ conferences, such as the International LGBTQ Leadership Summit, provide opportunities for activists to network, exchange ideas, and brainstorm innovative approaches to address challenges faced by LGBTQ communities worldwide. Collaborative initiatives enable activists to learn from each other's experiences, strengthen their advocacy efforts, and amplify their collective voices.

## Unconventional Solutions: Art and Culture

Art and culture have always been powerful tools for social change, and they play a significant role in the global fight for LGBTQ rights. Artists, writers, filmmakers, and performers use their creative works to challenge stereotypes, raise awareness, and foster empathy and understanding.

Artistic expressions can serve as a catalyst for social transformation by changing hearts and minds. Through films, documentaries, literature, visual arts, and performances, LGBTQ stories and experiences are highlighted, humanizing the struggles and triumphs of LGBTQ individuals and contributing to the growing acceptance and visibility of the community.

## Addressing Intersectionality

In the global fight for LGBTQ rights, it is essential to recognize and address intersectionality—the overlapping and interconnected nature of social identities and oppressions. LGBTQ individuals can face additional discrimination based on factors such as race, ethnicity, religion, disability, or socioeconomic status.

Activists working on LGBTQ rights understand the importance of intersectional approaches to advocacy. They strive to create inclusive spaces that recognize and value the experiences and contributions of individuals from diverse backgrounds. By acknowledging and addressing intersecting forms of discrimination, the fight for LGBTQ rights becomes more comprehensive and empowering.

## Continuing the Journey

While significant progress has been made in advancing LGBTQ rights globally, there is still much work to be done. The fight for equality and justice for all LGBTQ individuals continues to evolve, adapting to new challenges and emerging issues.

Moving forward, activists and allies must remain vigilant and committed to the cause. The fight for LGBTQ rights requires ongoing advocacy, education, and collaboration to ensure that every individual, regardless of their sexual orientation or gender identity, can enjoy the same rights and opportunities as their heterosexual and cisgender counterparts.

By working together, supporting local LGBTQ organizations, and challenging systemic and societal barriers, we can create a world where LGBTQ individuals are celebrated, respected, and embraced for who they are. The global fight for LGBTQ rights is a journey that carries tremendous significance, and it is one that we must all continue to support.

## The Role of Intersectionality in Activism

Intersectionality plays a crucial role in activism, especially in the fight for LGBTQ rights. It recognizes that individuals are not defined by a single identity, but instead, our lived experiences and oppressions are shaped by the intersection of multiple identities, such as race, gender, sexual orientation, and socioeconomic status. In this section, we will explore how intersectionality influences and strengthens the LGBTQ activist movement.

### Understanding Intersectionality

Intersectionality was coined by legal scholar Kimberlé Crenshaw in 1989 and has since become a powerful framework for understanding social justice issues. It recognizes that systems of oppression are interconnected, and the discrimination faced by individuals cannot be fully understood or addressed by considering only one aspect of their identity. For example, a white gay man may experience privilege due to his race while facing discrimination based on his sexual orientation. Conversely, a transgender woman of color may experience compounding forms of discrimination due to her gender identity, race, and socioeconomic status.

### Recognizing the Complexity of Identities

Intersectionality prompts us to recognize the complexity of people's identities and the unique challenges they face. LGBTQ activism that solely focuses on sexual orientation undermines the experiences of LGBTQ individuals who also contend with racial, gender, or other forms of oppression. By incorporating an intersectional lens, we come to understand that liberation cannot be achieved without addressing these interconnected systems of oppression.

## Advocating for Inclusive Policies

Intersectionality guides activists to advocate for policies that address the needs of all LGBTQ individuals, regardless of their intersecting identities. For example, an inclusive non-discrimination policy should consider the specific challenges faced by LGBTQ individuals of color, people with disabilities, or those from low-income backgrounds. By recognizing and addressing the unique oppressions faced by different groups within the LGBTQ community, activism becomes more holistic and effective.

## Challenging Privilege and Power Dynamics

Intersectionality challenges us to confront our privilege and power dynamics within the LGBTQ community and society as a whole. It encourages us to examine how some individuals may benefit from systems of oppression while others are marginalized. For activists, this means actively listening to and amplifying the voices of those from marginalized communities within the LGBTQ movement, and working to create spaces that are inclusive and equitable for all.

## Building Coalitions and Alliances

Intersectional activism emphasizes the importance of building coalitions and alliances with other social justice movements. By recognizing the intersecting forms of oppression faced by marginalized communities, activists can collaborate and work together towards common goals. For example, LGBTQ activists can join forces with feminist movements, racial justice organizations, or disability rights advocates to address shared issues and strengthen their collective impact.

## Addressing Systemic Issues

Intersectional activism challenges us to go beyond individual-level changes and address systemic issues that perpetuate discrimination and inequality. This requires understanding how intersecting identities intersect with larger power structures and institutions. Activists must advocate for systemic changes, such as comprehensive anti-discrimination laws, inclusive education curricula, and healthcare policies that address the unique needs of LGBTQ individuals from diverse backgrounds.

**Navigating Challenges**

Navigating intersectionality in activism is not without its challenges. A key challenge is ensuring that diverse voices are truly represented and leading the movement, rather than tokenizing or relegating them to the sidelines. It is also important to recognize and address tensions that may arise between different groups within the LGBTQ community, such as racial or gender-based divisions. By actively engaging in dialogue, actively listening, and centering the voices of marginalized individuals, activists can strive for a more inclusive and united movement.

In conclusion, intersectionality is a powerful framework that recognizes the complex and interconnected forms of oppression faced by individuals. In LGBTQ activism, intersectionality helps us understand and address the unique challenges experienced by LGBTQ individuals at the intersection of multiple identities. By recognizing the diversity within the LGBTQ community and building coalitions with other social justice movements, activists can create a more inclusive movement that addresses systemic issues and paves the way for a future of equality and justice for all.

## Embracing New Technologies for Advocacy

In today's digitally connected world, the power of technology is undeniable. As Omar Sharif Jr. continues his journey as an LGBTQ activist, he recognizes the immense potential of embracing new technologies for advocacy. By harnessing the capabilities of social media platforms, online resources, and innovative tools, Omar aims to amplify his voice, reach a wider audience, and inspire change on a global scale.

**The Digital Landscape of Activism**

The emergence of social media has revolutionized the way we communicate and share information. Platforms like Twitter, Facebook, and Instagram provide a space for individuals and organizations to connect, engage, and raise awareness about important causes. In the context of LGBTQ advocacy, these platforms serve as powerful tools for spreading inclusive messages, highlighting ongoing struggles, and mobilizing support.

In addition to social media, other digital technologies such as virtual reality (VR) and augmented reality (AR) have the potential to reshape the advocacy landscape. VR experiences can offer immersive, empathetic journeys that help people understand the challenges faced by LGBTQ individuals. AR, on the other hand, can bring visibility to the community by overlaying information, statistics, and personal stories in real-world environments.

## Harnessing Social Media for LGBTQ Activism

Social media platforms have become indispensable for modern activists, including Omar Sharif Jr. By utilizing these platforms strategically, he can maximize his impact and engage with a global audience. Here are some ways in which Omar embraces new technologies for advocacy through social media:

**Building an online presence:** Omar recognizes the importance of maintaining an active online presence to amplify his message. He regularly updates his social media profiles with informative content, personal stories, and calls to action. This not only keeps his followers engaged but also helps in fostering a sense of community among LGBTQ individuals.

**Engaging with followers:** Social media allows Omar to directly engage with his followers, creating meaningful connections and inspiring dialogue. By responding to comments, messages, and mentions, he fosters a sense of inclusivity and encourages others to share their own stories and experiences.

**Promoting LGBTQ events and initiatives:** Omar leverages his online platforms to raise awareness about LGBTQ events, conferences, and initiatives. By creating event pages, sharing information, and encouraging participation, he helps mobilize support for important causes.

**Connecting with other activists:** Social media networks provide a unique opportunity for activists to connect with like-minded individuals and organizations. Omar uses these platforms to collaborate with other activists, share resources, and amplify each other's messages, creating a united front in the fight for LGBTQ rights.

## Utilizing Online Resources

The internet serves as a valuable repository of knowledge and resources. Advocates like Omar Sharif Jr. recognize the importance of utilizing online platforms and tools to educate and empower individuals, regardless of their geographical location. Here are some ways in which Omar embraces new technologies for advocacy through online resources:

**Creating educational content:** Omar actively creates and shares educational content to raise awareness about LGBTQ issues. Through blog posts, articles, and videos, he tackles topics such as gender identity, discrimination, and mental health, providing a valuable resource for LGBTQ individuals, their allies, and the general public.

**Providing support networks:** Online support networks play a crucial role in empowering LGBTQ individuals and helping them navigate their journey. Omar collaborates with existing platforms and organizations to create safe spaces where individuals can come together, share experiences, seek advice, and find support.

**Offering digital tools:** Technology enables the development of various digital tools that can assist LGBTQ individuals in different ways. Omar promotes the use of LGBTQ-inclusive dating apps, mental health support apps, and online resources for legal rights and protections. The accessibility of these tools helps individuals overcome geographical constraints and find the support they need.

**Hosting webinars and online workshops:** Omar organizes webinars and online workshops to share knowledge, provide guidance, and answer questions from the LGBTQ community. These virtual events attract a diverse audience and allow for meaningful interactions and learning opportunities.

## Challenges and Considerations

While embracing new technologies for advocacy offers countless possibilities, there are also challenges and considerations to navigate. Omar Sharif Jr. understands the need to address these issues to ensure the responsible and effective use of technology in his activism. Here are a few challenges and considerations:

**Digital divide:** Not everyone has equal access to the internet and technology due to factors such as socioeconomic status or geographical location. Omar aims to bridge this digital divide by collaborating with organizations that provide resources and access to marginalized communities.

**Cybersecurity and privacy:** As an outspoken LGBTQ activist, Omar is aware of the potential risks associated with online platforms, such as cyberbullying, online harassment, and privacy concerns. He takes necessary measures to protect his own digital presence and advocates for better online safety measures for all users.

**Authenticity in the digital space:** In a world where social media can often perpetuate a curated version of reality, Omar emphasizes the importance of maintaining authenticity and transparency. He shares both the triumphs and challenges of LGBTQ activism, providing a realistic portrayal of the journey.

**Navigating algorithmic biases:** Online platforms operate using complex algorithms that can inadvertently perpetuate biases. Omar educates himself on these biases and actively works against them to ensure that his content reaches diverse audiences and does not reinforce stereotypes or discrimination.

## One Step Closer to a More Inclusive Future

As Omar Sharif Jr. embraces new technologies for advocacy, he recognizes their potential to create a more inclusive and accepting world. By harnessing the power of social media, online resources, and innovative tools, he amplifies his voice and reaches individuals who may otherwise be marginalized or isolated. Through responsible and strategic use of technology, Omar strives to break down barriers, challenge societal norms, and inspire change on a global scale.

In the next chapter, we will dive into the legacy Omar Sharif Jr. is building, the impact of his activism, and his vision for the future of LGBTQ and Middle Eastern advocacy.

## The Ongoing Journey of Omar Sharif Jr.

The journey of Omar Sharif Jr. as an LGBTQ activist and advocate is far from over. As he continues to make strides in promoting equality and acceptance, his ongoing journey is marked by a relentless dedication to effecting change for the better. In this section, we explore the challenges he faces, the progress he has made, and the future endeavors that lie ahead.

## Overcoming Challenges

Throughout his activism, Omar has faced numerous challenges that have tested his resolve and determination. As an openly gay advocate in the Middle East, he has often encountered social and cultural obstacles that inhibit progress. Despite these challenges, Omar remains steadfast in his commitment to fighting for the rights of the LGBTQ community.

One of the major ongoing challenges is combating prejudice and discrimination entrenched in society. Although progress has been made, widespread homophobia and transphobia persist in many parts of the world. Omar continues to work tirelessly to dismantle these barriers and foster a more inclusive society.

## Envisioning a More Inclusive Future

Looking ahead, Omar Sharif Jr. envisions a future where LGBTQ individuals are fully embraced and valued in all aspects of life. He believes that education and awareness are key drivers of change and continues to emphasize their importance in his activism.

Omar is actively involved in advocating for LGBTQ-inclusive education both locally and globally. He recognizes the power of knowledge in challenging stereotypes and prejudice. Through his initiatives, he strives to create safe spaces that foster understanding and acceptance for all.

## Emerging Issues and New Challenges

As society evolves, so do the challenges faced by the LGBTQ community. Omar Sharif Jr. recognizes the need to stay vigilant and adapt to emerging issues that affect the rights and well-being of LGBTQ individuals.

One area that demands attention is the intersectionality of oppressions. Omar acknowledges that individuals can face discrimination based on multiple identities, such as race, gender, and sexual orientation. He emphasizes the importance of addressing these intersecting forms of discrimination to build an inclusive movement that leaves no one behind.

Additionally, with the rapid advancement of technology, new challenges arise in the digital space. Cyberbullying, online harassment, and the spread of hate speech can have devastating effects on LGBTQ individuals. Omar advocates for responsible digital citizenship and works to create online spaces that are safe and supportive for the LGBTQ community.

## Collaborating for Change

Omar Sharif Jr. understands the power of collaboration and the collective impact it can have on advocacy efforts. He actively seeks partnerships with organizations, governments, and individuals who share his passion for equality and justice.

By joining forces with like-minded activists, Omar envisions creating a global network that amplifies the voices of LGBTQ individuals and promotes positive change. These collaborations span across borders and cultures, with the aim of fostering understanding and empathy worldwide.

### Empowering the Next Generation

Central to Omar Sharif Jr.'s ongoing journey is the empowerment of the next generation of LGBTQ activists. He recognizes the importance of passing the torch and inspiring future leaders to continue the fight for equality.

Through mentorship programs and educational initiatives, Omar strives to empower LGBTQ youth and equip them with the necessary tools to effect change. He believes that nurturing a new wave of activists is instrumental in shaping a future that is more inclusive and accepting.

### Conclusion

As Omar Sharif Jr. continues his ongoing journey as an LGBTQ activist, he remains a passionate advocate for equality, justice, and acceptance. Through collaborative efforts, education, and empowering the next generation of activists, Omar is committed to effecting change on a global scale.

His tireless dedication to challenging societal norms, promoting inclusivity, and envisioning a future free from discrimination ensures that his impact will not only be felt in the present but will create a lasting legacy for generations to come.

## Conclusion: A Hero for Our Times

### Celebrating Omar Sharif Jr.'s Contributions

In this final section, we celebrate the incredible contributions that Omar Sharif Jr. has made to the LGBTQ and Middle Eastern advocacy movements. His journey has been one of courage, resilience, and commitment to creating a more inclusive world. Let's delve into the impact he has had and why he is truly a hero for our times.

### A Trailblazer for LGBTQ Rights

Omar Sharif Jr. has been at the forefront of LGBTQ activism, boldly challenging societal norms and fighting for equal rights for all. His decision to publicly come out as gay was a watershed moment, inspiring countless individuals to embrace their own identities and live authentically. By sharing his story, he has shattered stereotypes and empowered LGBTQ communities around the world.

Sharif Jr.'s visibility as a gay man in the Middle East has been particularly groundbreaking. In a region where homosexuality is often stigmatized and even criminalized, his advocacy has shown that there is strength in embracing one's true self. By breaking cultural norms and speaking out against discrimination, he has paved the way for a more accepting and tolerant society.

## Using Media as a Platform for Change

Omar Sharif Jr. has harnessed the power of media and entertainment to advance the cause of LGBTQ rights. Through public speaking engagements, interviews, and social media presence, he has raised awareness about the challenges faced by LGBTQ individuals in the Middle East and beyond. His message of love, acceptance, and inclusivity has reached millions, fostering conversations and encouraging dialogue on a global scale.

Sharif Jr.'s involvement in the media and entertainment industry has also been instrumental in challenging stereotypes and misconceptions about LGBTQ individuals. By appearing in TV shows, films, and documentaries that depict LGBTQ characters and storylines, he has helped to normalize LGBTQ identities and experiences. Through his work, he has shown that diversity and representation matter, and that everyone deserves to have their stories told.

## Building Bridges between LGBTQ and Middle Eastern Advocacy

One of Omar Sharif Jr.'s most significant contributions has been his efforts to bridge the gap between LGBTQ and Middle Eastern advocacy. By focusing on the intersectionality of identities and issues, he has fostered understanding and collaboration between these two communities.

Through partnerships and collaborations with LGBTQ organizations in the Middle East, he has worked to create safe spaces and support networks for individuals who face discrimination and persecution. His advocacy has been instrumental in challenging oppressive laws and policies, and advocating for LGBTQ-inclusive education and healthcare.

Sharif Jr.'s work has also emphasized the importance of cultural sensitivity and respect. He has engaged with religious and community leaders, promoting dialogue and understanding between LGBTQ individuals and their families. Through his efforts, he has helped to break down barriers and foster a more accepting and compassionate society.

## Inspiring Future Generations of Activists

Omar Sharif Jr.'s contributions to LGBTQ and Middle Eastern advocacy will leave a lasting legacy for generations to come. His fearlessness, resilience, and

CONCLUSION: A HERO FOR OUR TIMES

unwavering dedication to creating a more inclusive world serve as an inspiration to future activists.

As a role model, Sharif Jr. has demonstrated the power of authenticity and living one's truth. He has shown that personal struggles can be transformed into sources of strength and resilience, fueling activism and creating meaningful change. His journey serves as a reminder that even in the face of adversity, one person can make an immeasurable impact.

## Preserving History for the LGBTQ Community

In addition to his advocacy work, Omar Sharif Jr. has worked tirelessly to preserve the history and stories of the LGBTQ community. Through his support of LGBTQ archives and museums, he ensures that the struggles, triumphs, and contributions of LGBTQ individuals are not forgotten.

By preserving this history, Sharif Jr. ensures that future generations have access to the stories of those who have fought for LGBTQ rights. He recognizes the importance of celebrating the achievements of activists who came before and acknowledging the ongoing work that is still needed.

## A Hero for Our Times

In conclusion, Omar Sharif Jr.'s contributions to LGBTQ and Middle Eastern advocacy have been nothing short of remarkable. Through his courage, visibility, and unwavering commitment, he has transformed lives, challenged societal norms, and paved the way for a more inclusive world.

His work serves as a testament to the power of authenticity, dialogue, and collective action. By bridging LGBTQ and Middle Eastern advocacy, he has brought communities together, fostering understanding and compassion.

Omar Sharif Jr.'s impact will continue to be felt for years to come. As we celebrate his remarkable journey, let us be inspired by his example and continue the fight for equality and acceptance for all.

## Reflecting on a Remarkable Journey

As we reach the end of Omar Sharif Jr.'s incredible journey, it is time to reflect on the remarkable impact he has had on LGBTQ and Middle Eastern advocacy. Throughout his life, Omar has faced numerous challenges and triumphs, leaving an indelible mark on the world. His journey serves as a testament to the power of authenticity, resilience, and unwavering dedication to advocating for equality and acceptance.

Omar's activism began with his decision to live authentically and embrace his LGBTQ identity. Coming to terms with his sexuality was not an easy process, as he grappled with the fear of rejection and the societal pressures ingrained within his cultural background. However, through the unwavering support of his close network of friends and family, Omar found the courage to break free from the confines of societal expectations and live his truth.

One of the most significant challenges Omar encountered was navigating the intersectionality of his LGBTQ identity and Middle Eastern cultural norms. The Middle East has a complex relationship with LGBTQ rights, often resulting in discrimination and persecution. However, through his advocacy work, Omar has been able to challenge cultural norms, break down barriers, and pave the way for a more inclusive society.

Omar's journey has been marked by impactful influences from trailblazers and historical figures within the LGBTQ community. He draws inspiration from those who have fought tirelessly for LGBTQ rights, not only in the Middle East but also globally. Omar recognizes the crucial role of his family in supporting his activism and acknowledges the power of collaboration with other advocates. By working together, Omar and his allies have amplified their voices and sparked meaningful change.

The rise of Omar Sharif Jr. as an LGBTQ icon has been a groundbreaking moment in the fight for equality. His decision to publicly come out has inspired countless others to embrace their identities without fear or shame. Omar's authenticity has become a driving force in his activism, showing others that it is possible to be true to oneself and effect change in society.

As an influential voice in the media and entertainment industry, Omar has used his platform to challenge stereotypes and misconceptions about the LGBTQ community. Through his work, he has shattered the notion that being LGBTQ is incompatible with Middle Eastern culture, promoting understanding and acceptance both locally and globally.

Education has been one of the cornerstones of Omar's activism. He recognizes the power of knowledge in breaking down barriers and promoting empathy. Omar has tirelessly advocated for LGBTQ-inclusive education, working to ensure that future generations have access to resources that foster acceptance and understanding.

Omar's legacy extends beyond his individual achievements. He has focused on building a sustainable movement that will continue to advocate for LGBTQ rights long after he has passed the torch to the next generation. By nurturing partnerships and collaborations, Omar has laid the foundation for ongoing progress and has left a lasting impact on LGBTQ activism worldwide.

Throughout his journey, Omar has faced personal and professional challenges, including threats and attacks from those who oppose his advocacy. However, he has found inner strength and resilience, overcoming these obstacles with determination and grace. Omar's ability to celebrate victories, both big and small, has fueled his unwavering commitment to his cause.

Recognizing the impact of policy and legislation on LGBTQ rights, Omar has engaged in lobbying efforts, collaborating with governments and NGOs to effect change at the institutional level. By leveraging his influence, he has made significant strides towards achieving full equality for the LGBTQ community.

Omar's contributions have been recognized and honored with various awards for LGBTQ activism. These accolades have served as a platform for spreading awareness and amplifying his message. He understands the importance of using recognition to further the cause, ensuring that the issues faced by the LGBTQ community remain at the forefront of conversations.

Reflecting on a lifetime of activism, Omar has experienced personal growth and learned valuable lessons along the way. He emphasizes the need for future activists to embrace empathy, perseverance, and the power of storytelling. Through his own journey, Omar has shown that activism is not limited to a single identity or cause but is interconnected and ever-evolving.

As Omar Sharif Jr.'s journey continues, his impact on the world of LGBTQ and Middle Eastern advocacy remains immeasurable. His commitment, passion, and ability to bridge cultures have been instrumental in fostering a more inclusive society. By inspiring future generations, expanding the Middle Eastern LGBTQ movement, and embracing new technologies for advocacy, Omar paves the way for a future where true equality is a reality.

In conclusion, Omar Sharif Jr.'s remarkable journey has served as a beacon of light in the fight for LGBTQ and Middle Eastern rights. His story reminds us of the power of authenticity, the strength of collective action, and the importance of fostering understanding and empathy. As we celebrate his contributions, we also celebrate the incredible potential for change that lies within each of us. Omar has left an indelible mark on the world, and his legacy will continue to inspire future generations to challenge the status quo and create a more inclusive and accepting world for all.

## The Legacy of LGBTQ and Middle Eastern Advocacy

Omar Sharif Jr.'s journey as an LGBTQ activist and advocate for Middle Eastern communities has left an indelible mark on both movements. Through his unwavering commitment and tireless efforts, he has contributed to the advancement of LGBTQ rights and the promotion of inclusivity in the Middle

East. This legacy serves as a beacon of hope and inspiration for future generations of activists.

One of the key aspects of Omar Sharif Jr.'s legacy is his ability to bridge LGBTQ and Middle Eastern advocacy. He understood the importance of acknowledging and addressing the unique challenges faced by individuals from both communities. By finding common ground and fostering dialogue, he brought together people from different cultures, backgrounds, and identities, working towards a shared goal of equality and acceptance.

In the Middle East, where LGBTQ rights have often been disregarded or even criminalized, Omar Sharif Jr. has advocated for change. He challenged cultural norms and social stigmas by openly embracing his LGBTQ identity. His courage empowered countless others to do the same, sparking a ripple effect that continues to create positive change in the region.

Omar Sharif Jr.'s advocacy work has also extended to creating LGBTQ-inclusive spaces and support networks in the Middle East. He recognized the importance of providing resources, education, and safe spaces for LGBTQ individuals to thrive and be themselves. By establishing LGBTQ centers and collaborating with local organizations, he laid the foundation for sustainable change and empowered the Middle Eastern LGBTQ community.

Part of Omar Sharif Jr.'s enduring legacy lies in his global impact. Through speaking engagements and participation in global LGBTQ conferences, he elevated the voices of queer activists from around the world. By amplifying their stories and experiences, he shed light on the similarities and shared struggles faced by LGBTQ individuals across borders.

Media has been a powerful tool in Omar Sharif Jr.'s advocacy efforts. He utilized social media platforms to reach a broader audience, challenging prejudices and misconceptions about LGBTQ individuals. By creating LGBTQ-inclusive content, he encouraged diverse representation and fostered understanding.

Education has been another critical component of Omar Sharif Jr.'s legacy. He recognized the power of knowledge in breaking down barriers and promoting acceptance. He advocated for LGBTQ-inclusive education, encouraging schools and institutions to embrace diversity and teach inclusivity. Through education initiatives, he empowered LGBTQ youth, equipping them with the tools to navigate a world that has not always been accepting.

The impact of Omar Sharif Jr.'s advocacy work is further reflected in the policy and legislation changes he helped initiate. He lobbied for LGBTQ equality, collaborating with governments and non-governmental organizations to push for legal protections and recognition of LGBTQ rights. His work paved the way for progressive reforms and brought attention to the systemic issues that needed to be addressed.

Omar Sharif Jr.'s achievements as an LGBTQ advocate have not gone unnoticed. He has been honored for his activism, receiving awards and recognition for his contributions to the LGBTQ community. These accolades serve as a platform to spread awareness about LGBTQ rights and advocate for change on a broader scale.

As Omar Sharif Jr. reflects on a lifetime of activism, he imparts valuable lessons to future generations of activists. His journey teaches us the power of authenticity, visibility, and collective action. He reminds us that change is possible, even in the face of adversity and cultural barriers. His legacy inspires us to continue the fight for LGBTQ rights and to work towards a more inclusive world.

In conclusion, Omar Sharif Jr.'s tireless advocacy work has left an indelible legacy in the realms of LGBTQ and Middle Eastern advocacy. By bridging communities, challenging norms, and amplifying voices, he has created a lasting impact. His work serves as a reminder of the power of individual bravery and collective action in driving change. As we look to the future, Omar Sharif Jr.'s legacy will guide us in the ongoing struggle for LGBTQ rights and inclusivity worldwide.

## Hope for a More Inclusive World

In this final section, we explore the hope that Omar Sharif Jr.'s activism brings for a more inclusive world. As the LGBTQ rights movement continues to gain momentum globally, it is essential to acknowledge the challenges ahead and the potential impact that can be made by individuals like Omar Sharif Jr.

## Continuing the Fight

Despite significant progress made in LGBTQ rights, we cannot overlook the fact that discrimination, prejudice, and human rights violations persist in many parts of the world. The fight for equality is far from over, and it requires dedicated individuals like Omar Sharif Jr. to continue pushing for change.

Omar's ability to bridge LGBTQ and Middle Eastern advocacy plays a crucial role in fostering understanding and acceptance across cultures. By highlighting the importance of cultural sensitivity and challenging misconceptions, he has paved the way for meaningful dialogues that can lead to positive change.

### Amplifying LGBTQ Voices

One of the key contributions Omar Sharif Jr. has made to the LGBTQ movement is using his platform to amplify the voices of marginalized communities. Through his public speaking engagements and collaborations, he has brought attention to the struggles and triumphs of LGBTQ individuals who face discrimination and persecution.

By sharing their stories, Omar has helped to humanize the LGBTQ experience and dispel stereotypes and misconceptions. This not only creates empathy and understanding but also empowers LGBTQ individuals to embrace their identities openly and without fear.

### Empowering the Next Generation

As an advocate for LGBTQ rights, Omar recognizes the importance of empowering the next generation of activists. Through his work in supporting LGBTQ-inclusive education and establishing safe spaces, he ensures that young LGBTQ individuals have the resources and support they need to thrive.

Moreover, he encourages LGBTQ youth to embrace their identities and push for change in their communities. By fostering an environment of acceptance and understanding, he inspires young activists to become champions for equality.

### The Role of Intersectionality

Omar Sharif Jr. recognizes that the fight for LGBTQ rights must go hand in hand with other social justice movements. Intersectionality, the understanding that different forms of oppression intersect and interact, is a guiding principle of his advocacy.

By acknowledging the interconnection of identities and forms of discrimination, Omar works towards creating a more inclusive and accepting world for everyone. He understands that achieving true equality requires addressing systemic inequalities and uplifting marginalized communities.

### Embracing New Technologies for Advocacy

In this digital age, technology has become a powerful tool for advocacy and activism. Omar Sharif Jr. harnesses the potential of social media and online platforms to reach a global audience, share resources, and mobilize support.

Through engaging content, Omar challenges prejudice and discrimination, educates the masses, and inspires others to take action. He leads by example, demonstrating how technology can be used to create real change in the quest for a more inclusive world.

## The Ongoing Journey

Omar Sharif Jr.'s journey as an LGBTQ activist is far from over. As he continues to navigate the challenges and triumphs of advocacy, his impact will continue to shape the future of LGBTQ rights.

With his commitment to building bridges between LGBTQ and Middle Eastern advocacy, amplifying marginalized voices, and empowering the next generation, Omar serves as an inspiration to activists around the world. His legacy will leave an indelible mark on the ongoing fight for a more inclusive world.

## Conclusion: A Hero for Our Times

In conclusion, Omar Sharif Jr. is more than just a LGBTQ icon or Middle Eastern advocate. He is a hero for our times, who embodies resilience, courage, and hope.

Through his determination to live authentically, he has transformed himself into a force for change. His ability to bridge LGBTQ and Middle Eastern advocacy offers a unique perspective that brings people together and challenges societal norms.

As we celebrate Omar's contributions, it is crucial to acknowledge that his work represents just a fraction of the progress needed to achieve true equality. However, his journey serves as a reminder that every individual has the power to make a difference.

Omar Sharif Jr.'s legacy will undoubtedly inspire future generations of activists to continue the fight for LGBTQ rights and a more inclusive world. With hope in our hearts and dedication to the cause, we can build upon his achievements and create a brighter future for all.

# Index

-doubt, 17
-up, 60

a Trevor Hero, 135
ability, 2, 4, 6, 10, 11, 14, 42, 50, 51, 54, 65–67, 78, 103, 105, 116, 118, 136, 140–142, 146, 166, 173, 175–177, 188, 190, 194, 205, 210, 212, 214, 245–247, 249
ableism, 65, 95, 148
absence, 21, 89
absurdity, 169
acceptance, 3, 5, 9, 11–13, 15–20, 22, 24–26, 28, 29, 31–35, 37, 40–44, 46, 48, 50–58, 61–65, 67, 69–73, 75–77, 79–81, 83, 85, 86, 100, 103–105, 109, 113, 115–117, 119, 120, 125, 126, 128, 131–134, 136, 140–142, 145, 148, 150, 151, 154–157, 160, 163, 164, 167, 169, 170, 172–188, 190, 192, 195, 196, 200, 201, 205, 206, 209–216, 219, 220, 222–225, 228–230, 232, 233, 239–244, 246–248
access, 21, 23, 31, 32, 52, 90, 96, 116, 126, 134, 151, 155, 160, 174, 176, 181, 186, 187, 204, 221, 243, 244
accessibility, 218
acclaim, 6
accolade, 136
account, 25, 145, 231
accountability, 204
accuracy, 171
achievement, 141, 196
acknowledgment, 231
act, 27, 33, 42, 48, 54, 105, 140, 142, 149, 159, 160, 222
action, 29, 32, 37, 42, 44, 50, 64–66, 76, 78, 98, 105, 120–122, 132, 137–139, 141, 143, 146, 147, 153, 158, 161, 168, 170, 175, 188–195, 202, 204, 205, 207, 214, 216, 224, 243, 245, 247, 248
activism, 2, 4–8, 10, 11, 13, 15, 16, 18, 26–29, 32, 33, 37–39, 41, 42, 46, 50, 53–56, 63, 65–73, 78, 92, 95–102, 104–106, 108–111, 113,

115, 118, 121, 122, 130–134, 136, 137, 139–147, 149, 153, 154, 156, 158–161, 165, 167–171, 173, 175, 176, 185–187, 189, 190, 192, 193, 197, 199, 201–207, 209–215, 217, 234–236, 238–241, 243–245, 247, 248
activist, 2, 6, 7, 9, 10, 15, 26, 27, 39, 41, 44, 57, 93, 94, 101–106, 135, 137, 140, 150–153, 156, 187, 193, 205, 210, 234, 236, 239, 241, 245, 249
activity, 32, 229, 232
actor, 1, 4, 6, 8, 14, 47, 73, 142, 176
adaptability, 206
adaptation, 99, 197
addition, 31, 43, 59, 64, 72, 110, 122, 129, 138, 140, 163, 165, 180, 184, 189, 200, 222, 243
address, 23, 30, 59, 60, 62, 63, 68, 69, 71, 77, 79, 83, 86, 89, 95 97, 99, 110, 111, 116, 118, 123, 126, 127, 130, 133, 157, 165, 166, 171, 174, 177, 180, 191, 197, 200, 204, 206, 230, 232, 233, 235, 236, 238
adherence, 47
administration, 90, 91
admiration, 6, 140
adoption, 114, 129
adulthood, 1
advancement, 156, 225, 240, 245
advantage, 164

advent, 167, 203
adversity, 11, 20, 39, 46, 51, 105, 107, 108, 110–113, 118, 144, 146, 149, 150, 195, 206, 210, 216, 243, 247
advertising, 169
advice, 12, 147
advocacy, 1, 2, 5–7, 9–11, 13, 15, 16, 18–20, 22–25, 27–38, 41–44, 46, 47, 49–53, 55–60, 63, 66–78, 91–94, 96, 98–101, 103, 104, 106, 108, 110–113, 115–125, 127, 128, 130–152, 154, 157–159, 161–163, 165–169, 173–175, 177, 182, 184, 188, 190–207, 209–216, 220, 221, 223–226, 231, 233, 234, 236–249
advocate, 1, 10, 11, 13, 15, 16, 18, 20, 22, 26, 30, 36, 37, 39, 41–44, 46, 49, 50, 57–59, 66, 71, 73, 76, 86, 95, 98, 99, 105, 109–111, 117, 119–121, 124, 126–128, 132, 134, 139, 141, 142, 144, 157, 161, 163–165, 167, 170, 171, 173, 179, 183, 184, 186, 187, 189, 190, 196, 197, 200, 203, 205, 209–211, 214, 229, 235, 239, 241, 244, 245, 247–249
affirmation, 62, 200
age, 1, 2, 4–6, 8, 10, 14, 41, 80, 120, 160, 164, 167, 173, 180, 186, 191, 196, 205, 224, 248

# Index

agency, 166
aid, 126, 166, 181
aim, 64, 70, 75, 87, 122, 123, 181, 183, 233, 240
Alexandria, 6
allure, 1
allyship, 65, 90, 134, 149, 162, 183, 184
amendment, 124, 126
amplification, 224
analysis, 92
answer, 191
anxiety, 14, 47, 200
appreciation, 184, 210
apprehension, 17
approach, 24, 30–32, 35, 36, 43, 44, 52, 53, 60, 63, 65–70, 73, 75, 80, 87, 93, 95, 99, 109, 110, 116, 118, 119, 130, 131, 148, 153, 154, 164–166, 169, 172, 188, 190, 192, 193, 196, 198, 200, 203, 212, 214–219, 221, 222, 227, 228, 231
approval, 18
area, 114, 182, 184, 240
array, 153
arsenal, 56, 76
art, 4, 10, 53, 73, 118, 161, 162, 172, 182, 187, 194, 222, 227, 228
artist, 172
aspect, 17, 26, 29, 30, 36, 47, 61, 62, 66–68, 70, 88, 109, 110, 113, 114, 117, 122, 125, 130, 131, 146, 147, 157, 167, 170, 176, 181, 183, 184, 190, 192, 216, 234

assistance, 31, 60, 110, 178, 179, 221, 230
atmosphere, 86
attention, 43, 49, 63, 64, 121, 127, 128, 133, 136–138, 140, 142, 143, 155, 161, 167, 222, 232, 240, 247, 248
attraction, 11, 17
audience, 27, 53, 56, 58–60, 62, 65, 78, 98, 120, 124, 127, 136, 137, 141, 142, 151, 154, 158–161, 167, 169, 171, 172, 174, 175, 181, 186–192, 196, 205, 218, 219, 224, 236, 237, 246, 248
Audre Lorde, 38
Australia, 203
authenticity, 9, 13, 18, 28, 45, 46, 48, 49, 52, 53, 55, 56, 98, 99, 104, 105, 109, 141, 147, 150, 170, 172, 187, 190, 195, 211, 213, 214, 243–245, 247
awakening, 56
award, 1, 136–139, 142
awareness, 28, 29, 31, 36, 38, 43, 50, 59, 60, 63, 67, 68, 70, 71, 75, 77, 78, 89, 91, 97, 109, 110, 112, 115–117, 120, 122, 124–127, 129–139, 141, 142, 148, 154, 158–163, 167, 170, 171, 176, 182, 183, 185, 186, 190, 192, 193, 198, 200, 201, 203, 209, 211, 214, 215, 218, 221–225, 228, 229, 232, 233, 236, 240, 242, 245, 247

backdrop, 8
background, 6, 23, 41, 55, 56, 101, 104, 164, 175, 189, 202, 213, 215, 244
backlash, 5, 25, 46, 49–51, 104, 109, 111, 120, 122, 140, 146, 169, 212
balance, 20, 26–28, 67, 69, 145, 162
balancing, 26–28, 42
bar, 203
barrier, 89, 109
battle, 13, 28, 103, 141, 231
beacon, 1, 5, 6, 20, 33, 39, 46, 51, 54, 140, 141, 179, 197, 202, 211, 213, 245, 246
beauty, 144
beginning, 18
behavior, 169
being, 4, 5, 14, 22, 23, 25, 26, 33, 34, 37, 45, 47–49, 51–54, 61, 87, 103–106, 108, 109, 111, 112, 116, 128, 131, 135, 137, 140–143, 145, 157, 169, 170, 178–180, 183, 186, 187, 212, 219, 224, 240, 244
belief, 27, 41, 46, 117, 209, 213, 216
belonging, 15–17, 34, 53, 79, 88, 117, 119, 121, 150, 177, 178, 180, 185, 188, 195, 209, 212, 224
benefit, 128, 178, 235
biography, 210
birth, 203
blend, 158
blueprint, 194
board, 197
body, 188, 189
box, 161

boy, 11, 14
brainstorm, 233
brainstorming, 27
bravery, 17, 150, 247
break, 5, 11, 18, 20, 24, 46, 52, 54, 57, 59, 60, 64, 71, 79, 86–88, 109, 117, 120, 134, 140, 150, 156, 165, 172, 173, 176, 183, 195, 205, 209, 224, 239, 242, 244
breakdown, 21
breaking, 1, 4, 9, 23, 25, 33, 34, 42, 44, 55, 129, 144, 145, 163, 167, 177, 183, 229, 242, 244, 246
breakout, 158
bridge, 2, 5, 7, 9, 13, 24, 34–36, 41, 42, 47, 50, 63, 68, 72, 97, 127, 134, 140, 141, 158, 163, 182, 190, 205, 212, 214, 216, 242, 245–247, 249
building, 32, 35–37, 43, 44, 69, 72, 75, 91 93, 96, 99, 111–113, 122, 123, 127, 129, 131, 133, 145, 147, 154, 156, 160, 166, 167, 185, 187, 195, 197, 198, 220–225, 228, 230, 232, 235, 236, 239, 244, 249
bullying, 10, 30, 87, 89, 91, 186, 190, 196, 204
burden, 14, 28, 49
bureaucracy, 112
burnout, 111

California, 38
call, 143, 170, 174
camaraderie, 178

*Index*

campaign, 91, 110, 115, 133
Canada, 1, 4, 114, 203
capacity, 15, 20, 150, 156, 160, 166, 221, 223, 225, 228, 230
capital, 93
care, 26, 28, 51, 104, 111, 113, 145
career, 27, 38, 42, 102, 106, 111, 135
carpet, 142
case, 41, 54, 62, 66, 68, 115, 132
catalyst, 7, 25, 28, 29, 46, 52, 64, 79, 85, 86, 126, 139, 141, 144, 150, 192, 214, 227, 228, 233
caucus, 165
cause, 16, 18, 25, 26, 49, 92, 97, 113, 121, 125, 130, 143, 147, 149, 161, 188, 191, 193–196, 200, 201, 206, 212, 216, 223, 231, 234, 242, 245, 249
celebration, 117, 122
celebrity, 127, 128, 142
censorship, 22
center, 60, 74, 179, 204
century, 203
challenge, 7–10, 16, 17, 19–22, 24, 29, 36, 37, 41–44, 46, 48, 52–54, 56, 58, 60–64, 67–72, 74, 75, 77, 79, 80, 85–88, 91, 95, 98, 99, 103, 104, 109, 110, 113, 116–122, 127, 133, 134, 141, 142, 144, 146, 148, 151, 152, 155, 156, 158, 161, 162, 169, 170, 172–176, 182–185, 195, 196, 201–206, 209, 211, 214, 216, 217, 219–222, 224, 228–233, 236, 239, 244, 245
chameleon, 14
champion, 76, 97, 124, 199
chance, 158, 160
change, 2, 5–7, 9, 16, 19, 20, 22, 24, 25, 28–30, 32–37, 41–44, 46, 49–56, 58, 60, 64–66, 68, 70–73, 75–78, 85, 86, 88, 94–99, 101, 103, 105, 108, 109, 113, 115, 116, 118–123, 125–154, 156, 157, 159, 161–164, 166, 167, 170–177, 180, 181, 185–187, 189, 190, 192–199, 201, 202, 204–207, 209–216, 219–228, 230, 232, 233, 236, 239–241, 243–249
changer, 170
channel, 50
chapter, 1, 4, 45–47, 49, 56, 94, 101, 153, 157, 164, 202, 209, 239
character, 61, 101, 146
charisma, 1, 4, 6
child, 1, 114
choice, 5, 18, 56, 61
chord, 1
cinema, 6
circle, 175, 177
cisgender, 88, 234
citizen, 57
citizenship, 240
city, 38, 179
class, 79, 90, 194
classism, 95
classmate, 10
classroom, 79
climate, 201, 202

coalition, 99, 198, 223
collaboration, 23, 29, 32, 35–37, 50, 55, 57, 66, 70, 71, 73, 74, 76, 91–93, 99, 100, 105, 109, 110, 118, 120, 122, 126, 133, 134, 139, 147, 149, 153, 164, 165, 167, 170, 172, 178, 181, 185, 193–196, 198, 206, 210, 218, 220, 225, 227, 228, 231, 232, 234, 240, 242, 244
collection, 39, 162
collective, 32, 37, 42, 44, 59, 66, 75, 76, 78, 91, 92, 94, 96, 98, 99, 105, 120–123, 128, 132, 141, 143, 146, 147, 157, 159, 163, 165, 168, 169, 186, 189, 195, 198, 202, 204–207, 214, 216–218, 224, 233, 235, 240, 243, 245, 247
color, 38, 39, 118, 202, 234, 235
combat, 34, 75, 76, 79, 95, 110, 155, 178, 183, 185, 232
comedy, 60
comfort, 165, 195, 216
commitment, 2, 5, 13, 18, 28, 29, 34, 38, 46, 51, 60, 61, 66, 67, 73, 78, 96, 98–101, 103, 104, 110, 117, 120, 128, 134, 135, 140–142, 144, 150, 151, 154, 157, 159, 184, 194, 195, 197, 199, 200, 202, 207, 210, 212, 213, 215, 222, 239, 241, 243, 245, 249
communication, 42, 72, 104, 124, 127, 146, 147, 155, 164, 169, 188, 190, 192, 224
community, 1, 2, 5, 7–10, 14–16, 21, 23–25, 27–34, 36, 38, 39, 41, 49, 50, 52, 53, 55–65, 67, 68, 71, 72, 74, 76, 77, 79, 80, 83, 86, 89–91, 93, 95, 96, 98, 99, 103–105, 108–110, 112, 115, 117–121, 123–136, 138–140, 142–145, 150–159, 161, 162, 168, 170, 171, 173–188, 191, 193, 195, 197, 199, 200, 202–204, 210–212, 217, 219, 220, 222–225, 228, 229, 233, 235, 236, 239, 240, 242–247
compassion, 10, 41, 63, 179, 184, 185, 193, 209, 211, 215, 243
competency, 178
complacency, 99
complexity, 14, 61, 62, 103, 184, 234
component, 188, 246
compromise, 42, 148
conclusion, 16, 18, 23, 29, 34, 37, 42, 44, 53, 93, 105, 111, 113, 118, 122, 130, 141, 147, 150, 152, 175, 192, 197, 204, 216, 225, 236, 243, 245, 247, 249
conference, 158, 190
confidence, 16, 32, 41, 86, 90, 147
conflict, 8, 14, 17, 103
conformity, 8, 47, 48
confrontation, 24, 119
confusion, 17
connection, 6, 27, 32, 33, 56, 59, 61, 63, 187, 188, 190–193

consciousness, 169
consent, 79, 87
conservatism, 220
consideration, 13, 130, 171
contact, 188
content, 43, 58–60, 64, 77, 97, 99, 141, 151, 155, 156, 164, 169–177, 181, 191, 246, 248
context, 7, 8, 24, 25, 37, 43, 66–68, 70, 71, 76, 78, 86, 121, 158, 192, 202, 214, 215, 223, 225, 236
continuation, 221
continuity, 225
contrast, 2
control, 26
conversation, 31, 62, 159, 165, 183, 191, 199
conviction, 189
coordination, 122
core, 96, 147
corner, 159
cornerstone, 2, 144
cost, 48
counseling, 64, 87, 111, 119, 178, 179, 186
country, 57, 80, 113–115, 223
courage, 11, 12, 15, 17, 19, 24, 28, 39, 41, 45, 48, 52, 104, 105, 109, 112, 140, 141, 150, 177, 189, 195, 209, 211, 213, 215, 216, 241, 243, 244, 246, 249
craft, 188, 231
creation, 43, 58–60, 66, 93, 138, 156, 160, 171, 174–177, 185, 200, 228

creative, 10, 43, 53, 105, 118, 222, 231, 233
creativity, 4, 172, 173
credibility, 101, 138, 139, 163, 187
crime, 127, 131
crisis, 135
criticism, 25, 49, 57, 104, 105
crowdfunding, 221
culmination, 11
culture, 3, 6, 7, 10, 24, 25, 28, 36, 41, 54, 58, 71, 72, 95, 130, 151, 161, 163, 179, 182, 218, 219, 223, 233, 244
curiosity, 4, 10, 41
curricula, 53, 62, 79, 86–89, 129, 180, 182, 183, 186, 196, 206, 214, 219, 235
curriculum, 36, 77, 80, 81, 83, 89, 90, 93, 120, 180, 183, 213, 224
cyberbullying, 99

Dan Savage, 133
dance, 26
day, 32
death, 126, 232
debate, 199
debunk, 29, 33, 79, 112, 185
decision, 1, 5, 14, 16–19, 26, 27, 33, 45, 47–49, 54, 77, 87, 91, 94, 104, 123, 126, 129, 139, 140, 164, 241, 244
decriminalization, 74, 109, 113, 119, 126, 129, 203, 212, 229, 232
dedication, 5, 38, 98, 100, 118, 120, 134, 137, 140, 142, 147, 152, 157, 159, 187, 196, 197, 199, 205, 206, 210,

211, 216, 239, 241, 243, 249
defiance, 65
delivery, 64
demand, 99, 121, 122
depression, 200
descent, 9
design, 89, 180
desire, 1, 5, 28, 37, 156, 188
destigmatization, 203, 204
destination, 99, 197
destruction, 218
determination, 2, 18, 24, 28, 29, 39, 42, 51, 57, 99–101, 103, 108, 109, 111, 112, 118, 134, 146, 149, 213, 215–217, 239, 245, 249
development, 36, 72, 74, 75, 89, 94, 124, 127, 129, 146, 221, 222, 225, 230
dialogue, 2, 6, 9, 24, 25, 29, 34, 35, 37, 41–43, 50, 51, 55, 56, 62, 63, 67–72, 74, 75, 77, 86, 91, 95, 110–112, 116, 119, 120, 123, 124, 127, 129, 138, 139, 150, 156, 163, 171, 174, 183, 184, 188, 189, 191, 193, 196–199, 201, 205, 210, 212, 215, 220, 228–231, 236, 242, 243, 246
difference, 5, 41, 42, 94, 108, 113, 136, 138, 140, 143, 157, 175, 193, 197, 207, 210, 211, 213, 216, 249
dignity, 46, 69, 98, 115, 121, 201, 232
dimension, 127
disability, 133, 171, 235

discipline, 8
discourse, 186, 199
discovery, 1, 8, 15, 16, 18–20, 28, 33, 45, 46, 52, 61, 140, 147, 150, 191, 192, 195
discrimination, 2, 8–10, 16, 19, 21, 23, 28, 30–32, 34, 38, 39, 59–62, 64–67, 69, 72, 74, 76, 79, 80, 87, 89–91, 97–99, 101, 110, 113, 114, 116–123, 126–131, 133, 134, 136, 141, 148, 151, 155, 156, 160, 169, 173–175, 177, 178, 180, 183, 185, 191, 193, 196, 198, 200–206, 209, 212, 214, 216, 218, 219, 222–224, 229, 231–235, 239–242, 244, 247, 248
discussion, 38, 95, 150, 190, 231
disparity, 145
disposal, 121
dissemination, 169
distance, 167
distress, 110, 196
diversity, 9, 33, 35, 37, 41, 53, 59, 61, 68, 77, 79, 83, 88, 91, 117, 121, 138, 174, 180, 188, 196, 212, 220, 236, 242, 246
divide, 50, 63, 97
documentation, 151, 218
door, 60, 183
doubt, 17
down, 1, 2, 5, 9, 25, 33, 34, 42, 44, 46, 51, 54, 55, 57, 59, 60, 64, 71, 79, 86–88, 109, 117, 120, 129, 134, 140, 144, 145, 153, 156,

# Index

    163–165, 167, 173, 176, 177, 183, 195, 205, 209, 219, 229, 239, 242, 244, 246
draft, 91
drag, 39
dream, 206
duality, 2, 4
duty, 14
dynamic, 13, 65, 173

ear, 27, 179
earth, 1
educating, 50, 64, 67, 148, 150, 187, 215
education, 22–24, 29, 53, 62, 71, 73–75, 77–81, 83–91, 93–96, 110, 112, 115, 116, 118–120, 122, 125, 127, 130–134, 140, 145, 156, 172, 176, 177, 180–185, 193, 196, 197, 199, 202, 204–206, 213, 214, 220, 222, 224, 229, 231, 232, 234, 235, 240–242, 244, 246, 248
educator, 90
effect, 5, 20, 56, 65, 75, 77, 105, 119, 120, 123, 128, 130, 136, 143, 144, 147, 149, 154, 162, 166, 186, 193, 194, 213, 241, 244–246
effectiveness, 80, 89, 133, 221, 223
effort, 26, 34, 75, 92, 96, 143, 157, 162, 195, 206
Egypt, 6
elder, 4
election, 115
element, 67, 92

emergence, 132, 236
emotion, 188
empathy, 2, 3, 9, 10, 13, 15, 16, 24, 25, 28, 31, 33–36, 43, 50, 51, 53, 55–58, 62–64, 68, 71, 72, 77–80, 83, 85–88, 95, 97, 99, 115, 116, 118, 120, 125, 133, 142, 144, 148, 154, 156, 160, 164, 170, 173, 174, 176, 179, 180, 182, 183, 185, 187, 188, 190, 191, 193, 194, 196, 200, 206, 212, 214, 215, 220, 224, 231, 233, 240, 244, 245, 248
emphasis, 39, 96
employment, 114, 116, 126, 131, 225
empowerment, 15, 17, 20, 31, 45, 46, 48, 52, 53, 87, 88, 91, 107, 110, 132, 140, 145, 150–152, 180, 205, 206, 222, 224, 225, 241
enactment, 229
encounter, 21, 22, 57
encouragement, 16, 48, 49, 58, 147
end, 32, 134, 243
endeavor, 73, 97, 199, 210
endpoint, 134
energy, 94, 104
enforcement, 110, 186
engagement, 61, 64, 66, 76, 91, 93, 94, 123, 127, 132, 151, 160, 171, 172, 211, 217, 224
entertainment, 1, 10, 14, 15, 33, 56, 58–60, 64, 72, 77, 111, 120, 127, 128, 164, 176, 184, 218, 242, 244

entrepreneurship, 225
entry, 3
environment, 4, 8, 9, 13, 21, 33, 41, 79, 81, 83, 85, 87–90, 95, 99, 109, 170, 178, 179, 182–186, 195, 197, 206, 213, 219, 224, 248
environmentalism, 202
epiphany, 28
epitome, 8
equality, 2, 6, 25, 26, 29, 34, 37, 39, 40, 43, 47, 55, 56, 58, 59, 61, 63–66, 69, 73–78, 88, 91, 93, 95, 96, 98–100, 105, 108, 110, 113–115, 117–119, 121–125, 127–129, 131–134, 136, 137, 139–143, 145–147, 150–153, 155, 157, 158, 163, 164, 167, 168, 177, 180, 182, 183, 187, 188, 192, 195, 197–204, 206, 207, 209, 210, 212–216, 220–222, 224, 225, 228–233, 236, 239–241, 243–249
era, 67
erasure, 89
essence, 172
establishment, 96, 129, 177, 200
esteem, 79, 170
ethnicity, 55, 67, 69
event, 28, 203
evidence, 24, 59, 65, 87, 123, 174, 230
evolution, 197, 202–204
example, 12, 15, 26, 28, 31, 42, 50, 62, 71, 74, 79, 87, 90, 93, 110, 121, 126, 129, 132, 137, 138, 142, 159, 164, 165, 172, 173, 179–182, 195–197, 199, 213, 215, 218, 234, 235, 243, 248
exception, 73
exchange, 9, 64, 138, 157, 165, 166, 198, 233
exclusion, 39, 116, 185, 204
exercise, 63
exhibition, 162
existence, 83
expectation, 8, 103
experience, 25, 36, 45, 51, 57, 58, 61, 69, 72, 94, 107, 116, 117, 130, 138, 154, 158, 172, 174, 176, 180, 204, 234, 248
expert, 129
expertise, 30, 70, 74, 92, 121, 123, 124, 126–128, 158, 162, 166, 181, 193, 218, 221
exploration, 13, 16, 19
exposure, 9, 97, 109, 142, 156
expression, 4, 10, 19, 22, 53, 118, 122, 152, 161, 182, 192, 204, 220, 222, 228, 231
eye, 15, 20, 26, 188, 197

facade, 14
face, 10–12, 14, 18, 20, 21, 23, 34, 36, 37, 39, 46, 49–51, 55, 57, 64, 67, 69, 73, 79, 85–87, 89, 92, 97, 103, 105, 108–111, 113, 115, 118, 122, 125, 133, 144, 145, 149, 150, 160, 177, 185, 186, 195–197, 200, 201, 204–206, 210, 211, 216, 219, 222, 224, 229,

*Index* 261

    231, 232, 234, 240, 242, 243, 247, 248
fact, 61, 192, 247
faith, 61, 201, 202
fame, 1, 6, 8, 140
family, 2, 4–17, 19, 21, 27, 28, 41, 42, 47, 48, 103, 104, 140, 162, 178, 189, 244
father, 8
façade, 17
fear, 5, 14, 17, 19, 28, 34, 41, 45, 47, 50, 98, 103, 107, 134, 151, 165, 185, 201, 211, 216, 222, 232, 244, 248
fearlessness, 211, 242
feature, 117
feedback, 171
feeling, 32, 41, 45, 63
field, 73, 159
fight, 6, 11, 26, 28, 29, 34, 37–41, 43, 46, 47, 56–58, 63, 65, 72, 73, 77, 78, 91–93, 95–99, 104, 110, 113–116, 118, 121, 122, 133, 134, 137, 138, 140, 141, 143, 145, 153, 155–157, 164, 166, 167, 173, 175, 177, 180, 183, 187, 192, 194, 195, 197, 199, 201, 202, 204, 206, 207, 209, 210, 213–216, 221, 222, 230–234, 241, 243–245, 247–249
fighting, 10, 38, 43, 65, 100, 105, 111, 136, 147, 151, 195, 197, 202, 210, 214, 239, 241
figure, 4, 8, 33, 38, 39, 47, 49, 71, 77, 92, 104, 140–142, 146, 160, 164, 215
film, 6, 53, 138, 161, 162, 164, 174, 184, 222, 228, 231
fire, 5
firm, 110
flame, 47
focus, 30, 68, 69, 89, 91, 106, 157, 190, 203, 204, 224
force, 9, 30, 41, 42, 53, 65, 121, 122, 145, 159, 194, 198, 215, 216, 244, 249
forefront, 5, 25, 31, 34, 56, 68, 71, 96, 98, 116, 132, 137, 141, 186, 199, 206, 241, 245
form, 67, 80, 158, 166, 169, 187, 230
format, 169
formation, 132, 203
formulation, 74
foster, 18, 31, 33, 36, 43, 44, 50, 53, 62, 66–68, 70, 72, 77, 86, 88, 90, 94, 99, 109, 112, 115, 117, 118, 139, 148, 151, 154–157, 160, 163, 164, 170, 171, 173, 179, 180, 182, 183, 185, 190, 192, 200, 201, 206, 210, 212, 214, 221, 222, 225, 227–229, 231, 233, 240, 242, 244
fostering, 9, 12, 13, 16, 22, 23, 34–37, 41, 44, 51–53, 55, 63–66, 69, 70, 73, 75, 78, 79, 83, 85, 87, 88, 90, 91, 95, 96, 110, 113, 116, 118, 120, 124, 127, 131–133, 136, 139, 144, 145, 147, 150, 151, 156–158, 160, 161, 164, 167, 172, 173,

178–180, 182–184, 187, 191, 193, 195, 199, 201, 205, 206, 209, 210, 218, 219, 222–224, 230, 232, 240, 242, 243, 245–248
foundation, 5, 9–11, 13, 37, 42, 50, 60, 80, 91, 100, 133, 149, 213, 225, 244, 246
fraction, 249
framework, 8, 19, 25, 36, 39, 68, 69, 79, 126, 163, 220, 234, 236
France, 113
freedom, 17, 22, 49, 104, 220
front, 60, 72, 99, 122, 123, 149, 162, 163, 192, 198, 210, 221, 223, 228
fuel, 50, 101, 104, 210
fulfillment, 14, 18, 27, 48, 147
funding, 93, 156, 179, 180, 200, 221, 223
fundraising, 60, 179, 193, 221
future, 2, 6, 10, 11, 23, 28, 29, 34, 37–39, 58, 60, 66, 73, 76, 78, 80, 85, 88, 91–96, 98–100, 115, 120, 121, 131, 134, 137, 141, 144–147, 149–152, 157, 159, 162, 173, 177, 190, 194, 199, 202, 204, 206, 207, 209–211, 213–217, 219, 222, 225, 228, 231, 233, 236, 239–241, 243–247, 249

gain, 27, 40, 79, 87, 116, 138, 185, 217, 223, 247
game, 170
gap, 2, 5, 9, 13, 24, 29, 41, 42, 62, 63, 66, 71, 72, 127, 163, 205, 212, 214, 216, 242
garner, 123, 124, 127, 129, 161
gathering, 12
gay, 5, 9, 15, 18–23, 38, 47, 49, 54, 57, 106, 138, 140, 150, 173, 203, 211, 234, 239, 241
gender, 8, 14, 23, 24, 30, 32, 35, 37, 38, 43, 50, 52, 55, 62, 66, 69, 71, 79, 83, 86, 88, 90, 96–98, 110, 114–117, 120, 121, 127, 130–133, 145, 153, 156, 163, 171, 182, 183, 185, 194, 198, 200, 201, 203, 204, 211, 212, 214, 215, 220, 228, 229, 231, 232, 234, 236, 240
generation, 48, 77, 91, 93, 95, 143, 145, 197, 206, 207, 212, 241, 244, 248, 249
glamour, 1, 45
glitz, 1, 45
globalization, 67
globe, 54, 76, 156, 164, 211
glossary, 181
goal, 55, 121, 129, 182, 189, 232, 246
government, 72, 119, 123, 127, 129, 221
grace, 6, 49, 245
grandfather, 1, 4, 6–8, 41
grandson, 1, 4, 14, 47, 142
grant, 114, 163, 221
gratitude, 48
greatness, 4
ground, 9, 67–70, 75, 112, 156, 191, 196, 223, 230, 246

## Index

groundbreaking, 37, 39, 101, 241, 244
groundwork, 29, 35, 222
group, 3, 16, 91, 121
growth, 3, 11, 15, 18, 20, 71, 94, 96, 107, 140, 144, 146, 147, 150, 197, 219, 221, 245
guest, 90
guidance, 12, 27, 30–32, 60, 72, 80, 94, 107, 110, 112, 150, 179, 180, 184, 197, 212, 221
guilt, 17

hall, 91, 93, 191
hand, 33, 67, 126, 190, 191, 202, 248
happiness, 5, 14, 18, 140
harassment, 87, 89, 99, 106, 112, 113, 130, 132, 169, 219, 229, 232, 240
harm, 17, 28, 185
harmony, 27, 202
Harvey Milk, 38, 87, 115, 137
hashtagging, 170
hate, 21, 49, 50, 99, 127, 131, 169, 203, 240
hatred, 110
haven, 17, 41
head, 46, 49, 56, 61, 63, 71, 109, 131, 146
healing, 222
health, 14, 31, 32, 52, 77, 79, 87, 89, 95, 111, 116, 133, 135, 157, 178, 181, 186, 197, 200, 202
healthcare, 116, 126, 127, 131, 132, 134, 178, 200, 204, 235, 242
heart, 42, 187
heartbeat, 132
Helem, 121
help, 10, 27, 34, 36, 58, 62, 67, 68, 79, 86, 87, 90, 94, 112, 117, 118, 123, 127, 133, 138, 162, 166, 171, 178, 181, 185–187, 189, 191, 200, 221–224, 230
heritage, 1–6, 8, 9, 41, 140, 210
hero, 38, 100, 207, 210, 215, 241, 249
heteronormativity, 133, 150
hiding, 13–15, 18, 19, 47, 56, 140
high, 48, 58, 79, 90, 111, 133, 137, 164, 196, 200
history, 7, 62, 79, 83, 86–90, 92, 94, 95, 148, 151, 152, 171, 180, 193, 202, 210, 214, 217–219, 243
Hodges, 132
Hollywood, 6, 45
home, 41, 57
homelessness, 39, 186
homophobia, 59, 75, 85, 109, 116–118, 141, 155, 169, 174, 240
homosexuality, 11, 17, 19, 22, 49, 54, 61, 68, 109, 113, 115, 119, 126, 129, 203, 204, 211, 212, 219, 229, 230, 232, 241
honesty, 18
honor, 2, 7, 8, 39, 137–139, 219
hope, 1, 5, 6, 20, 23, 33, 34, 38, 39, 46, 51, 54, 56, 113, 120, 133, 139–141, 143, 144, 146, 150, 164, 175, 177, 179, 194, 197, 202, 206,

211–213, 216, 219, 246, 247, 249
horizon, 219
hostility, 104, 116
household, 4
housing, 114, 116, 126, 131
hub, 60
humanity, 2, 3, 56, 62, 64, 133, 144, 146, 163, 183, 215, 220
humility, 70
humor, 60, 161, 169
hurdle, 99

icebreaker, 32
Iceland, 114
icon, 1, 6, 45, 46, 49, 140, 154, 164, 174, 202, 244, 249
identification, 115
identity, 1, 3–8, 14, 16–20, 24, 28, 29, 32, 33, 37, 41, 42, 45–47, 50–53, 55, 56, 61, 65, 69, 71, 79, 83, 86, 88, 96, 98, 104, 105, 114, 116, 117, 120, 121, 130, 131, 140, 146, 148, 156, 163, 177, 182, 183, 185, 195, 201, 204, 211–213, 215–217, 229, 231, 232, 234, 244–246
ignorance, 34, 50, 185
image, 14, 104
imagination, 155
imagine, 47
impact, 1, 3, 4, 6, 7, 16, 18, 22, 24, 29, 30, 33, 34, 37, 38, 41, 42, 44–47, 49, 51, 53, 56, 58, 62–66, 73, 76, 78–80, 83, 86, 87, 89, 92, 93, 95–100, 103, 105, 111, 113, 115–117, 122–124, 133–137, 140–145, 147–151, 153–159, 162, 163, 168, 170, 172, 174–177, 179–182, 184, 186, 187, 189–193, 196–202, 205–207, 209–213, 215, 217, 220, 221, 225, 226, 235, 237, 239–241, 243–247, 249
implementation, 84, 89, 119, 127, 129, 130, 170, 223
importance, 2, 3, 5, 7–9, 13, 14, 16, 18–20, 24–27, 29–33, 38, 39, 41–43, 50, 53–55, 58, 59, 61, 62, 65–68, 71–73, 77, 81, 83, 86, 88–91, 93–96, 99, 105, 110–113, 119, 120, 123, 125, 127, 129–131, 139, 142–149, 151, 153–156, 159, 160, 163, 170, 174, 175, 177, 180, 183, 184, 186, 188, 190, 193–198, 200, 201, 204–206, 210, 212, 214, 216, 219, 222, 225, 229, 233, 235, 237, 240–243, 245–248
impression, 4
imprint, 4
imprisonment, 126, 232
improvement, 81
inclination, 8, 10
inclusion, 39, 54, 60, 67, 69, 89, 136, 142, 160, 165, 181, 185, 192, 204, 209, 212, 225
inclusivity, 58, 59, 64, 69, 77, 86, 88–91, 95, 105, 110, 117, 120, 122, 125–128, 134,

# Index

138, 146, 152, 174, 179, 183, 192, 206, 231, 241, 242, 245–247
income, 201, 235
increase, 23, 79, 115, 123, 128, 218
indignation, 10
individual, 1, 7, 12, 16, 19, 20, 27–29, 42, 44, 54, 65, 93, 95–97, 111, 116, 141–144, 146, 151, 158, 188, 189, 198, 201, 202, 205, 210, 211, 213, 216, 222, 234, 235, 244, 247, 249
industry, 1, 6, 14, 15, 33, 56, 58–60, 64, 72, 77, 111, 120, 127, 128, 164, 176, 184, 242, 244
inequality, 10, 122, 128, 171, 198, 201, 235
influence, 1, 6, 7, 38, 59, 61, 72, 77, 92, 99, 111, 119, 124–128, 133, 142, 143, 153, 160, 161, 163, 164, 175–177, 181, 186, 205, 212, 220, 221, 223, 245
information, 10, 29, 31, 50, 53, 61, 62, 71, 72, 79, 80, 83, 87, 88, 90, 98, 116, 127, 133, 167, 169, 175, 178, 180, 183, 185, 187, 193, 218, 220, 236
initiative, 75, 133, 179
injustice, 95, 122
innovation, 111
input, 93, 129, 171
insight, 40, 151
inspiration, 5, 9, 13, 19, 20, 25, 33, 37, 39, 41, 45, 53, 54, 56, 66, 73, 80, 98, 103, 113, 131, 137, 141, 144, 146, 150, 157, 159, 175, 198, 199, 209, 212, 213, 243, 244, 246, 249
instance, 129, 138, 163, 165, 169, 188, 190
institution, 80
interconnectedness, 9, 65, 66, 95, 130, 167, 194, 198, 201, 203, 205, 214
interconnection, 248
interest, 189
internet, 67, 165, 203, 237
interpretation, 230
intersect, 95, 198, 214, 235, 248
intersection, 6, 62, 172, 202, 204, 234, 236
intersectionality, 9, 23, 29, 39, 55, 62, 65–67, 95, 97, 110, 111, 130, 133, 143, 145, 153, 157, 193, 198, 201, 214–216, 230, 231, 234, 236, 240, 242, 244
intervention, 135
introduction, 124, 223
introspection, 19, 27, 146, 188
investment, 199
involvement, 29, 30, 32, 39, 59, 93–95, 159, 174, 178, 184, 185, 194, 195, 219, 242
isolation, 8, 11, 17, 19, 21, 23, 30, 34, 47, 72, 79, 90, 178, 194, 195, 205
issue, 115, 200

Johnson, 38
journal, 3
journalism, 138

journey, 1, 2, 4, 5, 7–20, 25, 27–29, 31, 33, 34, 37, 39, 41, 44–47, 49, 51–59, 61, 62, 64, 66, 71, 73, 78, 92, 93, 95–99, 101, 103–106, 108, 109, 111–113, 118, 120, 131, 134, 137, 140, 141, 143–147, 149–152, 157, 164, 174, 179, 181, 182, 189, 191, 192, 194, 195, 197, 199, 202, 205–207, 209–211, 213, 215, 216, 225, 228, 234, 236, 239, 241, 243–245, 247, 249
joy, 26, 51, 111, 117
judgment, 5, 14, 17, 26, 41, 185, 201
justice, 2, 5, 10, 11, 43, 69, 73, 78, 93, 95, 110, 113, 118, 131, 133, 134, 137, 143, 145, 147, 150, 151, 153, 162, 167, 193, 198, 199, 201, 202, 210, 213, 214, 216, 233–236, 240, 241, 248

Kimberlé Crenshaw, 234
knowledge, 10, 30, 32, 62, 65, 78–80, 86, 88, 89, 92, 94, 95, 116, 120, 122, 124, 147, 148, 157, 159, 160, 166, 167, 180, 182, 187, 206, 214, 215, 219, 221, 225, 230, 233, 237, 240, 244, 246

lack, 21, 61, 79, 80, 89, 160, 196, 225, 229
landmark, 115, 132

landscape, 8, 20, 28, 36, 59, 68, 75, 76, 92, 99, 103, 113, 131, 144, 197, 219, 220, 228
language, 138, 171, 188, 190, 192
law, 110
layer, 14, 103
leadership, 11, 91, 94, 160, 225
learning, 67, 77, 197, 198, 213
Lebanon, 121
legacy, 1, 6, 7, 14, 38, 39, 47, 60, 66, 73, 78, 91–93, 96, 103, 137, 144, 145, 147, 150–152, 157, 177, 202, 205, 207, 210, 211, 213, 215, 239, 241, 242, 244–247, 249
legalization, 114, 203
legislation, 32, 38, 74, 77, 99, 115, 119, 123, 124, 127, 131, 141, 151, 190, 223, 230, 245, 246
lens, 234
lesson, 87, 90, 180, 197
level, 2, 16, 26, 46, 65, 73, 80, 101, 128–130, 132, 149, 159, 166, 188, 189, 195, 206, 222, 223, 235, 245
leverage, 42, 92, 99, 120, 121, 128, 139, 143, 163, 186, 206, 221
levity, 60
liberation, 54, 105, 234
life, 2, 4–6, 10, 12, 14, 16–18, 20, 26–28, 33, 38, 44–49, 51, 54, 62, 104, 131, 137, 140, 145, 151, 155, 162, 179, 184, 188, 189, 191, 192, 196, 240, 243
lifeline, 8, 165, 181

# Index

lifetime, 144–146, 245, 247
light, 2, 6, 15, 33, 52, 54, 61, 62, 64, 78, 129, 136, 142, 152, 155, 158, 160, 169, 173, 176, 198, 200, 217, 245, 246
line, 24
lineage, 7
listening, 27, 35, 43, 57, 74, 154, 179, 235, 236
literature, 39, 53, 79, 87, 89, 95, 117, 138, 161, 180, 218, 233
litigation, 221, 232
living, 14, 16–20, 28, 39, 46, 48, 49, 52, 54, 148, 177, 202, 215, 243
lobby, 125, 131, 186, 232
lobbying, 77, 121–128, 151, 203, 222, 223, 245
location, 164, 181, 237
loneliness, 178
Lorde, 38, 39
loss, 18
love, 5, 9, 13–15, 18, 41, 42, 46, 48, 61, 100, 103, 117, 134, 150, 175, 177, 185, 188, 242
low, 79, 235

mainstream, 58, 111, 160, 164, 170, 173, 174, 217, 218
making, 4, 5, 27, 36, 41, 51, 56, 60, 87, 91, 94, 95, 109, 118, 127, 129, 140, 147, 165, 188, 189, 199, 215, 219, 220, 231
man, 5, 7, 15, 17, 18, 47, 49, 150, 173, 234, 241
manner, 24, 223
marginalization, 19, 39, 97, 130, 160, 177, 200, 202, 224, 229, 231
mark, 39, 58, 63, 97, 100, 144, 150, 177, 209, 213, 215, 243, 245, 249
market, 6
marriage, 114, 125, 132, 203, 204
Marsha P. Johnson, 38, 39, 87
masculinity, 8
matter, 77, 113, 206, 216, 242
mean, 17, 67
means, 1, 10, 26, 35, 67, 79, 148, 160, 164, 165, 197, 218, 235
media, 10, 15, 31, 33, 34, 36, 43, 49–51, 56, 58–61, 64, 66, 70, 72, 73, 77, 78, 91, 97, 98, 110, 111, 115, 119, 120, 124, 127, 129, 138, 141, 142, 147, 151, 154–156, 159–161, 163–171, 173–177, 184, 186, 191, 196, 198, 199, 203, 205, 211, 214, 220, 224, 236, 237, 239, 242, 244, 246, 248
medium, 73, 228
member, 1, 4, 9, 41, 56, 91, 103
memory, 1, 7, 218
mentee, 94
mentor, 94
mentorship, 30, 60, 77, 80, 90, 94–96, 145, 186, 212, 221, 225, 241
merit, 138
message, 15, 38, 55, 58, 60, 65, 117, 128, 139, 141, 147, 151, 154, 155, 162, 164, 167,

174–177, 186–192, 196, 242, 245
messaging, 104
Michel Dimitri Chalhoub, 6
Middle East, 54, 222, 228, 231
Middle Eastern, 1, 4, 6–11, 14, 16, 19, 28, 34, 41, 47, 93, 103, 104, 109, 118, 120, 140, 150, 189
midst, 27, 48, 111
milestone, 98, 114, 115, 204
mind, 13, 47, 51, 99
mindedness, 215
mindfulness, 26
mindset, 146, 215, 216
misconception, 54, 61
misinformation, 50, 61, 63, 224, 229
mission, 1, 5, 9, 26, 29, 49, 74, 76, 96, 135
misunderstanding, 166
mix, 68
mixture, 17
mobilization, 221
model, 104, 140, 164, 177, 210, 212, 213, 243
moment, 14–16, 18, 28, 45, 48, 54, 56, 241, 244
momentum, 56, 97, 203, 232, 247
monolith, 35
Montreal, 1, 4
morale, 194
mother, 48
motivation, 41, 50, 57, 194
movement, 4, 22, 29, 35, 38, 39, 42, 57, 67, 68, 70, 91–94, 96, 97, 101, 103, 110, 113, 114, 118, 121, 122, 132, 133, 137–139, 141–143, 147, 148, 151, 154, 157, 159–162, 164–167, 189, 192–194, 197, 198, 203, 204, 206, 209–211, 215, 219, 221, 223, 225, 230, 234–236, 240, 244, 245, 247, 248
movie, 1, 115
multimedia, 191
multitude, 23
Muna, 62
music, 118, 172, 192, 222, 228, 231
musician, 172
myth, 61

name, 6
narrative, 6, 25, 51, 62, 67, 75, 151, 188
nation, 36
nature, 5, 10, 30, 37, 97, 148, 153, 162, 169, 202, 206, 218
navigation, 27, 220
need, 10, 13, 14, 20, 26, 29, 31, 47, 51, 56, 62, 64, 66, 67, 71, 78, 89, 96, 98, 104, 119, 123, 124, 132, 134, 145, 148, 153, 156, 161, 176–178, 180, 181, 184, 200, 201, 214, 238, 240, 245, 248
negativity, 50, 51, 104, 112, 169
Netherlands, 114
network, 15, 17, 27, 49, 50, 90, 92, 110, 112, 121, 132, 156, 160, 161, 165, 184, 233, 240, 244
networking, 60, 94, 158, 166, 221
New York City, 113, 132, 203
news, 59, 174
noise, 215

# Index

notion, 61, 244

obstacle, 109, 110
offense, 166, 232
office, 38
official, 38
Omar, 1, 2, 8, 10–20, 26–29, 41–44, 49–53, 58–63, 74, 75, 96–98, 103–108, 111–113, 119–121, 135–137, 142, 143, 146–159, 173–175, 180–182, 195–202, 209–213, 236, 237, 239–241, 243–245, 247–249
Omar Jr., 1, 4, 5, 8, 9, 42
Omar Jr.'s, 4–6, 8, 9
Omar Sharif, 1, 4, 6, 8, 14, 41, 47
Omar Sharif Jr., 1, 2, 4, 6–11, 13, 14, 16, 17, 19, 20, 23–34, 41–51, 54–58, 60, 61, 63, 66, 68, 71–78, 86, 88, 91–113, 116, 118, 120, 122–130, 134–147, 153–164, 167–169, 173–177, 180–184, 187–194, 197–202, 205, 207, 210, 213–216, 225–229, 231, 236–244, 246–249
Omar Sharif Jr.'s, 2, 6, 9, 12, 13, 15–18, 20, 29–32, 37, 41, 42, 44, 47, 53–58, 63, 65–67, 70, 73, 76, 78, 96, 98–100, 106, 109, 110, 113, 118, 122, 124, 125, 127, 128, 136, 137, 141, 143, 144, 146, 147, 150, 152–159, 162, 164, 170, 174–177, 181, 184, 189, 199, 202, 205–207, 209–213, 215, 216, 241–243, 245–247, 249
Omar Sharif's, 6
Omar Sharif, 1
on, 1–10, 12, 14–16, 18, 20, 22, 23, 25, 28, 29, 32–34, 36–39, 41–56, 58–65, 67–69, 71, 73, 76, 78, 80, 83, 86, 87, 89, 91–94, 96–101, 103, 104, 106, 108–111, 113–115, 117, 119, 121, 122, 124, 126–131, 134, 136, 138, 139, 141, 142, 144–155, 157–170, 172, 173, 175–178, 181, 186–190, 193, 195–205, 207, 209, 211–213, 215, 216, 219, 220, 222–224, 230–234, 236, 239–247, 249
one, 1, 4, 11, 13, 19, 20, 24, 26–29, 32–34, 38, 41, 45, 46, 49, 52, 54, 56, 61, 66, 93, 95, 96, 103, 105, 110, 111, 121, 131, 134, 140, 141, 145, 154, 157, 165, 169, 181, 183, 195, 197, 198, 207, 210, 211, 213, 216, 222, 228, 234, 240, 241, 243, 244
online, 14, 31, 32, 72, 78, 91, 99, 106, 111, 112, 133, 154, 159, 161, 165, 168–170, 173, 181, 182, 184, 186, 187, 191, 198, 224, 236, 237, 239, 240, 248

op, 155, 174, 199
opinion, 59, 60, 63, 66, 72, 77, 111, 123–125, 127, 134, 155, 173, 176, 205, 223
opportunity, 9, 16, 27, 50, 58, 114, 142, 151, 165, 173, 185
opposition, 9, 57, 75, 86, 101, 124, 169
oppression, 8, 9, 21, 23, 38, 39, 55, 65, 95, 134, 148, 201, 203, 214, 234–236, 248
optimism, 146, 194
option, 14
order, 14, 23, 26, 27, 73, 116, 123, 128, 130, 180, 183, 190, 217
organization, 121, 135, 181
organizing, 5, 36, 64, 87, 121, 122, 124, 132, 182, 185, 191, 193, 203, 220
orientation, 16, 24, 26, 28, 29, 32, 37, 45, 50, 61, 69, 71, 83, 86, 96, 98, 114, 116, 117, 120, 121, 130, 131, 156, 163, 182, 183, 185, 212, 215, 229, 232, 234, 240
ostracism, 9, 14, 21
ostracization, 219
other, 11, 17, 32, 33, 36, 38, 42–44, 59, 65, 69, 72, 95, 99, 105, 118, 123, 126, 128–133, 136, 142, 145, 147, 148, 153, 154, 158, 166, 171, 173, 176, 185, 190, 192, 198, 201, 203–205, 210, 216, 218, 220, 228, 233–236, 244, 248
outlet, 222
outlook, 4

outpouring, 46
outreach, 97, 133, 154
ownership, 87, 96, 132, 193

pain, 10
pair, 96, 221
panel, 31, 32, 59, 158, 174, 183, 190, 199, 212, 220
paradigm, 167
parent, 114
part, 32, 47, 51, 65, 105, 132, 151, 206, 217, 218, 232
participant, 38
participation, 58, 109, 157–159, 171, 246
partnering, 24, 30, 36, 43, 64, 69, 76, 86, 93, 99, 126, 128, 163, 186, 204, 221, 230
partnership, 72, 92, 210
passion, 2, 4, 10, 29, 73, 150, 189, 198, 199, 202, 210, 216, 240, 245
past, 92, 99, 210
path, 1, 4, 6, 7, 11, 12, 16, 51, 101, 102, 105, 108, 111, 112, 139, 150, 152, 164, 216
pathway, 53
patience, 9, 13, 105
peace, 27
peer, 90
penalty, 232
people, 7, 15, 16, 33, 34, 42, 46, 48, 51, 52, 63, 65, 67, 69, 86, 95, 97, 103, 122, 133, 135, 137, 140, 142, 154–156, 168, 175, 180, 185, 188, 190, 191, 193, 195, 196, 199, 202, 203, 217, 228,

230, 232, 234, 235, 246, 249
perception, 58, 73, 80
performance, 87, 161, 197
perpetuation, 89
persecution, 17, 28, 98, 165, 202, 216, 218, 242, 244, 248
perseverance, 25, 51, 75, 112, 120, 134, 144, 146, 149, 209, 215, 216, 245
persistence, 86
person, 4, 9, 10, 27, 38, 96, 103, 116, 154, 207, 210, 243
persona, 26
personality, 155
perspective, 4, 9, 18, 95, 147, 169, 172, 176, 249
philanthropic, 177
picture, 188, 195, 213
place, 15, 31, 201
plan, 90, 123
planet, 201
planning, 75, 91–93, 122, 178, 180, 221
platform, 2, 5, 7, 16, 18, 24, 29, 33, 34, 42, 46, 57, 59, 61, 63, 77, 95, 96, 98, 111, 116, 117, 119, 120, 122, 127–129, 135–137, 139, 141–143, 150, 151, 153, 154, 157, 159–162, 164, 167–169, 171, 174, 176, 184, 198, 201, 211, 214, 216, 220, 224, 229, 244, 245, 247, 248
play, 7, 10, 22, 32, 71, 86, 112, 114, 117, 126–128, 133, 137, 139, 142, 161, 169, 177, 180, 185, 187, 189, 191, 218, 219, 221–223, 226, 229, 233
poet, 38
poetry, 162, 192
point, 17, 113, 132, 203
police, 113, 132, 203
policy, 34, 36, 60, 63, 66, 68, 74, 75, 81, 91, 109, 116, 118, 119, 121–124, 127–132, 134, 139, 141–143, 145, 150–152, 186, 187, 203, 204, 212, 213, 223, 225, 232, 235, 245, 246
politician, 38
pool, 92, 128, 181
population, 131, 140
position, 76, 154, 189
possibility, 209
potential, 5, 16, 17, 34, 47, 49, 67, 85, 86, 98, 110, 115, 140, 147, 167, 173, 192, 198, 199, 224, 236, 239, 245, 247, 248
poverty, 39, 202
power, 1, 5–7, 13, 16, 20, 25, 29, 31–34, 36, 37, 41–43, 46, 48, 49, 51, 53–58, 67, 70, 72, 73, 77–79, 86, 88–90, 92, 95, 97–99, 101, 105, 111, 112, 118, 120–123, 128, 132, 136, 141, 142, 144–147, 151, 152, 154, 155, 159, 160, 163, 166, 167, 170, 171, 173–176, 180–187, 189, 192, 194, 195, 198, 199, 202, 204, 205, 209, 211, 213–215, 222, 228, 231, 235, 236, 239, 240, 242–247, 249

practice, 201
precedent, 132, 195
prejudice, 2, 14, 16, 21, 28, 34, 46, 64, 95, 113, 116, 122, 131, 141, 156, 170, 173–175, 178, 183, 185, 191, 193, 205, 209, 224, 239, 240, 247, 248
presence, 4, 6, 51, 54, 59, 63, 66, 106, 115, 142, 151, 158, 159, 161, 173, 174, 184, 199, 205, 220, 242
present, 74, 90, 206, 241
presentation, 196
presenter, 176
preservation, 151, 152, 210, 219
press, 142
pressure, 8, 14, 19, 23, 45, 103, 127, 138, 222
prevention, 133, 135
pride, 8, 46, 55, 117, 210, 217
principle, 42, 248
privacy, 26
privilege, 2, 7, 8, 62, 133, 234, 235
process, 11, 19, 52, 67, 97, 144, 162, 171, 194, 206, 244
production, 43, 164, 171
professional, 15, 16, 51, 72, 89, 101, 103–105, 111, 133, 144, 145, 216, 244
profile, 58, 111, 137, 164
program, 93
progress, 18, 25, 29, 34, 35, 37, 39, 41, 61, 67, 72, 73, 76, 77, 92, 95, 97–99, 109, 112–114, 116, 119, 127, 131, 134, 136–139, 141, 143, 144, 148, 158, 159, 171, 175, 185, 187, 194, 199, 204, 205, 210, 214, 216, 217, 222, 225, 233, 239, 244, 247, 249
project, 162
promise, 98, 100
promotion, 245
prosecution, 232
prospect, 47
protection, 114, 131, 204, 212
public, 7, 15, 20, 25–28, 31, 33, 38, 45, 49, 50, 52, 59–61, 63, 65, 66, 72, 77, 99, 104, 106, 109–111, 114, 115, 123–125, 127, 128, 131, 133, 134, 138, 141, 142, 146, 147, 155, 160, 164, 171, 173, 174, 176, 178, 186–190, 195, 199, 200, 205, 212, 217, 218, 223, 224, 242, 248
purpose, 5, 20, 27, 28, 121, 122, 147, 216
pursuit, 25, 75, 134, 144, 147, 151, 167, 202, 212, 214
push, 42, 50, 57, 72, 74, 76, 123, 128, 129, 134, 139, 173, 202, 212, 216, 229, 231, 246, 248

quality, 11, 26, 179
queen, 39
queerness, 62
quest, 29, 128, 182, 216, 249
question, 10, 25, 28, 73, 146, 174, 183, 185, 228
quo, 8, 10, 52, 54, 202, 216, 245

race, 38, 55, 62, 67, 69, 97, 110, 130, 171, 194, 201, 234, 240

# Index

racism, 65, 95, 148
raid, 203
raising, 50, 60, 63, 67, 68, 70, 112, 117, 122, 126, 148, 154, 215, 218, 223, 228, 229, 232
rally, 139
range, 32, 111, 132, 155, 165, 178–181, 192, 201, 230
reach, 15, 16, 48, 56–59, 73, 78, 92, 98, 110, 127, 133, 136–138, 142, 143, 154, 158, 161, 162, 167, 169, 173, 175–177, 181, 186, 191, 192, 196, 198, 203, 205, 218, 219, 221, 224, 226, 236, 243, 246, 248
reality, 108, 245
realization, 17, 28, 29
realm, 7, 169, 170
recognition, 14, 35, 62, 67, 114, 125, 131, 132, 134, 136–139, 141–144, 150, 152, 204, 212, 231, 232, 245–247
record, 219
reflection, 24, 27, 28, 52, 67, 105, 146, 147, 188
reform, 76, 121, 143, 229
refuge, 30, 64
refugee, 198
region, 20, 22, 35, 43, 64, 68, 71–75, 119, 158, 184, 211, 212, 219, 220, 223, 225, 227–231, 241, 246
regret, 18
rejection, 14, 16, 17, 19, 21, 41, 47, 48, 204, 205, 244
relationship, 12, 94, 104, 244
relaxation, 111
religion, 7, 44, 62, 67, 69, 110, 130, 194, 201, 231
reminder, 8, 12, 16, 17, 20, 37, 51, 78, 95, 105, 136, 137, 146, 147, 152, 159, 206, 207, 213, 217, 243, 247, 249
repeal, 124, 126, 223
report, 112
repository, 237
representation, 1, 6, 7, 33, 34, 43, 53, 58, 64, 72, 77, 79, 80, 115, 117, 119, 126, 129, 130, 157, 160, 166, 170, 172, 174, 217, 242, 246
representative, 110, 143
reprisal, 232
request, 91
research, 59, 87, 124, 154, 190
resilience, 1, 6, 11–13, 17, 20, 29, 32, 39, 40, 45, 46, 49–51, 62, 65, 73, 98, 99, 101, 103, 105, 108–113, 117, 118, 133, 144, 146, 147, 149, 159, 175, 186, 189, 195, 204, 206, 210, 213, 215–217, 222, 224, 225, 241–243, 245, 249
resistance, 48, 50, 68, 72, 75, 85, 86, 89, 101, 112, 122, 125, 127, 197
resolve, 146, 239
resource, 32, 60, 72, 90, 181, 218, 221
respect, 2, 8, 25, 35–37, 42, 44, 50, 67, 70, 71, 73, 79, 83, 88, 90, 98, 115, 120, 130, 140, 155, 196, 212, 232, 242
response, 78, 203
responsibility, 8, 41, 91

result, 48, 61, 72, 112, 132, 141, 172, 205
richness, 9, 41, 174, 184
right, 15, 42, 125, 142, 151, 175, 197, 215
rise, 46, 99, 164, 216, 244
risk, 49, 67, 165, 220
Rivera, 39
road, 131–134
roadmap, 92
role, 4, 7, 10, 14, 32, 34, 36, 38, 41, 42, 44, 48, 59, 63–65, 68–72, 74, 79, 80, 83, 86, 87, 90, 92, 94, 104, 109, 112, 114, 116, 117, 121, 123, 125–128, 132, 133, 137, 139–143, 145, 146, 151, 155–157, 161, 164, 165, 169, 173, 177, 180, 182, 184, 185, 187–189, 191, 203, 205, 206, 210–213, 218–224, 226, 229, 230, 232–234, 243, 244, 247
room, 188
root, 4, 95, 122
ruling, 132, 204

safe, 14, 16, 17, 22, 30, 32, 35, 41, 43, 51, 52, 57, 64, 66, 68, 71–73, 77, 79, 87, 88, 90, 91, 95, 96, 99, 112, 116, 117, 119, 130, 132, 135, 140, 148, 150, 156, 170, 177–180, 182, 183, 185–187, 189, 193, 195–197, 200, 201, 203, 205, 207, 209, 212, 219, 224, 225, 230–232, 240, 242, 246, 248
safety, 37, 106, 108, 112, 146
Sarah, 16
Saudi Arabia, 62
scale, 2, 28, 43, 45, 63, 64, 76, 78, 97, 98, 100, 121, 141, 142, 151, 153, 154, 157, 159, 160, 162, 164–167, 173, 186, 190, 196, 207, 230, 232, 236, 239, 241, 242, 247
schedule, 104
scholar, 234
school, 10, 30, 79, 89–91, 196, 219, 224
schooling, 80
scope, 168, 198, 199
screen, 1, 4, 6
script, 192
scrutiny, 20, 26
secrecy, 14, 28, 47, 49
secret, 14
section, 7, 13, 14, 16, 18, 20, 23, 26, 28, 29, 32–34, 37, 39, 42, 45, 46, 49, 51, 53, 58, 61, 63, 66, 70, 76, 78, 83, 86, 88, 91, 96, 98, 101–103, 106, 108, 111, 116, 118, 122, 128, 131, 137, 141, 144, 146, 147, 157, 159, 162, 167, 170, 173, 177, 180, 182, 185, 187, 194, 197, 200, 202, 205, 211, 213, 219, 223, 225, 234, 239, 241, 247
security, 110
seek, 30, 50, 51, 94, 111, 112, 145, 149, 180, 181, 187, 194,

# Index

200, 221
segment, 32
self, 1–3, 5, 8, 10–20, 26, 28, 32, 33, 39, 45, 46, 48, 49, 51, 52, 54, 58, 61, 62, 67, 79, 103–105, 111, 113, 115, 140, 145–147, 150, 152, 170, 186, 191, 192, 195, 213, 242
sensation, 1
sense, 2, 5, 8, 10, 11, 13, 15–18, 26–28, 31, 34, 41, 46, 48, 52, 53, 57, 63–65, 72, 78, 79, 87, 88, 90, 95, 99, 117, 119, 121, 124, 132, 146, 147, 150, 154, 158, 168, 177, 178, 180, 183, 185, 187–195, 206, 209, 210, 212, 215–217, 222, 224, 232
sensitivity, 9, 25, 35, 66–71, 73–75, 89, 119, 130, 158, 163, 164, 166, 171, 178, 184, 228, 242, 247
series, 91
serve, 13, 20, 30, 37, 66, 72, 78, 95, 103, 117, 122, 126, 131, 135–137, 139, 143, 152, 157, 159, 171, 173, 177, 178, 194, 206, 222, 226, 228, 233, 236, 243, 247
service, 132
set, 2, 4, 20, 25, 29, 39, 98, 101, 132, 166, 218
setting, 26, 93, 195
sex, 74, 79, 87, 113, 114, 117, 119, 125, 126, 131, 132, 203, 204, 212, 213, 220, 229, 232

sexism, 65, 95, 148
sexuality, 2, 11–13, 15, 17–19, 33, 35, 38, 47, 52, 54, 61, 79, 89, 103, 109, 140, 201, 204, 228, 244
shame, 17, 34, 52, 244
shape, 24, 47, 60, 66, 68, 85, 87, 100, 123, 127, 136, 141, 142, 147, 173, 202, 206, 210, 211, 215, 230, 249
share, 9, 15, 22, 24–26, 30, 32, 34–36, 49, 54, 56–60, 73, 92–96, 112, 113, 120, 128, 138, 139, 143, 148, 154, 156, 157, 159–162, 164–166, 168, 169, 173, 178, 183, 185, 186, 189, 193–195, 198, 211, 216, 224, 226, 228, 233, 236, 240, 248
Sharif, 4, 8, 26, 45–47, 175–177
Sharif Jr., 33, 34, 64–66, 101, 103, 140, 141, 162–164, 193, 194, 206, 243
Sharif Jr.'s, 65, 101, 140, 241, 242
sharing, 2, 18, 24, 25, 27, 29, 31, 33, 34, 36, 44, 46, 51, 54, 55, 57, 59, 61, 62, 64, 65, 68, 72, 90, 92, 94, 99, 109–112, 122–125, 133, 138, 142, 146–148, 150, 151, 154–158, 160, 167, 173, 175, 176, 187, 189, 191, 192, 195, 197, 203, 205, 206, 209, 210, 212, 213, 217, 218, 230, 241, 248
shift, 18, 34, 65, 87, 155, 167, 206
show, 115

side, 15
sight, 27
significance, 9, 16, 33, 53, 66, 73, 86, 112, 123, 144, 156, 159, 161, 162, 185, 195, 217, 234
silencing, 22
silver, 1, 6
situation, 12, 48
skepticism, 151
society, 2, 5, 10, 14, 16, 17, 20, 23–25, 29, 33, 37, 41, 44, 46, 47, 52, 53, 55, 58, 61–63, 65, 66, 70, 71, 77, 80, 83, 85, 88, 89, 95, 104, 109, 115, 116, 121, 122, 124, 127, 128, 131, 133, 134, 136, 137, 139, 142, 143, 145–147, 150, 155, 160, 170, 172, 175, 176, 180, 182–185, 189, 190, 194, 197, 199, 200, 209, 212, 219, 220, 224, 225, 228, 229, 231, 235, 239, 240, 242, 244, 245
socio, 20, 30, 201
solace, 8, 10, 14, 16, 19, 29, 150, 175, 200
solidarity, 23, 39, 57, 64–66, 78, 95, 110, 112, 117, 121, 132, 134, 146, 147, 153, 154, 158, 165, 168, 178, 192, 193, 195, 230, 232
solution, 27
source, 20, 41, 157
sovereignty, 36
space, 14, 24, 25, 29, 32, 41, 43, 51, 52, 57, 90, 110, 112, 122, 148, 157, 168, 178, 180, 183, 189, 205, 212, 220, 228, 236, 240
Spain, 115
spark, 29, 31, 34, 59, 99, 136, 161, 164, 174, 228
speaker, 90, 157, 176, 187–189
speaking, 8, 10, 25, 29, 31, 50, 55, 57, 59, 65, 66, 124, 138, 141, 147, 153, 155, 156, 187–190, 209, 212, 242, 246, 248
specific, 30, 36, 47, 66, 67, 93, 97, 123, 158, 178, 186, 190, 199, 200, 229, 235
speech, 99, 188, 240
spirit, 1, 2, 100, 157, 159, 199, 210, 215–217
spirituality, 61
spokesperson, 104
sponsorship, 179
spotlight, 1, 48, 56
spread, 135, 138, 142, 163, 175, 190, 192, 240, 247
staff, 79, 89, 90, 130
stage, 2, 4, 15, 49, 142, 159, 204
stance, 25
stand, 8, 10, 31, 55, 58, 60, 65, 136, 146, 168, 177
star, 1, 4
start, 4
state, 14, 17
statement, 173
status, 8, 10, 12, 23, 52, 54, 63, 67, 69, 97, 110, 115, 127, 128, 130, 140–142, 201, 202, 216, 231, 234, 245
step, 12, 15, 48, 49, 71, 93, 113, 114, 136, 137, 177, 180, 195, 229

stereotype, 3, 61
sterilization, 115
stewardship, 202
stifling, 28
stigma, 5, 9, 14, 21, 89, 119, 170, 172, 200, 219, 228, 232
stigmatization, 177, 229
stone, 134, 142
Stonewall, 38, 39, 113
story, 1, 7, 9, 11–13, 15, 16, 18, 20, 25, 29, 34, 45, 46, 51, 54, 56–58, 62, 77, 95, 101, 105, 111, 120, 129, 142, 147, 151, 195, 197, 206, 207, 209, 211, 213, 241, 245
storytelling, 2–4, 6, 31, 51, 53, 68, 73, 77, 80, 87, 95, 99, 161, 167, 172, 173, 176, 182, 188, 194, 195, 198, 245
strategy, 3, 69, 70, 86, 98, 111, 112, 121, 124, 129, 179, 220
strength, 5, 15, 16, 20, 39, 42, 46, 48, 49, 51, 52, 96, 99, 104, 105, 111–113, 146, 147, 149, 159, 177, 189, 195, 210, 241, 243, 245
stress, 111
structure, 2, 50
struggle, 8, 13–15, 17, 19, 25, 39, 45, 47, 48, 57, 95, 99, 103, 136, 140, 194, 200, 206, 216, 225, 247
student, 87, 90
style, 59, 65, 155
subject, 26
success, 14, 41, 57, 87, 91, 96, 157, 166, 168, 170, 175, 219, 225

suicide, 133, 135, 200
suit, 71, 113, 114
sum, 121
support, 6, 8, 10, 14–17, 19–23, 27–32, 34, 37, 39, 41–43, 46, 48–53, 60, 64, 68, 69, 71, 72, 76, 77, 80, 83, 87, 90, 91, 94, 96, 100, 104, 105, 108–112, 115, 117–121, 123–126, 128–133, 135, 136, 138–140, 145, 147, 148, 151, 154–156, 158, 161, 165–171, 175–182, 184–188, 191, 193, 195–198, 200, 201, 204–206, 216, 219, 221–225, 228, 230, 234, 236, 242–244, 246, 248
surgery, 115
surrounding, 9, 20, 28, 41, 52, 58, 60, 61, 109, 112, 119, 120, 165, 176, 200, 211
survey, 80
sustainability, 91–93, 96, 179, 221, 223
Sweden, 114
Sylvia Rivera, 39
symbol, 56, 139, 206
system, 19, 27, 53, 96, 110, 112, 126

taboo, 2, 8, 11, 17, 19, 21, 42, 203
tactic, 222
talent, 1, 4, 6, 59, 60, 73
talk, 58, 109, 190
Tammy Baldwin, 115
tapestry, 4, 40
target, 49, 76, 167, 229

task, 8, 26, 34, 37, 73, 84, 104, 219, 220, 222
teaching, 88, 95, 120, 180
team, 92
tech, 99
technology, 78, 97, 98, 181, 186, 187, 191, 192, 196–199, 214, 224, 225, 236, 238–240, 248, 249
teenager, 2
television, 115, 138, 174, 184, 218
tension, 104, 188
term, 91, 97, 122, 194, 221, 224, 225
terminology, 171, 190
terrain, 5
Terry Miller, 133
testament, 13, 20, 55, 67, 101, 105, 136, 141, 147, 150, 189, 202, 204, 207, 209, 214, 243
The Middle East, 219, 223, 244
the Middle East, 2, 7, 8, 14, 15, 19–25, 28, 33, 35–37, 43, 44, 49, 54, 57, 62–64, 68, 71–74, 76, 93, 98–100, 109, 118–120, 140, 145, 146, 151, 153, 157–159, 163, 173, 174, 187, 188, 193, 199, 201, 209, 211, 212, 214, 219–223, 225, 226, 228–231, 239, 241, 242, 244, 246
the Middle Eastern, 67, 70, 71, 158, 184, 211
the United Kingdom, 203
the United States, 114, 132, 179
theater, 53, 118, 222, 228, 231
theme, 2, 87
therapy, 111

thinking, 10, 78, 88, 105, 112, 199
thirst, 10
thought, 109, 118, 155, 175, 188, 222
thrive, 27, 85, 88, 130, 134, 177, 202, 206, 232, 246, 248
time, 4, 25–28, 35, 38, 47, 48, 67, 70, 99, 104, 105, 121, 167, 216, 243
timeline, 93
today, 39, 160, 167, 173, 186, 191, 236
tokenism, 87
tolerance, 9, 95, 119, 140, 182
toll, 14, 17, 47, 103
tool, 10, 24, 46, 60, 62, 71, 76, 78, 85, 86, 88, 94, 108, 118, 129, 133, 139, 141, 145, 157, 160, 161, 166, 167, 172, 181, 182, 184, 185, 190, 198, 246, 248
torch, 94–96, 241, 244
touch, 60, 192
town, 91, 93, 191
track, 94
traction, 138, 231
tradition, 8, 35
trailblazer, 11, 38, 118, 164
training, 80, 86, 89, 93, 130, 132, 178, 181, 183, 196, 197, 213, 224, 230
transfer, 221
transformation, 52, 86, 149–152, 214, 233
transgender, 38, 39, 62, 114–116, 133, 134, 138, 200, 202, 204, 234
translation, 165

*Index* 279

transphobia, 59, 72, 75, 85, 116–118, 141, 155, 174, 240
travel, 165
triumph, 17
trust, 35, 44, 46, 69, 70, 73, 75, 127, 162, 187, 188, 228
truth, 13, 46, 52, 54, 55, 61, 209, 243, 244
turmoil, 15, 103
turn, 50
turning, 17, 107, 113, 132, 203

U.S., 38
umbrella, 143
uncertainty, 47
understanding, 2, 5, 6, 8–10, 12, 13, 15, 16, 18, 24, 25, 27–37, 39, 41–44, 46, 50, 51, 53–55, 57, 58, 61–64, 66–71, 74, 75, 77–81, 83, 85–90, 95, 97, 99, 109, 112, 115, 116, 118–120, 124, 125, 127, 130–133, 140, 142, 144–148, 150, 154–158, 160, 162, 164, 166, 170, 171, 174, 176, 178, 180–185, 187–190, 192, 193, 195–197, 200, 201, 203–206, 210–212, 214–218, 220, 223–225, 228, 229, 231–235, 240, 242–248
undertaking, 37
unhappiness, 18
uniqueness, 52
unity, 2, 13, 16, 38, 43, 57, 78, 96, 117, 147, 154, 206
university, 16
up, 1, 4, 6–11, 14, 16, 18, 19, 28, 31, 41, 47, 54, 55, 58, 60, 62, 65, 103, 120, 156, 164, 177, 183, 195, 220
upbringing, 1, 2, 4, 7, 9
uprising, 38, 39, 113
urgency, 123, 124, 155, 193
use, 28, 43, 59, 80, 133, 142, 143, 145, 156, 161, 162, 167, 169, 173–175, 177, 196, 222, 227, 231, 233, 238, 239
user, 169
utilization, 175, 177

validation, 80, 88, 142
value, 41, 44, 89, 147, 181, 233
variety, 45
victory, 48
video, 172
view, 218, 219
violence, 19, 21, 89, 106, 112, 116, 122, 133, 134, 185, 204, 220, 229, 232
visibility, 23, 33, 34, 38, 49, 56–60, 72, 86, 115, 117, 127, 129, 134, 136–140, 142, 160, 166, 167, 169, 172, 174, 184, 203, 204, 211, 213, 214, 220, 222, 228–230, 233, 241, 243, 247
vision, 57, 92, 133, 143, 209, 211, 239
visual, 53, 118, 161, 162, 172, 182, 189, 191, 192, 231, 233
voice, 5, 6, 8, 10, 25, 41, 42, 46, 55–58, 61, 65, 120, 123, 128, 132, 139, 142, 147, 159, 165, 176, 195, 205,

210, 211, 213, 236, 239, 244
volunteering, 5
vulnerability, 18, 27, 28, 57, 187, 189, 190

walk, 32
wave, 113, 132, 213, 241
way, 1, 5, 11, 18, 24, 29, 30, 37–39, 44, 46, 49, 51, 58, 61, 63, 67, 68, 73, 76, 80, 86, 87, 92, 94, 95, 104, 108, 109, 115, 120, 131, 137, 138, 143, 150, 151, 165, 169, 174, 182, 184, 188, 190–192, 194, 199, 201, 205, 209, 211–213, 216, 219, 221, 222, 228, 236, 242–247
wealth, 147
web, 14, 37
weight, 14, 47
well, 5, 8, 14, 26, 30, 37, 47, 48, 51, 66, 87, 92, 103, 106, 108, 110, 111, 116, 122, 123, 128, 129, 131, 132, 135, 140, 145, 157, 169, 170, 174, 178–181, 186, 212, 219, 224, 240
whole, 83, 124, 143, 178, 193, 235
willingness, 10, 11, 17, 54, 57, 67, 70, 71, 99, 105, 174, 213
wisdom, 94, 146, 147
wit, 60, 169
woman, 14, 38, 62, 234
work, 9, 10, 13, 16, 20, 23–25, 29–32, 35, 37, 38, 41, 42, 46, 47, 49–53, 55, 63, 65–67, 70, 72, 73, 75, 76, 78, 90, 96, 98, 99, 101, 104, 106, 112–115, 118–122, 125, 126, 131, 135–140, 142–146, 148, 150–154, 156–159, 161–163, 167, 175, 176, 182–184, 189, 191, 192, 194–199, 201, 204, 209, 210, 213–217, 219, 220, 229–233, 235, 240, 242–244, 246–249
workplace, 181, 225
workshop, 31, 32
world, 1, 2, 4–7, 10, 13, 15, 17, 18, 25, 29, 33, 34, 37–39, 41, 42, 45–48, 51, 53, 56, 57, 59, 64–68, 73, 76, 78, 79, 86, 88, 91, 94–101, 103, 110, 111, 113, 114, 118, 121, 125, 128, 131, 134, 136, 137, 139–141, 143–147, 150, 152–154, 157–159, 161–165, 167, 170, 175, 177, 184, 187, 190, 192, 194, 197–202, 205, 207, 210, 211, 213–217, 231–234, 236, 239–241, 243, 245–249
worldview, 8, 146
worth, 67, 112
writer, 38
writing, 155, 199, 221

year, 121
youth, 5, 30–32, 39, 77, 79, 80, 83, 85, 87–91, 94–96, 133, 135, 140, 186, 187, 190, 196, 197, 199, 204, 206, 212, 213, 241, 246, 248

zone, 216